MW01065185

Southern California

BEACH
Recipe

Recipes from Favorite Coastal Restaurants – Malibu to Laguna Beach

by
Joan Stromquist and Carl Stromquist

Tierra Publications

Tierra Publications
2801 Rodeo Road
Suite B-612
Santa Fe, New Mexico 87505
(505) 983-6300

Additional copies may be obtained by contacting Tierra Publications. For your convenience, order forms are included in the back of the book.

Cover design by James Finnell
Chama Graphics
Santa Fe, New Mexico

Photographs by Carol Westcott
Santa Fe, New Mexico

Library of Congress Catalog Card Number:

90-70729

ISBN: 0-9622807-3-9

Printed in the United States of America

Acknowledgements

This cookbook is dedicated to the talented chefs and restaurant owners of Southern California who so generously took time from their busy schedules to provide us with these outstanding recipes.

We give our thanks to Carol Westcott for her involvement in selecting the restaurants, obtaining recipes, and interviewing the chefs. A rare combination of qualities was required for the successful completion of this task, including a good sense of humor, patience, perseverance, a knowledge of gourmet cooking, and a love of great restaurants. We also thank Carol for her contribution of the photographs in this book.

To Jim Finnell, a Santa Fe artist, we give our praise for his creation of the visually striking cover.

For her work in proofreading and editing, we thank Sonya Moore.

And, finally, we thank our golden retriever "Kona", whose playful antics and constant affection were a stabilizing force during some rocky times.

Joan Stromquist

Carl Stromquist

Restaurant Addresses

Antoine
Le Meridien Hotel
4500 MacArthur Blvd.
Newport Beach, CA 92660
(714) 476-2001

Bayside 240
Portofino Inn
260 Portofino Way
Redondo Beach, CA 90277
(213) 379-8481

BeauRivage
26025 Pacific Coast Highway
Malibu, CA 90265
(213) 456-5733

Califia
Radisson Plaza Hotel
1400 Parkview Avenue
Manhattan Beach, CA 90266
(213) 546-7511

Caruso & Me
383 West 5th Street
San Pedro, CA 90731
(213) 833-0683

Chez Melange
1716 Pacific Coast Highway
Redondo Beach, CA 90277
(213) 540-1222

Coral Cafe
Sheraton at Redondo Beach
300 North Harbor Drive
Redondo Beach, CA 90277
(213) 318-8888

Eats
411½ Main Street
El Segundo, CA 90245
(213) 640-3287

Erika's
15300 Sunset Blvd.
Pacific Palisades, CA 90272
(213) 454-3703

Fennel
1535 Ocean Avenue
Santa Monica, CA 90401
(213) 394-2079

Five Crowns
3801 East Coast Highway
Corona del Mar, CA 92625
(714) 760-0331

The Golden Truffle
1767 Newport Blvd.
Costa Mesa, CA 92627
(714) 645-9858

La Rive Gauche
320 Tejon Place
Palos Verdes Estates, CA 90274
(213) 378-0267

Mangiamo
128 Manhattan Blvd.
Manhattan Beach, CA 90266
(213) 318-3434

Papadakis Taverna
301 West 6th Street
San Pedro, CA 90731
(213) 548-1186

Papa Garo's
1810 S. Catalina
Redondo Beach, CA 90277
(213) 540-7272

Pascal
Plaza Newport
1000 Bristol St. at Jamboree
Newport Beach, CA 92660
(714) 752-0107

Patrick's Roadhouse
106 Entrada Drive
Santa Monica, CA 90402
(213) 459-4544

Pavilion
Four Seasons Hotel
690 Newport Center Drive
Newport Beach, CA 92660
(714) 760-4920

Rebecca's
2025 Pacific Avenue
Venice Beach, CA 90291
(213) 306-6266

The Rex
2100 West Oceanfront
Newport Beach, CA 92663
(714) 675-2566

Rockenwagner
1023 West Washington Blvd.
Venice, CA 90290
(213) 399-6504

Royal Khyber
1000 Bristol St. at Jamboree
Newport Beach, CA 92660
(714) 752-5200

Saddle Peak Lodge
419 Cold Canyon Road
Calabasas, CA 91302
(213) 456-7325

Sausalito South
3280 N. Sepulveda Blvd.
Manhattan Beach, CA 90266
(213) 546-4507

Sorrento Grille
370 Glenneyre Street
Laguna Beach, CA 92651
(714) 494-8686

Towers
Surf & Sand Hotel
1555 South Coast Highway
Laguna Beach, CA 92651
(714) 497-4477

Valentino
3115 Pico Blvd.
Santa Monica, CA 90405
(213) 829-4313

West Beach Cafe
60 North Venice Blvd.
Venice, CA 90291
(213) 823-5396

Whale & Ale Pub Restaurant
327 West Seventh Street
San Pedro, CA 90731
(213) 832-0363

Table of Contents

6

10

Food Categories

Appetizers

Sauces, Condiments, and Dips

Soups

Southern California
BEACH
Recipe

Archway Entrance to Pier, Santa Monica

Antoine

Newport Beach

Located in Le Meridien Hotel, the beautifully appointed Antoine offers a French cuisine that rivals some of the finest restaurants in Europe.

Menu

*Gratineed Oysters
with Diced Apples in a
Calvados Sabayon*

*Sautéed Prawns
with Fried Leeks in
Prawn-Carrot Sauce*

*Antoine's Cream of
Mushroom Soup and
Chicken-Hazelnut Quenelles*

*Rack of Lamb with
Chanterelles and Lentils in
a Port Wine Sauce*

*Stilton Mille-Feuille
with Golden Raisins and
Warm Walnuts*

*Warm Pineapple Mousse
with Toasted
Shredded Coconut*

Chef de Cuisine Roy Breiman says, *"This is very simple, but very good! The hardest part is opening the oysters, so see if you can coax your fish man into doing it. The preferred apple to use is the Golden Delicious."*

Gratineed Oysters with Diced Apples in a Calvados Sabayon

1	cup heavy cream
3	egg yolks, lightly beaten
2	tablespoons Calvados
16	fresh oysters in the half shell
2	apples, peeled and finely diced *(reserve in cold water with juice of 1 lemon)*

In a small bowl place the heavy cream and whisk it for 3 to 5 minutes, or until it is softly whipped.

Add the egg yolks and the Calvados, and whisk them in.

In each oyster half shell place the diced apple. Place the oyster meat on top. Cover it with the cream mixture.

Place the oysters on a flat sheet and broil them for 1 to 2 minutes, or until the cream mixture is golden.

serves 4

Sautéed Prawns with Fried Leeks in Prawn-Carrot Sauce

Sautéed Prawns with Fried Leeks

16	**large prawns** *(heads on)*, **peeled and deveined** *(reserve the heads and shells for the Prawn-Carrot Sauce – recipe on next page)*
	salt
	pepper
¼	**cup olive oil**
3	**cups peanut oil**
1	**leek, washed and finely julienned**
	Prawn-Carrot Sauce *(recipe on next page)*

Season the prawns with the salt and the pepper. Refrigerate the prawns for 1 hour.

In a large skillet place the olive oil and heat it on medium high until it is hot. Add the chilled prawns and sauté them for 2 minutes on each side, or until they are just done. Set them aside and keep them warm.

In a large saucepan place the peanut oil and heat it on medium until it is hot *(350°)*. Add the leeks and fry them for 1 minute, or until they are golden brown. Remove them with a slotted spoon and place them on paper towels to drain. Lightly season them with the salt.

In each of 4 medium-sized plates with high rims place ½ cup of the Prawn-Carrot Sauce. Place 4 prawns on top of the sauce, in a circular pattern. Place the fried leeks on top.

serves 4

"Once people try this dish they will order it time and time again. The recipe was given to me by our consulting chef in France, who has a two-star restaurant in Versailles."

"When you fry the leeks be very careful that the oil is not too hot, because otherwise they will get black and taste bitter. You want them golden brown and crisp. You can test the temperature by dipping a little piece of leek in the oil to see what happens."

"Peanut oil cooks items at a high heat very nicely. It has an acid in it that somehow makes it the best for deep-frying vegetables. Do not use olive oil!"

"A nice garnish for this dish would be some diced fresh tomatoes that have first been peeled and seeded. I didn't put this in the recipe because I wanted to make it seem as simple as possible to make. But if you want to do it, great, because they really will add a nice color and set the dish off perfectly. We cut the tomatoes into little diamond shapes."

Prawn-Carrot Sauce

3	**tablespoons olive oil**
2	**cups shells and heads of prawns** *(reserved from the Sautéed Prawns with Fried Leeks recipe on previous page)*
1	**onion, diced**
4	**carrots, sliced**
1	**leek, washed and diced**
1	**cup white wine**
1	**pint heavy cream**
3	**tablespoons butter, cut into small pieces**
	salt *(to taste)*
	pepper *(to taste)*

In a medium saucepan place the oil and heat it on medium high until it is hot. Add the shells and heads of the prawns, and sauté them for 4 minutes. Remove them and set them aside.

Add the onions, carrots, and leeks. Sauté them for 5 minutes.

Return the prawn shells and heads to the pan. Sauté the ingredients for 3 minutes.

Add the white wine. Cook the ingredients for 4 to 6 minutes, or until the liquid is reduced to ¼.

Add the heavy cream. Cook the ingredients on low heat for 12 to 15 minutes, or until the liquid is reduced to ½.

Remove the prawn shells and heads with a slotted spoon and discard them.

Place the sauce in a food processor and blend it. Strain the sauce and return it to the pan.

While whisking constantly, add the pieces of butter one at a time.

Season the sauce with the salt and the pepper.

"Try to get prawns that have the heads on because they will give the sauce a better flavor. If you can get some lobster shells, then that would be even better. You might try asking your fish man at the market to save some for you."

"When you make the sauce be sure that the shells are completely removed before you blend it. If you leave any shells in that will be very bad, because they will taste bitter, they will discolor the sauce, and they will look awful."

"If the sauce is too thick, then you can add some more cream. If it is too thin, then you can reduce it further."

"There is that moment of truth when the customer is ready to sign their credit card slip and the thought crosses their mind, 'Wow! Was it worth the money?' We always want the answer to be 'yes!' We are an expensive restaurant and so our food and service must be first class all the way."

Antoine

Antoine's Cream of Mushroom Soup and Chicken-Hazelnut Quenelles

Antoine's Cream of Mushroom Soup

4	tablespoons butter
20	medium mushrooms, sliced
¼	cup sherry
3	cups chicken stock *(recipe on page 297)*
2	cups heavy cream
¾	cup sherry
	salt *(to taste)*
	pepper *(to taste)*
	Chicken-Hazelnut Quenelles *(recipe on next page)*
2	tablespoons hazelnuts, skins removed *(see chef's comments on this page for instructions)*, **and chopped**

In a large skillet place the butter and heat it on medium high until it has melted. Add the mushrooms and sauté them for 4 to 5 minutes, or until they are brown. Add the ¼ cup of sherry and deglaze the pan.

Add the chicken stock. Cook the ingredients on medium heat for 12 to 15 minutes, or until the liquid is reduced by ½.

Add the heavy cream and stir it in. Cook the soup for 10 to 12 minutes, or until the liquid is reduced by ½.

In a small saucepan place the ¾ cup of sherry. Cook it on medium high heat for 4 to 6 minutes, or until it is reduced by ¾.

Add the reduced sherry, salt, and pepper to the soup, and stir them in.

In each of 4 individual serving bowls place 3 of the Chicken-Hazelnut Quenelles. Ladle the soup on top. Sprinkle on the hazelnuts.

serves 4

"This soup has three main flavors that complement each other very well.....the mushrooms, the sherry, and the chicken. By combining these flavors a wonderful new fourth flavor is created. You could combine these three flavors in other ways. For instance, you could have sautéed chicken with sherried mushrooms, which would give you a complete dish rather than a soup."

"To roast the hazelnuts you should place them on a sheet pan and put them in a 400° oven for 2 or 3 minutes, or until the outside skin starts to break away. Rub the hazelnuts together so that the outer dark skins flake off. You do not want to toast them, you just want the skin to loosen up."

"To create something from nothing makes me happy."

Chicken-Hazelnut Quenelles

2	chicken breasts, skin and bones removed
	salt
	pepper
2	eggs
1	tablespoon butter, softened
¼	cup heavy cream
¼	cup hazelnuts, skins removed *(see chef's comments on previous page for instructions)*, **and chopped**
2	**cups chicken stock** *(recipe on page 297)*

In a food processor place the chicken breasts, salt, and pepper. Purée them until a smooth consistency is achieved. Add the eggs one at a time and blend them in well. Add the butter and blend it in.

With the food processor still running, slowly add the heavy cream so that it is mixed in well.

In a medium bowl place the puréed chicken mixture. Add the hazelnuts and mix them in. Place the mousse in the refrigerator so that it chills.

Remove the chilled mousse and, using 2 spoons, form it into 12 egg-shaped quenelles.

Place the chicken stock in a medium saucepan and heat it on medium high until it almost reaches a boil. Place the quenelles in the stock and cook them for 3 minutes. Turn them once during the cooking process.

serves 4

"The most difficult part in preparing this soup recipe is the making and cooking of the quenelles. A quenelle is an egg shaped item that the French use a lot in their cooking. They make for a wonderful presentation. Here we use quenelles that are made with chicken mousse."

"Cooking is like a puzzle. You have a variety of ingredients to use, and you must figure out how to put them together so that they are interesting and tasty."

"When people come to Antoine, I want them to leave the rest of the world behind them.....to forget about their bills, traffic, problems, and worries. Here I want them to feel pampered, well taken care of, and deeply satisfied."

Rack of Lamb with Chanterelles and Lentils in a Port Wine Sauce

Rack of Lamb with Chanterelles

½   cup honey
2   medium racks of lamb
¼   cup fresh thyme, finely chopped
2   tablespoons butter
12 chanterelle mushrooms, cleaned and diced
    salt *(to taste)*
    pepper *(to taste)*
    Lentils *(recipe on next page)*
    Port Wine Sauce *(recipe on next page)*

Spread the honey evenly over the racks of lamb. Sprinkle on the thyme.

Preheat the oven to 475°. Place the racks of lamb in a baking pan and roast them for 15 to 18 minutes, or until they are golden brown and soft to the touch. Remove the lamb and let it rest.

In a small skillet place the butter and heat it on medium high until it has melted. Add the chanterelle mushrooms and sauté them for 3 to 4 minutes, or until they are tender. Season them with the salt and the pepper.

Slice the racks of lamb between the bones.

In the center of each of 4 individual serving plates place a portion of the Lentils. Spoon the Port Wine Sauce around them. Place the lamb on top of the Lentils. Place the mushrooms around the lamb.

serves 4

"There is a wonderful combination of flavors in this dish. The lamb cooked with the honey and fresh thyme is outstanding!"

"In cooking the lamb you should not worry if some of the honey burns. It will run off the lamb and onto the pan, and when it cooks in a hot oven it turns black and caramelizes. But the honey that stays on the lamb does not turn black. So if you see some smoke coming out of your oven, don't worry!"

"In cooking it is important that you treat the ingredients with the utmost respect. This is true for each step involved in making the dish.....from the initial selection of the product to the final presentation. If you put this kind of energy into your cooking, then the people who finally eat the dish will be able to feel that energy. It is a spiritual thing."

Lentils

6	slices bacon, chopped
1	carrot, chopped
1	onion, chopped
½	pound lentils, soaked for 2 hours and drained
1	quart chicken stock *(or as needed)* – *(recipe on page 297)*
1	tablespoon fresh thyme, chopped
½	teaspoon salt
⅓	teaspoon pepper

In a medium large saucepan place the bacon and fry it on medium high heat for 1 to 2 minutes.

Add the carrots and onions. Sauté them for 3 to 4 minutes, or until they are tender and the bacon is brown.

Add the lentils, chicken stock, thyme, salt, and pepper.

Bring the liquid to a boil and then reduce it to a simmer. Cook the lentils for 1 hour, or until they are tender. Add more chicken stock if necessary.

serves 4

Port Wine Sauce

½	cup shallots, finely sliced
1	large bottle Tawny Port
3	cups veal stock *(recipe on page 151)*
	salt *(to taste)*
	pepper *(to taste)*

In a medium saucepan place the shallots and the Tawny Port. Heat them on medium low for 20 to 30 minutes, or until the liquid is reduced to ¼.

Add the veal stock and cook the ingredients for 20 to 30 minutes, or until the liquid is reduced to ¼.

Add the salt and the pepper, and stir them in.

Strain the sauce.

Stilton Mille-Feuille with Golden Raisins and Warm Walnuts

¼	cup golden raisins
¼	cup port wine
¼	pound Stilton cheese
4	tablespoons butter, softened
½	cup heavy cream
1	sheet puff pastry, cut into twelve 2" circles
1	tablespoon butter, melted
⅔	cup walnuts, finely ground *(reserve 12 large pieces for the garnish)*

Place the raisins in the port wine and marinate them for ½ hour. Drain the raisins and gently pat them dry with paper towels.

Place the Stilton cheese in a food processor and blend it. Add the softened butter and blend it in. Add the heavy cream and blend it in until the mixture is very smooth.

Remove the mixture from the food processor and place it in a bowl. Add the marinated raisins and mix them in well.

Preheat the oven to 350°. Place the puff pastry circles on a greased sheet pan. Prick them with a fork. Place another baking sheet on top of the pastry. Bake them for 8 to 10 minutes, or until they are golden brown.

On each of 4 small plates place 1 circle of the puff pastry. In this order, place 3 tablespoons of the cheese mixture, one pastry round, 3 tablespoons of the cheese mixture, and one pastry round. Brush the top with the melted butter. Evenly sprinkle on the ground walnuts.

Place the stacked pastry in the refrigerator for 10 minutes so that they chill.

Heat the remaining whole walnuts in the oven for 1 minute and place them around the mille-feuilles.

serves 4

"This is a cheese course that usually follows the entrée, before the dessert course. It is a small serving and it goes on a plate that is a little bit bigger than a saucer. Mille-Feuille means 'a thousand layers', which refers to the way a puff pastry is made."

"The trickiest part is to make sure that the dough layers are flat when you bake them. This is why you put a sheet pan on top. We use puff pastry because it has a delicate and fragile flavor, but you could also use phyllo dough."

"When you refrigerate this the cheese should be a little hard on the outside and soft on the inside. You have two different textures in the cheese this way, and it makes for a wonderful, sensuous surprise when you bite into it."

"You don't have to use raisins and walnuts. You could use black currants, chives, or different kinds of nuts."

Antoine

Warm Pineapple Mousse with Toasted Shredded Coconut

1	fresh pineapple, peeled, cored, puréed, and strained
½	cup heavy cream
6	egg yolks
1	tablespoon cornstarch
½	cup sugar
¼	cup water
6	egg whites
¼	cup coconut, shredded
2	tablespoons powdered sugar

In a medium saucepan place the pineapple purée and the heavy cream, and stir them together. Heat the mixture on medium for 8 to 10 minutes, or until it is reduced to a syrup. Keep it warm.

In a small bowl place the egg yolks and the cornstarch, and beat them together.

Add the egg yolks to the cream mixture. While whipping constantly, cook the mixture for 6 to 8 minutes, or until it is the consistency of a medium whipped cream. Set it aside.

In a small saucepan place the sugar and water, and heat them on low until the mixture reaches 115°.

In a medium bowl place the egg whites. Beat them with an electric mixer on low speed for 2 to 3 minutes, or until they are frothy. Turn the electric mixer on high, and while continuing to beat the egg whites slowly pour the sugar-water mixture down the side of the bowl. Continue to beat the mixture for 8 to 10 minutes more, or until the meringue is very shiny and the bottom of the mixing bowl is cool.

Add the cream mixture to the meringue, and gently fold it in.

Preheat the oven to 400°. In each of 4 small soufflé dishes place the mixture so that the dishes are half-filled. Add the shredded coconut. Fill the dishes up with the remaining mixture. Sprinkle the powdered sugar on top. Bake the mousse for 8 to 10 minutes, or until it is set. Remove it from the oven.

Place the mousse under a preheated broiler for 30 seconds, or until the sugar is caramelized.

serves 4

"You will love this dessert! It's a great recipe, and you can substitute other kinds of fruit, like passion fruit, guava, or orange."

"If your meringue does not look really thick and shiny, then try it again."

"When I was twenty years old I had a hard time deciding what to do with my life. I wanted to be an artist, but I couldn't draw, and I also wanted to travel. So I decided to try cooking, and that was the correct choice because not only did it provide an outlet for my creative urges, but it also allowed me to work in different places in Europe and in America."

"It's important for me to be of service to others. This fulfills me."

Antoine

Sailboats, Marina del Rey

Bayside 240
Redondo Beach

Located at the popular Portofino Inn, Bayside 240 serves an imaginative seafood cuisine in a light and airy dining room that boasts a spectacular 180˚ view!

Executive Chef Thomas Tompkins says, *"People absolutely love this appetizer. It's one of those dishes that just melts in your mouth, and it's simple to make."*

Crab Loaf with Cheese Sauce

3	cups half and half
3	tablespoons butter
1	green bell pepper, seeded and diced medium
½	medium white onion, diced medium
2	tablespoons garlic, diced
1	teaspoon fresh thyme, chopped
3	tablespoons flour
1	pound cheddar cheese, grated
1	pound crab meat, shells picked out
4	6" sourdough roundettes
4	tablespoons Herb Butter *(recipe on page 31)*
1	cup cheddar cheese, grated

In a medium saucepan place the half and half. Bring it to a simmer and keep it warm.

In another medium saucepan place the butter and heat it until it has melted. Add the bell peppers, onions, garlic, and thyme. Sauté the ingredients for 5 to 6 minutes, or until they are tender.

Add the flour, and stir it constantly for 5 minutes. While continuing to stir constantly, slowly add the warm half and half. Make sure that no lumps form. Simmer the sauce for 20 minutes. Add the 1 pound of cheese and stir it in so that it is melted. Add the crab and stir it in. Keep the sauce warm.

Hollow out the sourdough loaves. Rub the inside of each loaf with the Herb Butter. Preheat the oven to 350°. Bake the loaves for 5 minutes, or until they are toasted.

Fill the loaves with the crab-cheese sauce. Sprinkle on the 1 cup of grated cheese. Bake the loaves for 5 minutes, or until the cheese melts and the sauce is hot.

serves 4

Ahi and Vegetable Roll with Soy Marinade

Ahi and Vegetable Roll

4	5-ounce ahi fillets, skin removed
2	teapoons wasabi, mixed with water to make a spreadable paste
1½	cups jicama, julienned into ⅛" strips
½	red bell pepper, julienned into ⅛" strips
2	scallions, sliced into ⅛" rings
8	snow peas, strings removed
4	tablespoons dark sesame oil
½	cup Soy Marinade *(recipe on next page)*
4	tablespoons wasabi, mixed with water to make a thick paste
4	tablespoons pickled ginger

Place each ahi fillet between 2 sheets of plastic wrap. Pound them with a meat mallet until they are ¼" thick. Remove the top sheet of the plastic wrap.

Spread the 2 teaspoons of wasabi paste on top of the fillets.

On the edge of each fillet place ¼ of the jicama, red bell peppers, scallions, and snow peas. Roll the ahi up very compactly. Tightly roll the plastic around the ahi roll and twist the ends. Place the rolls in the refrigerator for 30 minutes. Remove the plastic.

Heat a large non-stick sauté pan on high until it is very hot. Add the dark sesame oil and the ahi rolls. Sear them for 45 seconds. Slice the ahi rolls into ½" thick slices at a 45° angle.

On each of 4 individual serving plates spread on the Soy Marinade. Place the sliced ahi pieces on top. Garnish the plate with some of the 4 tablespoons of wasabi paste and some of the pickled ginger.

serves 4

"This dish is like sushi because the fish is raw in the middle, even though it is seared. We have a lot of customers who frequent sushi bars, and they say that they really like this item. It's one of our best sellers, but then you have to remember that this is California, and California people are really into eating raw fish."

"The only trick here is in rolling up the ahi in the plastic wrap. The first 360° roll of the wrap around the fish must be very tight, and there can be no wrinkles in the plastic. The finished roll of fish should be 1 inch to 1½ inches in diameter, and 5 inches to 6 inches long."

"My feeling about fresh fish is that if you are willing to serve it raw, then it must be extremely fresh, because there is no way to disguise the flavor. I think that to truly enjoy and understand the flavor of any kind of fish you need to eat it raw as well as cooked."

"This marinade is a very versatile product. You can use it with shellfish, chicken, and beef. It can be a dip, a basting mixture for barbecuing, or a marinade. If you do use it as a marinade, then don't leave the item in it for more than an hour or two, because the acidity from the pineapple will cook it. Keep the sauce refrigerated and it will last for several weeks."

Soy Marinade

1	cup pineapple juice
2	tablespoons soy sauce
2	tablespoons dark sesame oil
1	teaspoon scallions, finely chopped
1	teaspoon garlic, finely chopped
1	teaspoon fresh ginger, finely chopped
½	teaspoon crushed red chile peppers

In a small bowl place all of the ingredients and mix them together. Store the marinade in the refrigerator.

makes 1¼ cups

"The Herb Butter is a great thing to have on hand because it will add a lot of flavor to whatever you are cooking. It's wonderful with shrimp, steak, and cooked vegetables."

"You need to rinse the parsley in a cheesecloth and then squeeze out the water, because otherwise it will turn the butter green."

"I have always loved to cook and I have always had a natural aptitude for it. When I was a cub scout I used to get lots of merit badges for cooking!"

Herb Butter

2	pounds unsalted butter, room temperature
2	tablespoons garlic, chopped
2	lemons, freshly squeezed
2	tablespoons parsley, chopped and rinsed in a cheesecloth
2	tablespoons fresh chives, thinly sliced
2	tablespoons shallots, minced
2	tablespoons fresh basil, thinly julienned
2	tablespoons fresh thyme, chopped
½	teaspoon salt

In a medium bowl place all of the ingredients and blend them together.

Lobster and Cream Cheese Egg Rolls with Serrano Sweet and Sour Sauce

Lobster and Cream Cheese Egg Rolls

6   ounces scallops
2   eggs
⅓   cup heavy cream
6   ounces cream cheese
2   tablespoons fresh chives, chopped
2   tablespoons fresh shallots, chopped
1   tablespoon garlic, chopped
1   tablespoon fresh tarragon, chopped
1   tablespoon fresh basil, chopped
6   ounces lobster meat, diced into ½" pieces
    salt *(to taste)*
    pepper *(to taste)*
12   egg roll skins
3   cups peanut oil
    Serrano Sweet and Sour Sauce *(recipe on next page)*

In a food processor place the scallops and purée them.

Add the 2 eggs and the heavy cream, and beat them in well. Set the mixture aside.

In a medium bowl place the cream cheese and beat it until it is very soft.

Add the scallop mixture, chives, shallots, garlic, tarragon, and basil. Mix the ingredients together so that they are well incorporated.

Add the lobster and gently mix it in *(don't break up the pieces)*. Season the mixture with the salt and the pepper.

Place one egg roll skin on a board so that a corner is facing towards you. Place 2 ounces of the mixture on the closest ⅓ of the skin. Roll the skin ½ way up. Fold in the 2 outside corners. Continue to roll it up. Brush some of the beaten egg on the far corner to seal the egg roll. Repeat this process with the remaining egg roll skins.

(continued on next page)

"I developed this recipe because I wanted to take an ordinary egg roll, which usually is about 95% vegetables inside, and make it more up-town by using lobster. The dish is very popular, and people feel that they are getting a good deal when they eat it because the egg rolls are so rich and full of lobster. They are delicious!"

"In making the egg rolls there is one thing to watch out for. When you fold over the two outside corners, be sure that the folds are nice and straight. If you don't, then, as one of my previous Oriental instructors pointed out, your egg roll will look like it has dog ears!"

"I use Canadian lobster that comes in cans and is frozen. You can use any kind of shellfish that you want."

In a large saucepan place the peanut oil and heat it on medium high until it is hot *(350°)*. Deep-fry the egg rolls for 6 to 7 minutes, or until they are crisp and golden brown. Drain them on paper towels.

Serve the egg rolls with a small bowl of the Serrano Sweet and Sour Sauce for dipping.

serves 6

Serrano Sweet and Sour Sauce

2	tablespoons dark sesame oil
¼	cup fresh pineapple, diced into ¼" pieces
3	serrano chile peppers, seeds removed *(optional)*, and finely minced
1	teaspoon garlic, finely minced
1	teaspoon shallots, chopped
¼	cup distilled white vinegar
2	tablespoons Dijon mustard
½	cup orange marmalade

In a medium skillet place the dark sesame oil and heat it on medium high until it is hot. Add the pineapple, serrano chile peppers, garlic, and shallots. Sauté the ingredients for 3 to 4 minutes, or until they are soft.

Add the vinegar, mustard, and orange marmalade. Stir the ingredients together and simmer them for 10 minutes.

Place the sauce in the refrigerator so that it chills.

"To me, the beauty of being a chef is not what I can do, but rather it is what I can teach others to do. There is no greater feeling than teaching someone to do something perfectly."

"This is a great tasting sauce that is very simple to make. You can use it with a lot of different things, and it's especially good with chicken. The serrano chile peppers give it a bite, but you can control the heat by not using the seeds."

"I like to use fruit jellies as a base when I make fruit sauces, and then add different ingredients to it. That way I don't have to mess with fruit pectin."

Crispy Lamb Chops
with Thyme Sauce

Crispy Lamb Chops

12	lamb chops, well trimmed
	salt
	pepper
1	large potato, peeled and grated
1	egg
1	tablespoon fresh basil, thinly sliced
4	cups vegetable oil
	Thyme Sauce (recipe on next page)
4	sprigs fresh thyme

Season the lamb chops with the salt and the pepper, and set them aside.

In a medium bowl place the potato, egg, and basil. Add a dash of the salt and the pepper. Mix the ingredients together well.

Squeeze the mixture together with your hands to remove any excess water.

Firmly pack the potato mixture around the lamb chops so that they are coated.

In a large saucepan place the vegetable oil and heat it on medium high until it is hot (350°). Deep-fry the coated lamb chops for 5 to 7 minutes, or until the crust is crisp and golden brown, and the lamb is cooked to the desired doneness.

On each of 4 individual serving plates place the Thyme Sauce. Place 3 lamb chops on top. Garnish the dish with a sprig of thyme.

serves 4

"My Sous Chef, Charles Frankenfield, developed this recipe. When he first told me about it he was somewhat hesitant, because the lamb chops are deep-fried, and that is really different. It's kind of like taking fresh salmon and deep-frying it. Anyway, he made the dish and I tasted it, and it was outstanding! The flavor of the lamb and the crispiness of the potatoes go really well together with the richness of the Thyme Sauce."

"The only tricky thing is how to tell when the lamb chops are done. You are deep-frying them and they have a crust, and so you can't feel them with your finger. I would recommend cooking one according to the prescribed time and then testing it with an internal thermometer. Medium would be 135° to 140°. This way you will know if the other chops should be cooked for a longer or shorter time."

"If you don't reduce the wine enough, then the acidity will separate the sauce when you add the cream. If this happens you can fix the sauce by straining it, and then running it in the blender. Actually, a lot of chefs will put the sauce in a blender even if it hasn't separated, and then add the pieces of butter. European chefs tend to look down on this practice.....they say that it is cheating. But I don't have a problem with it because I think that it gives the sauce a smoother consistency and a nicer sheen."

"I love working in California because the people are so responsive to new things. Once I worked with a chef in Texas who was a Californian, and he would make all of these wild and different dishes which he called 'Left Coast Food'. The younger people enjoyed the things that he made. But the older, more traditional people wanted their food prepared in the ways they were used to. They wanted their shrimp served in a shrimp cocktail, and not in some weird way they had never seen before."

Thyme Sauce

6	sprigs fresh thyme
1	cup white wine
1	tablespoon garlic, chopped
1	tablespoon shallots, chopped
1	bay leaf
1	lemon, juiced
½	cup heavy cream
½	pound cold butter, cut into small pieces
	salt *(to taste)*
	pepper *(to taste)*

In a small saucepan place the thyme, white wine, garlic, shallots, bay leaf, and lemon juice. Heat the ingredients on medium low and let them cook for 12 to 15 minutes, or until the liquid is reduced to ⅓.

Add the heavy cream and simmer it for 12 to 15 minutes, or until the liquid is reduced to ½.

While whisking constantly, add the pieces of butter one at a time.

Season the sauce with the salt and the pepper.

Strain the sauce.

Cajun Grilled Snapper with Linguini and Veracruz Sauce

Cajun Grilled Snapper with Linguini

4	6-ounce snapper fillets
2	tablespoons cajun spice
12	ounces linguini, cooked al dente
2	cups Veracruz Sauce *(recipe follows)*

Lightly dust the snapper fillets with the cajun spice. Grill them for 2 to 3 minutes on each side, or until they are just done.

On each of 4 individual serving plates place the linguini so that it covers ⅔ of the plate. Place a snapper fillet on the other part of the plate. Ladle the Veracruz Sauce over the linguini and the snapper.

serves 4

"If you love pasta and you love fish, then you will certainly love this dish. It's flavorful, healthy, and easy to make. Try to get a good kind of snapper. Don't use the Pacific red snapper, if possible. Any lean, flaky fish will work with this recipe, like sea bass or grouper."

Veracruz Sauce

¼	cup vegetable oil
1	large onion, slivered
1	green bell pepper, seeds removed, and slivered
2	tablespoons garlic, chopped
2	tablespoons capers
12	small green olives, stuffed with pimiento
1	cup white wine
3	cups tomatoes, chopped
	salt *(to taste)*
	pepper *(to taste)*

In a medium saucepan place the vegetable oil and heat it on medium until it is hot. Add the onions, green bell peppers, garlic, capers, and olives. Sauté the ingredients for 12 to 15 minutes, or until they are soft and golden brown.

Add the white wine. Cook the ingredients for 4 to 6 minutes, or until the liquid is reduced by ½. Add the tomatoes. Simmer the ingredients for 30 to 45 minutes, or until they are cooked into a thick sauce. Season the sauce with the salt and the pepper.

"This is a great tasting sauce that makes a nice variation from the normal marinara sauce that is so often served with pasta. The most important thing in making this is to be sure to get the onions, garlic, and bell peppers nice and brown, because this will caramelize them and the natural sugars will be released."

"I came up with this recipe when I worked at another restaurant. We were designing a menu for Cinco de Mayo and I wanted to do a traditional Mexican dessert in a slightly different way. There is a basic ratio for making flan which is 8 eggs to 1 quart of milk. So I substituted 1 cup of Kahlua for one of the cups of milk."

"There are times when I will devote half a day to creating new recipes, and I go into a whole other world. I forget all of my worries and I become completely absorbed in what I am doing. It's fun to cook.....I love it! I almost look forward to a cook calling in sick because it means that I get to work the line. Being an Executive Chef has a lot of responsibilities that occupy my time, so I am not able to cook as much as I would like."

"In the United States there is a big diversity in the styles of cooking and I like to combine them in my own cooking. You cannot put a label on my style of cooking other than to say that I am just an American, and I pretty much do whatever I want. If it works, great, and if it doesn't work, I'll try something else."

Kahlua Caramel Flan

2	cups sugar
¼	cup water
8	eggs
½	cup sugar
3	cups milk
1	cup Kahlua
1	cup fresh berries

In a small saucepan place the 2 cups of sugar and the water. Heat the ingredients on medium high and cook them for 20 to 25 minutes, or until the sugar is golden brown.

In each of 8 individual baking cups pour the caramelized sugar so that it is ½ " high. Set the cups aside.

In a medium bowl place the eggs and beat them so that the yolks are combined with the whites.

Add the ½ cup of sugar, milk, and Kahlua. Whisk the ingredients together so that they are well blended.

Pour the mixture into each of the 8 cups with the caramelized sugar.

Preheat the oven to 250°. Place the cups in a large baking pan. Fill the pan with hot water so that it is halfway up the cups. Bake the flan for 45 to 60 minutes, or until it is set.

Let the flan cool to room temperature.

Place it in the refrigerator so that it chills.

Run a paring knife around the inside edge of each cup to loosen the flan. Invert it onto a small serving plate. Pour the caramelized sugar on top of the flan. Garnish the dish with the fresh berries.

serves 8

Sails, Newport Beach

BeauRivage

Malibu

Chic, colorful, and romantic, the BeauRivage offers a spectacular Pacific Ocean view which is surpassed only by its incredible Mediterranean cuisine.

Menu

Neptune Gazpacho

BeauRivage Salade Exotique with Chutney Vinaigrette

Stuffed Artichokes with Saffron

Broiled Herbed Quails with Gnocchi Romana

Sambousek of Lamb

Fresh Tuna Ragoût with Fennel

Crêpes Delice with Mangoes

Basic Crêpes

Lemon Cheese Tart

Crème Fraîche

Owner Daniel Forge says, *"This recipe is not designed for a fancy restaurant, but rather for the average cook at home who wants to prepare a simple, refreshing soup."*

Neptune Gazpacho

2	cups tomato juice
2	cups clam juice
1	cucumber, peeled, seeded, and diced
3	scallions, thinly sliced
2	tablespoons virgin olive oil
2	tablespoons red wine vinegar
1	tablespoon sugar
1	tablespoon fresh dill, chopped
1	clove garlic, crushed and chopped
4	ounces cream cheese, frozen hard and then coarsely grated
1	avocado, peeled, pitted, and diced medium
½	teaspoon tabasco sauce
¾	cup bay shrimp, cooked

In a large bowl place all of the ingredients except for the shrimp. Gently mix the ingredients together.

Place the soup in the refrigerator and chill it overnight.

Serve the soup in chilled serving bowls and garnish it with the bay shrimps floating on top.

serves 8

BeauRivage Salade Exotique with Chutney Vinaigrette

BeauRivage Salade Exotique

4	hearts of palm, quartered
4	Belgian endives, cut at an angle into ½" wide pieces
2	bunches watercress, well chopped
4	large tomatoes, sliced medium
	Chutney Vinaigrette *(recipe follows)*
1	tablespoon fresh chives, chopped

On a large serving platter place the hearts of palm, Belgian endives, watercress, and tomato slices. Arrange these items in an attractive way.

Spoon the Chutney Vinaigrette over the salad.

Sprinkle on the chives.

serves 8

"I came up with this recipe maybe 20 years ago. It is a beautifully colored salad with the white hearts of palm, the green endive and watercress, and the red tomato."

"Be sure to arrange all of the salad items very artfully on the plate. You can be creative, and no matter what you come up with, your guests will think it looks wonderful!"

Chutney Vinaigrette

1	lemon, juiced
¼	teaspoon curry powder
1	teaspoon red wine vinegar
½	teaspoon English dry mustard
½	teaspoon salt
¼	teaspoon white pepper
½	cup virgin olive oil
½	cup Major Grey Chutney, chopped

In a small bowl place the lemon juice, curry powder, red wine vinegar, dry mustard, salt, and white pepper. Mix the ingredients together well.

Add the olive oil and whisk it in well.

Add the chopped chutney and mix it in.

Chill the dressing in the refrigerator.

"There is an unusual, exotic taste to this dressing that will really make the salad extraordinary."

Stuffed Artichokes with Saffron

8	**large artichokes, stems removed** *(reserve the stems)*
4	**tablespoons heavy cream**
4	**tablespoons sour cream**
2	**pinches saffron**
1	**cup parsley, chopped**
2	**egg yolks**
	salt *(to taste)*
	pepper *(to taste)*
2	**lemons, juiced**
16	**anchovy fillets, finely chopped**
1	**cup bread crumbs**
1	**teaspoon garlic powder** *(or to taste)*
¼	**cup virgin olive oil**
¼	**cup water** *(or as needed)*

Peel the artichoke stems and then chop them. Set them aside.

In a medium bowl place the heavy cream and the sour cream, and mix them together.

Add the saffron, parsley, egg yolks, salt, pepper, lemon juice, anchovies, bread crumbs, and chopped artichoke stems. Mix the ingredients together well.

Spread the artichoke leaves apart and very carefully place the mixture between the leaves. Sprinkle on the garlic powder between the leaves.

In a wide and deep, heavy skillet place the oil and heat it on medium low. Place the stuffed artichokes in the skillet so that they are in an upright postion. Cover the pan tightly and cook the artichokes for 15 minutes.

Add the water and cook them for another 30 minutes *(add more water if necessary as time goes on)*, or until they are tender.

serves 8

"If you like artichokes you will just love this dish! But, I must warn you that they are a little bit messy to eat. So, tie a serviette around your neck, and then go to work!"

"People always cut off the stem of the artichoke and then they throw it away. But what they don't realize is that the stem is some of the best part. It is an extension of the artichoke heart and it tastes wonderful. I love the artichoke heart.....you eat it at the very last, like it is the dessert of the artichoke."

"I remember many years ago when my wife and I were returning from our honeymoon in San Francisco. We were driving down Highway 1, near Castroville, which is the 'Artichoke Capital of the World'. All of a sudden we came upon hundreds of artichokes lying in the middle of the road.....they had fallen off a farming truck. So I gathered up as many as would fit in our car, and took them home to Los Angeles. So many beautiful artichokes..... was I ever thrilled!"

Broiled Herbed Quails with Gnocchi Romana

Broiled Herbed Quails

16	quails, split down the back and flattened
½	cup olive oil
	salt
	pepper
	dried rosemary
	dried thyme
8	sprigs fresh sage
⅓	cup cognac
¼	cup white wine
1	tablespoon butter
	Gnocchi Romana *(recipe on next page)*

In a large baking pan place the quails. Brush them thoroughly with the olive oil, both inside and out. Season the quails with the salt, pepper, rosemary, and thyme. Place 1 sprig of sage under each quail.

In a preheated oven broil the quails for 6 to 7 minutes, or until the top side is browned. Turn the quails over and place the sage sprigs on top. Broil the quails for another 5 minutes.

Remove the pan from the oven and place it on the burner over a high heat. Sprinkle on the cognac and flambé it. Pour on the white wine.

Remove the quails and set them aside.

Add the butter and stir it with the pan juices to make a sauce.

On each of 8 individual serving plates place 2 of the quails and the sprigs of sage. Pour the sauce over the quails and serve them with a side of the Gnocchi Romana.

serves 8

"Quail is one of my favorite foods. Every time I go to Italy the first thing I do is to go to a restaurant and eat 3 or 4 of them. It is a wonderful bird."

"This recipe might look long and complicated, but it is not hard to do at all. The secret to the good taste lies in the fresh sprigs of sage. When you put the sprigs of sage on top of the quails in the oven they get dark and crisp, and they taste delicious!"

"I don't really like quails when they are boned. They are so small that they lose all of their juiciness if the bones are removed."

"In Mexico they have wonderful quail. There is a special restaurant in Tijuana that I love to go to. They know me so well there, that as soon as they see me at the door they say, 'Ahh.....we have to get some quail for you to eat!' "

Gnocchi Romana

1	quart milk
⅓	cup butter
1	pinch cayenne pepper
⅛	teaspoon nutmeg
1	pinch salt
10	ounces semolina *(wheat hearts)*
8	egg yolks, whipped
⅓	cup Parmesan cheese, freshly grated
⅓	cup butter, melted
¼	cup Parmesan cheese, freshly grated

"You can't miss with this recipe. It's very tasty and it goes well with the quail. The only trick is to keep stirring it and don't let it stick to the bottom of the pan."

In a large saucepan place the milk and bring it to a boil over low heat. Add the first ⅓ cup of butter, cayenne pepper, nutmeg, and salt.

While stirring constantly, slowly sprinkle in the semolina. Continue to stir the mixture for 5 to 7 minutes more, or until it is of a smooth consistency.

Add the whipped egg yolks and stir them in so that they are well incorporated.

Add the ⅓ cup of Parmesan cheese and mix it in well.

In a greased baking dish pour in the paste *(it should be 1" thick)*. Smooth it out with a spatula. Cover the pan and let the paste cool.

Preheat the oven to 350°.

"Our restaurant serves a Mediterranean cuisine, which means that we serve foods from all of the countries that border the Mediterranean Sea. That includes Italy, Spain, southern France, Greece, Corsica, Albania, and so on around to North Africa."

Cut the gnocchi into squares *(or rounds)*. Place them in a buttered pan. Brush on the melted butter and sprinkle on the ¼ cup of Parmesan cheese. Bake them for 7 to 10 minutes, or until they are lightly browned.

serves 8

Sambousek of Lamb

1   tablespoon vegetable oil
1   tablespoon onion, finely chopped
1   tablespoon celery, finely chopped
1   tablespoon carrot, finely chopped
½   teaspoon salt
1   pound lean ground lamb
½   teaspoon ground cumin
1   pinch cayenne pepper
¼   cup dry white wine
1   tablespoon parsley, chopped
1   teaspoon fresh mint, chopped
24 4" phyllo dough squares
1   egg, beaten

In a heavy skillet place the oil and heat it on medium until it is hot. Add the onions, celery, carrots, and salt. Sauté the ingredients for 1 to 2 minutes, or until the vegetables start to become tender.

Add the lamb, cumin, and cayenne pepper. Sauté the ingredients together for 5 to 6 minutes, or until the meat is browned.

Move the ingredients to one side of the pan. Place the empty side over a high heat. Pour the wine into the empty side, bring it to a boil, and flambé it.

Mix the wine together with the solid ingredients. Cover the pan and reduce the heat to medium. Cook the mixture for 5 minutes, or until it has a uniform, paste-like consistency (for a stuffing).

Add the parsley and mint, and mix them in.

Remove the pan from the heat and let the mixture cool.

In the center of each phyllo dough square place a small amount of the mixture. Bring the 4 corners together, twist them, and then firmly pinch them together.

Preheat the oven to 325°. On a lightly greased baking sheet place the stuffed phyllo squares. Brush on the beaten egg. Bake the squares for 8 to 10 minutes, or until they are golden brown.

serves 8

"This is a very nice and spicy appetizer that is popular in the Middle Eastern countries. It is made with lamb, but you can substitute turkey or chicken if you prefer."

"The finished product will look like little purses. They become very crispy when you bake them and they look really pretty. This recipe calls for 3 little purses per person, to be served as an appetizer, but you can serve more of them and have them be an entrée."

"Phyllo dough comes frozen and is available at your local market. It is as good as you could make it yourself, I think, and infinitely easier. It will keep frozen for months, and you can peel off the sheets as you need them."

Fresh Tuna Ragoût with Fennel

3	pounds fresh tuna, sliced into 8 pieces, ½" thick
1	lemon, juiced
½	cup olive oil
¼	cup parsley, chopped
½	cup olive oil
2	medium red onions, sliced into thin rings
3	pounds fresh fennel bulbs, cut in half and minced
2	tablespoons garlic, crushed
¼	teaspoon salt
½	teaspoon crushed red peppers
1	pinch saffron
¼	teaspoon ground ginger
	water *(as needed)*
24	Calamata olives
1	lemon, juiced
⅓	cup parsley, chopped

"This is a recipe from Tunisia in North Africa. I was traveling there and had it in a restaurant. It was so good that I asked for the recipe."

"This recipe calls for a little pinch of saffron, which is a very expensive ingredient, as you well know. Right now it costs about $60 an ounce. I keep my saffron locked up with my jewels! It has a flavor all of its own, which I can't describe. You have to taste it. It is the pistil of a flower and it has to be picked by hand. People spend hours and hours gathering it to acquire one ounce."

"The fennel bulb has an anise flavor. However, it is not that strong, especially when you cook it. It adds a nice, subtle background taste to the ragoût."

In a medium bowl place the tuna, the juice of the first lemon, the first ½ cup of olive oil, and the ¼ cup of parsley. Let the tuna sit for 20 minutes. Turn the tuna over and let it sit for another 20 minutes.

In a large, heavy sauté pan place the other ½ cup of olive oil and heat it on medium high until it is hot. Add the onions and the fennel. Cover the pan and reduce the heat to low. Cook the vegetables for 10 to 15 minutes, or until they are tender.

Add the marinated tuna, garlic, salt, crushed red peppers, saffron, and ginger. Cover the ingredients with water.

Cover the pan and simmer the ingredients for 15 minutes.

Add the olives and bring the liquid to a boil.

Sprinkle on the juice of the other lemon and the ⅓ cup of parsley. Serve the fish right out of the sauté pan.

serves 8

Crêpes Delice with Mangoes

1½	teaspoons sugar
⅛	cup water
1½	teaspoons Kirsch
1	ripe mango, peeled and sliced into 8 pieces
2	teaspoons sugar
¼	cup unsalted butter, softened
½	teaspoon orange rind, grated
¼	teaspoon lemon rind, grated
½	orange, juiced
¼	lemon, juiced
8	Basic Crêpes *(recipe on following page)*
⅛	cup Cointreau
⅛	cup Tuaca
⅛	cup Kirsch
	Crème Fraîche *(recipe on page 49)*

In a small bowl place the 1½ teaspoons of sugar, the water, and the 1½ teaspoons of Kirsch. Mix the ingredients together. Add the sliced mango and let it marinate for 2 hours.

In another small bowl place the 2 teaspoons of sugar, butter, grated orange rind, grated lemon rind, orange juice, and lemon juice. Mix the ingredients together well to make a sauce.

Place 1 mango slice on each crêpe and roll it up.

Add the marinade to the sauce and stir it in.

Preheat the oven to 300°. On each of 4 individual oven-proof serving plates place 2 of the rolled crêpes. Pour the sauce over the crêpes. Place the plates in the oven for 5 to 7 minutes, or until they are hot *(do not burn the crêpes)*.

In a small saucepan place the Cointreau, Tuaca, and the ⅛ cup of Kirsch. Bring the ingredients to a boil. Pour the liquid over the heated crêpes and flambé them. Serve the Crème Fraîche on the side.

serves 4

"Mangoes are somewhat difficult to slice. They are slippery and you have to know how to work with the fiber."

"This is a wonderful dessert that is not too terribly rich. It is very elegant, and when you flambé the crêpes you have an impressive presentation for your guests."

"A lot of movie stars live in Malibu and so we have many famous people who come to our restaurant. But we don't make a big fuss over them because they don't want to be bothered. There are restaurants where movie stars go to be seen, but they come here because they feel comfortable, they know they will be well taken care of, and they love our food."

Basic Crêpes

5	eggs
2	cups milk
1½	cups sifted flour
⅓	cup sugar
⅛	teaspoon salt
½	teaspoon vanilla
½	teaspoon orange zest *(outer orange part grated off)*
¼	teaspoon lemon zest *(outer yellow part grated off)*
⅛	cup Cointreau
2	tablespoons clarified butter

"You may need practice making the crêpes before you really get the hang of it. So don't worry if you ruin the first 2 or 3 that you try to make. If the recipe makes too many crêpes, then freeze the leftovers."

"I really love flavors! I like to use the flavors from a lot of different countries, and I believe in using the best ingredients that I can put my hands on.....even if it's just butter or olive oil."

In a medium bowl place the eggs and milk, and beat them together.

In another medium bowl place the flour, sugar, and salt. Stir them together.

While stirring constantly, slowly add the egg-milk mixture to the flour. Stir the batter until it is smooth.

Add the vanilla, orange zest, lemon zest, and Cointreau. Stir them in well. Cover the bowl and place it in the refrigerator for ½ hour.

Lightly coat a non-stick crêpe pan with some of the clarified butter. Heat it on medium high until it is hot. For each crêpe pour in 3 tablespoons of the batter. Quickly tilt the pan so that the batter covers the bottom. Cook the crêpe for 35 to 40 seconds or until it is lightly browned. Turn it over and cook the other side for 15 seconds.

Let the crêpes cool on a rack. Stack them with pieces of waxed paper in between each one.

makes 8 to 10 crêpes

Lemon Cheese Tart

12	ounces short pastry dough
2	pounds cream cheese, softened
⅓	cup sugar
3	egg yolks
2	lemons, zested *(outer yellow part grated off)* **and juiced**
3	tablespoons cornstarch dissolved in 2 tablespoons of water
3	egg whites
1	pinch salt
3	tablespoons sugar

Preheat the oven to 350°.

Roll out the short pastry dough. Place it in a buttered springform pan, 9½" wide and 2" high. Fill the bottom with dried beans. Bake the dough for 10 to 15 minutes, or until it is barely cooked. Remove the dried beans and set the crust aside.

In a medium bowl place the cream cheese and the ⅓ cup of sugar, and whip them together.

Add the egg yolks, lemon zest, lemon juice, and the cornstarch-water mixture. Mix the ingredients together well.

In a small bowl place the egg whites, salt, and the 3 tablespoons of sugar. Whip the ingredients together until the egg whites form stiff peaks.

Gently fold the egg whites into the cheese mixture.

Preheat the oven to 300°.

Pour the mixture into the pre-baked shell and bake it for 30 minutes. Let the tart cool.

serves 8 to 10

"Our pastry chef is Genevieve Boyer, and she is a real dynamo in the kitchen! She does the work of two men and we are really lucky to have her."

"This dessert is almost like a custard, although when it comes out of the oven it will be puffed up, more like a soufflé. But then as it cools it will fall some."

"You can soften the cream cheese in a microwave."

Crème Fraîche

| 1 | tablespoon plain yogurt |
| 1 | quart whipping cream |

In a medium bowl place the yogurt and cover it with plastic wrap. Let it sit at room temperature for 6 hours.

Add the whipping cream to the yogurt and mix them together so that they are well blended.

Cover the bowl with plastic wrap and let the mixture sit at room temperature overnight.

Store the crème fraîche in the refrigerator.

"Crème fraîche is called for in many recipes, so it's a good thing to know how to make it. Serve it with some fresh berries.... it's wonderful!"

"When you enter the BeauRivage you feel as if you have been transported to an elegant restaurant in Europe. We sit on 5½ acres overlooking the beautiful Pacific Ocean. Marlon Brando came here the other day for the first time. He looked around, and said, 'I didn't know that such a place existed in the United States!' This is the truth.....he really said that!"

Entrance, Anderson House, Malibu

Califia
Manhattan Beach

In the Radisson Plaza Hotel you will find a modern French cuisine served in the elegant and beautifully decorated Califia restaurant.

Chef Tim Owen says, *"This soup is very light and healthy. For a more attractive garnish you can make a chiffonnade of basil. Stack the leaves on top of each other, roll them up tightly, and then slice them very thin."*

Roasted Eggplant Soup

1	**large eggplant**
2	**red bell peppers**
2	**large tomatoes**
3	**tablespoons olive oil**
1	**onion, chopped**
8	**cloves garlic, minced**
1	**teaspoon cumin**
1	**quart chicken stock** *(recipe on page 297)*
½	**cup heavy cream**
	salt *(to taste)*
4	**tablespoons fresh basil, thinly sliced**

Roast the eggplant, bell peppers, and tomatoes by holding them over an open flame *(or broil them)* so that they are black all over. Remove the skins. Remove the seeds from the bell peppers and the tomatoes. Chop the eggplant, bell peppers, and tomatoes. Set them aside.

In a medium large saucepan place the olive oil and heat it on medium high until it is hot. Add the onions and sauté them for 3 to 4 minutes, or until they are tender.

Add the roasted eggplant, bell peppers, and tomatoes. Stir the ingredients together.

Add the garlic, cumin, and chicken stock. Simmer the ingredients for 45 minutes.

Add the cream and stir it in.

Pour the soup into a blender and purée it so that it is smooth.

Season the soup with the salt. Garnish it with the sliced basil.

serves 4

Blue Crab Cakes
with Cayenne Mayonnaise

Blue Crab Cakes

1	stalk celery, finely chopped
1	bunch green onions, finely chopped
1	bunch parsley, finely chopped
1	egg
1	tablespoon Dijon mustard
¾	cup mayonnaise
2	lemons, juiced
½	teaspoon salt
½	teaspoon pepper
1	4¼-ounce box of Carr's Water Biscuits, ground
1	pound Blue Crab meat
4	tablespoons butter *(or as needed)*
	Cayenne Mayonnaise *(recipe on next page)*
2	lemons, wedged

In a medium bowl place the celery, green onions, parsley, egg, mustard, mayonnaise, and lemon juice. Mix the ingredients together well.

Add the salt, pepper, and ground biscuits. Gently mix the ingredients together with your hands so that they are well combined. Carefully fold the crab meat into the mixture. Let the mixture sit for ½ hour in the refrigerator.

Form the mixture into patties.

In a large skillet place the butter and heat it on medium until it has melted. Sauté the crab cakes for 3 to 4 minutes on each side, or until they are golden brown.

Serve the crab cakes with the Cayenne Mayonnaise and the lemon wedges.

serves 8

"Blue crabs are voracious little guys. They are very aggressive and territorial, and they pinch your toes on the beach!"

"These crab cakes are not breaded or deep-fried, so they are very light. There are crackers in the mixture to bind it together. If you can't find Carr's Water Biscuits you can use saltine crackers."

"You add the crab meat after the other ingredients have been mixed together, and then you gently fold it in. Be careful not to mush up the crab meat.....you want to maintain its integrity."

"This is presented as an appetizer in the recipe because of the size of the portions, but it also would be great for lunch. You can make the cakes any size you want. Once I made them the size of silver dollars and served them at a large party. I had someone standing there cooking them to order, and the people really enjoyed that."

Cayenne Mayonnaise

1	red bell pepper, roasted, peeled, and seeded
2	egg yolks
1	tablespoon white wine vinegar
1	lemon, juiced
1½	teaspoons capers
6	cloves garlic
8	anchovy fillets
1½	teaspoons cayenne pepper
1	cup salad oil
	salt *(to taste)*

In a blender place the roasted red bell pepper, egg yolks, white wine vinegar, lemon juice, capers, garlic, anchovy fillets, and cayenne pepper. Blend the ingredients together so that they are smooth.

With the blender still running, slowly dribble in the salad oil so that a mayonnaise is formed. Correct the seasoning with the salt *(and more lemon juice)* if necessary.

"Crab cakes come from the East Coast. They are usually breaded and deep-fried, and they are served with rich tartar sauce. So I came up with this recipe as an alternative. The consistency is much lighter, and the flavors are wonderful. The anchovies and capers blend together very well, and they balance out the hotness of the cayenne pepper and the tartness of the lemon."

"The anchovies are salty, so you should only add salt to the mayonnaise after you taste it. And don't be afraid of the flavor of the anchovies..... they blend in perfectly. It's like with a Caesar salad.....the anchovy is an essential background flavor, but it doesn't stand out and say, 'Hey, taste me! I'm an anchovy!' "

"I rarely make anything at home. If I open a carton of yogurt I am really doing well!"

Heart of Romaine
and Watercress
with Basil Anchovy Sauce

Heart of Romaine and Watercress

1	cup Basil Anchovy Sauce *(recipe follows)*
2	heads Belgian endive, washed and dried
2	hearts of romaine, split in half
2	bunches watercress
4	cherry tomatoes, quartered and seeds removed

On each of 4 individual salad plates pour ¼ cup of the Basil Anchovy Sauce. Spread it around evenly.

Place 4 endive spears on the plate so that they are facing in the same direction.

Place one of the halved hearts of romaine on top of the endive spears, so that just their tips are showing.

Place the watercress at the stem end of the romaine.

Place the tomato quarters on the romaine.

serves 4

Basil Anchovy Sauce

1	cup Chablis
½	cup white wine vinegar
8	cloves garlic, chopped
2	shallots, chopped
6	anchovy fillets
1	bunch basil
2	egg yolks
1	lemon, juiced
¼	cup extra virgin olive oil
	salt *(to taste)*
	pepper *(to taste)*

(continued on next page)

"This salad is essentially like a Caesar salad, except that the presentation and the dressing are different. By not tossing the ingredients together the presentation is greatly enhanced over that of a tossed salad. It looks beautiful when it is all put together. The various lettuces sit on top of the sauce so you can see how beautiful they are."

"The sauce is a mayonnaise, with one wine reduction to start with. When you put the basil leaves in the blender with the hot reduction, they turn bright green. The flavors are wonderful, and they blend together perfectly. Again, you don't have to worry about the taste of the anchovies standing out."

"Creativity is involved in putting together an entire dish. There must be beauty, color, and integrity. In other words, don't put something on the plate just because it has the right color or shape. It also must make sense flavor-wise. Otherwise, it will be shocking or bizarre."

In a small saucepan place the Chablis, white wine vinegar, garlic, shallots, and anchovies. Heat the ingredients on medium low and simmer them for 8 to 10 minutes, or until the liquid is reduced to ¼ cup. Strain the liquid.

In a blender place the basil and the strained, reduced liquid. Purée the ingredients until they are smooth.

Add the egg yolks and the lemon juice, and purée them. While the blender is running, slowly add the olive oil.

Season the sauce with the salt and the pepper.

Court Bouillon

2	quarts water
½	cup carrots, chopped
½	cup celery, chopped
1	small onion, chopped
¼	cup parsley, chopped
1	bay leaf
1	tablespoon fresh thyme, chopped
1	tablespoon fresh basil, chopped
2	cloves garlic
10	black peppercorns
1	teaspoon salt
¼	cup white wine vinegar
¼	cup white wine

"Court bouillon is used mainly for cooking fish and shellfish. Foods that are cooked in the liquid will absorb the flavor of the ingredients in the bouillon."

"I learned to be my own judge as to what tastes good, and to trust that other people will like what I like."

In a large saucepan place all of the ingredients. Bring the liquid to a boil and then simmer it for 30 minutes. Let it cool.

Strain the broth.

Steamed King Salmon with Basil Sauce

Steamed King Salmon

1½ pounds salmon fillet, trimmed and sliced diagonally into
     12 strips, 1" wide and 4" long
12   leaves of spinach
1   cup Basil Sauce *(recipe follows)*
1   head Belgian endive
2   ounces salmon caviar

On each strip of salmon place a spinach leaf. Fold the salmon strip over on top of itself. Place the salmon in a steamer and cook it for 2 minutes, or until it is just done.

On each of 4 individual serving plates place ¼ of the Basil Sauce. Artfully arrange three of the salmon strips and three endive spears on top. Garnish the dish with the caviar.

serves 4

Basil Sauce

1   tablespoon butter
6   shallots, thinly sliced
4   cloves garlic, thinly sliced
1   cup Chablis
1   cup clam juice
¼   cup white wine vinegar
¼   cup heavy cream
1   lemon, juiced
2   sticks sweet butter, cut into pieces
½   bunch basil, stems removed
     salt *(to taste)*

In a medium saucepan place the 1 tablespoon of butter and heat it on medium high until it has melted. Add the shallots and garlic. Sauté them for 2 to 3 minutes, or until the shallots are tender. Add the Chablis, clam juice, and white wine vinegar. Cook the ingredients for 15 to 20 minutes, or until it is reduced to ¼ cup.

(continued on next page)

"This is an elegant looking plate when it is put together. The only difficulty lies in determining how long to cook the salmon. You want all of the juices to be inside the fish. If you see any white fat seeping out then you have cooked it too long. Cook it so that it is medium rare, because it will continue to cook until you eat it."

"You can buy salmon caviar in the refrigerated gourmet section of your market. It's not too expensive and it makes an attractive garnish."

"The Basil Sauce is beautiful and it goes together with the salmon very well. It will be light green in color, and it looks so pretty next to the pink salmon and the dark green spinach."

Add the heavy cream and the lemon juice. Reduce the heat to low and simmer the ingredients for 1 to 2 minutes, or until the liquid starts to thicken.

Raise the heat to medium. While whisking constantly, add the pieces of butter one at a time.

Strain the sauce into a blender. Add the basil leaves. Purée the sauce and then season it with the salt. Add some water if the sauce is too thick.

Marinated Gulf Shrimp with Cellophane Noodles

"These shrimp have an interesting Oriental twist to them, and they are delicious! This is a perfect thing to serve on a large platter at a buffet."

2	**quarts court bouillon** (*recipe on page 55*)
16	**jumbo gulf shrimp**
¼	**cup lime juice, freshly squeezed**
2	**tablespoons fresh ginger, chopped**
1	**bunch cilantro, chopped** (*reserve 4 sprigs for the garnish*)
2	**green onions, chopped**
1	**teaspoon Szechwan peppercorns, crushed**
1	**teaspoon salt** (*or to taste*)
1	**teaspoon Oriental Mixed Chile Powder**
¾	**cup salad oil**
5	**drops dark sesame oil**
½	**pound cellophane noodles, cooked**
1	**cup red cabbage, finely shredded**
1	**carrot, finely julienned and quickly blanched**

"Cellophane noodles are made out of bean threads, and when you cook them they turn clear."

In a large saucepot place the court bouillon. Bring it to a boil over high heat. Add the shrimp and poach them for 2 minutes. Remove the shrimp and place them in the refrigerator so that they chill. Peel and devein the shrimp. Leave the tails on.

"I think you can find the Szechwan peppercorns fairly easily. The Oriental Mixed Chile Powder might be harder to locate. I buy it in an Oriental store in my neighborhood."

In a medium bowl place the lime juice, ginger, cilantro, green onions, crushed Szechwan peppercorns, salt, Oriental Mixed Chile Powder, salad oil, and sesame oil. Let the mixture sit for 24 hours. Strain the marinade into another bowl. Add the shrimp and let them sit for ½ hour.

In each of 4 individual serving bowls pour the marinade. Place the noodles on top. Add the red cabbage and the carrots. Place 4 shrimp on top, with the tails pointing to the center of the bowl.

serves 4

Rack of Lamb in Mustard Crust with Northern White Beans

Rack of Lamb in Mustard Crust

1	sprig rosemary, chopped
2	cloves garlic, chopped
½	cup Chablis
4	tablespoons Dijon mustard
4	tablespoons extra virgin olive oil
	salt
	pepper
2	9-rib racks of lamb, well trimmed and cut between each third bone
4	tablespoons sweet butter *(or as needed)*
	Northern White Beans *(recipe on next page)*

In a small saucepan place the rosemary, garlic, and Chablis. Cook the ingredients on medium heat for 4 to 6 minutes, or until the liquid is reduced to 2 tablespoons.

Pour the mixture into a blender and purée it. Add the mustard and blend it in. With the blender still running, slowly dribble in the olive oil. Season the mustard paste with the salt and set it aside.

Season the lamb with the salt and the pepper. Coat both sides with the mustard paste.

In a large sauté pan place the butter and heat it on medium high until it has melted. Add the lamb racks and sauté them for 2 to 3 minutes on each side, or until they are lightly browned.

Preheat the oven to 450°. Place the lamb racks in a baking pan and roast them for 10 minutes, or until they are medium rare. Turn the lamb so that all sides are evenly browned.

Remove the lamb racks from the oven and place them on a warm plate. Let them rest for 5 minutes. Slice the lamb between each bone.

On each of 6 individual serving plates place the Northern White Beans. Place the lamb on top.

serves 6

"People usually don't think of cooking a rack of lamb at home because they are used to ordering it in a restaurant. But it's very easy to do and it is the perfect thing to serve at a nice dinner party. Ask your butcher to remove the chine bones."

"This dish is our number one best seller. Try it..... you'll love it!"

"I always strive to make my dishes healthy, even though the people who come to the restaurant might want to splurge."

"For me, cooking is both a challenge and a frustration. You never know how many customers are going to come and you don't know what they are going to order when they get here. So there is a continual guessing game in so far as what to prepare, and how much to prepare. This is a real challenge, because no matter how carefully you predict, you can still be completely wrong. When this happens we do a lot of running around in the kitchen!"

Northern White Beans

¼   **cup extra virgin olive oil**
½   **onion, diced**
¼   **pound pancetta** *(Italian style bacon)*, **diced**
1   **bratwurst, diced**
1   **chicken leg, boned, skin removed, and diced**
¾   **cup dried Northern White Beans, soaked in water overnight and drained**
1   **large tomato, peeled, seeded, and diced**
2   **cups chicken stock** *(recipe on page 297)*
2   **bay leaves**
½   **bunch thyme, chopped**
     salt *(to taste)*
     pepper *(to taste)*

In a medium saucepan place the olive oil and heat it on medium high until it is hot. Add the onions and sauté them for 2 to 3 minutes, or until they are tender.

Add the pancetta, bratwurst, and chicken. Sauté the ingredients for 5 minutes.

Add the soaked beans, tomatoes, chicken stock, bay leaves, and thyme.

Simmer the beans for 1½ hours, or until they are tender. Add the salt and the pepper, and stir them in.

Remove the bay leaves and strain off the liquid *(reserve it for a future use)*.

serves 6

"These beans can be made the day before. They are one of those wonderful dishes that tastes even better the next day. The recipe is based on a French dish in which the French housewife uses all of her leftover scraps of meat and juices from the last couple of days."

"Beans are normally bland tasting, but in this dish they are rich and delicious! Use any other leftover items that you have in your refrigerator. You can use another kind of sausage, but it must be a hearty one."

"As a chef I am being judged every single day by our customers, depending upon how much they enjoyed the food. This is part of the challenge!"

Sunset, Manhattan Beach

Caruso & Me
San Pedro

Fashioned after a neighborhood Italian *trattoria*, Caruso & Me has the perfect atmosphere in which to enjoy its delicious Italian and Mediterranean cuisine.

Menu

Caruso's Italian Mushrooms

Greek Salad

Tortellini con Pomodoro à la Caruso

Scampi with Angel Hair Pasta

Grilled Sea Bass with Capers

Grilled Marinated Lamb Loin Chops and Baby Vegetables

Fresh Mango Sorbetto with Coulis of Raspberries

Owner and chef, Louis "Bif" Caruso says, *"This is one of the best appetizers that you will ever taste..... and it couldn't be simpler to make!"*

Caruso's Italian Mushrooms

8	large shiitake mushrooms, stems removed
2	tablespoons olive oil
1	teaspoon lemon juice
1	teaspoon balsamic vinegar
½	teaspoon mixed dried herbs
1	tablespoon fresh tomatoes, diced
1	tablespoon sun-dried tomatoes, diced
2	black olives, sliced
1	tablespoon Parmesan cheese, freshly grated
1	tablespoon mozzarella cheese, grated

In a medium bowl place the mushrooms, olive oil, lemon juice, balsamic vinegar, and herbs. Let the mushrooms marinate for 1 hour.

Place the mushrooms on a baking sheet. Sprinkle on the fresh tomatoes and the sun-dried tomatoes. Place the sliced olives on top.

Sprinkle on the Parmesan and mozzarella cheeses.

Place the mushrooms under a preheated broiler for 1 minute, or until the cheese has melted.

serves 4

Greek Salad

2	cups red wine vinegar
2	cups extra virgin olive oil
2	cups white wine
2	pounds button mushrooms
16	green olives
24	Greek olives
12	cloves garlic, chopped
12	small shallots, chopped
2	teaspoons fresh tarragon, finely chopped
½	teaspoon salt
8	large leaves of butter lettuce
4	green onions, sliced and cut into 2" long pieces
2	carrots, julienned
4	parsley sprigs
2	lemons, cut into wedges

In a large saucepan place the red wine vinegar, olive oil, and white wine. Cook the ingredients on medium high heat for 4 to 6 minutes, or until the liquid is caramel colored and reduced by ½.

Add the mushrooms, green olives, Greek olives, garlic, shallots, tarragon, and salt. Simmer the ingredients for 4 to 6 minutes, or until the liquid is reduced by ½. Let the mixture cool.

On each of 4 individual serving plates place 2 of the lettuce leaves. Spoon on the cooked vegetables with the juice.

Sprinkle on the onions and carrots. Garnish the dish with the parsley and the lemon wedges.

serves 4

"This is a wonderful, festive dish that is full of delicious flavors from the Mediterranean. It's almost like an Italian antipasto. Serve this with some good bread for lunch.....and have fun eating it!"

"I have been involved in cooking and racing cars since 1948, and I love them both equally. I am probably the only person in the United States, or maybe even the whole world, who is both a Certified Chief Mechanic and a Certified Executive Chef. In 1967 we raced at Indianapolis and had a 7th place finish."

Tortellini con Pomodoro
à la Caruso

3	tablespoons extra virgin olive oil
½	onion, finely chopped
1⅓	pounds tomatoes, blanched, peeled, seeded, and coarsely chopped
2	cloves garlic, finely chopped
2	tablespoons dry white wine
	salt *(to taste)*
	pepper *(to taste)*
1	teaspoon fresh basil leaves, chopped
1	pound tortellini, cooked al dente
⅔	cup Parmesan cheese, freshly grated

In a medium saucepan place the olive oil and heat it on medium high until it is hot. Add the onions and sauté them for 2 to 3 minutes, or until they are translucent.

Add the chopped tomatoes, garlic, and white wine. Bring the ingredients to a boil and then reduce the heat to low. Simmer the sauce for 10 minutes, or until it is nicely thickened.

Add the salt, pepper, and basil, and stir them in.

Add the sauce to the cooked tortellini and toss it in so that all of the pasta is well coated.

Add ½ of the Parmesan cheese and mix it in well.

Sprinkle the remainder of the Parmesan cheese on top.

serves 4

"We make our own sun-dried tomatoes because the commercial ones are too salty. We slice Roma tomatoes in half, sprinkle on a bit of salt, and put them in the oven on top of a rack. We leave them there for many hours with just the pilot light on, until they get all shriveled and dried out. Then we chop them up and store them in olive oil with some basil and garlic."

"This is a very simple, light dish that can be quickly prepared. There is no cream in it and it is good for you to eat. I love dishes like this.....ones that taste good but at the same time are light and healthy."

"I'll bet that you didn't know that the shape of tortellini pasta is modeled after the navel of Venus de Milo."

64

Scampi with Angel Hair Pasta

1	tablespoon sweet butter
2	tablespoons extra virgin olive oil
12	cloves garlic, finely chopped
4	teaspoons parsley, finely chopped
4	shallots, finely chopped
½	cup scallions, finely chopped
24	large shrimp, peeled and deveined
¼	teaspoon paprika
⅛	teaspoon salt
⅛	teaspoon pepper
¼	cup dry white wine
½	pound angel hair pasta, cooked al dente
1	tablespoon sweet butter
1	lemon, cut into 4 wedges

In a large skillet place the first tablespoon of butter and the olive oil. Heat them on medium high until the butter has melted and the oil is hot. Add the garlic, parsley, shallots, and scallions. Sauté the ingredients for 3 to 4 minutes, or until the garlic is limp but not browned.

Add the shrimp, paprika, salt, and pepper. Gently stir the shrimp for 2 to 3 minutes, or until they are halfway done.

Add the white wine and simmer the sauce for 2 to 3 minutes, or until the liquid is almost absorbed and the shrimp are pink.

Gently toss the cooked angel hair pasta with the second tablespoon of butter.

On each of 4 individual serving plates place a serving of the pasta. Place the shrimp on top. Pour on the sauce. Garnish the dish with the lemon wedges.

serves 4

"When you are simmering the shrimp in the wine be sure that you do not overcook them. You might have to remove the shrimp from the pan and then cook the sauce a little longer by itself so that it reduces enough."

"When people come to my restaurant I want them to savor the food and really enjoy themselves. I also want them to feel completely relaxed.....like they are guests in my own home. I never want them to feel like customers."

"Chefs don't stir what they are sautéing. Rather, they shake the pan and flip the ingredients around. You can practice doing this at home by using a piece of dry toast. Once you get the hang of it, it's great!"

Caruso & Me

Grilled Sea Bass with Capers

"This fish dish looks very classy on the plate. It's a great thing for dieters because even though it is low in calories, the shallots, capers, wine, lemon juice, and olive oil give it an excellent flavor. Two years ago I lost 68 pounds, so I am very conscious of the food that I prepare."

"Rinse the capers before you use them and that will get rid of the vinegar taste."

"Cooking and car racing have a lot of similarities. To be good at either one you need to be well organized, have strong concentration, and love what you are doing!"

1	teaspoon olive oil
1	teaspoon shallots, finely chopped
1	tablespoon capers
½	teaspoon parsley, finely chopped
1	tablespoon white wine
1	teaspoon lemon juice, freshly squeezed
1	tablespoon olive oil
1	tablespoon lemon juice, freshly squeezed
4	sea bass fillets, 1½" thick
1	lemon, cut into 4 wedges

In a small saucepan place the teaspoon of olive oil and heat it on medium until it is hot. Add the shallots and sauté them for 3 to 4 minutes, or until they are tender. Add the capers, parsley, white wine, and the teaspoon of lemon juice. Cook the sauce for 1 minute. Set it aside and keep it warm.

In a small bowl place the tablespoon of olive oil and the tablespoon of lemon juice. Set it aside.

In an outdoor grill build a fire with charcoal briquettes. Let the fire burn down to hot coals.

Place the sea bass fillets on the grill. Baste them with the olive oil and lemon juice. Cook the fillets for 4 to 5 minutes on each side, or until they are just done.

On each of 4 individual serving plates place a fish fillet. Pour the sauce over the fish. Garnish the dish with a lemon wedge.

serves 4

Grilled Marinated Lamb Loin Chops and Baby Vegetables

3	cups extra virgin olive oil
1	lemon, juiced
⅓	bunch fresh rosemary, finely chopped
⅔	bunch fresh thyme, finely chopped
5	cloves garlic, minced
3	shallots, minced
1	teaspoon parsley, chopped
8	double lamb loin chops
4	baby carrots, peeled and blanched
4	baby turnips, peeled and blanched
4	baby zucchini, blanched
2	Japanese eggplants, sliced, salted, and drained

In a medium bowl place the olive oil, lemon juice, rosemary, thyme, garlic, shallots, and parsley. Add the lamb chops and marinate them overnight in the refrigerator.

Remove the lamb chops from the marinade and set them aside.

Add the blanched vegetables to the marinade and let them sit for 1 hour.

Grill *(or broil)* the lamb chops for 3 to 4 minutes on each side, or until they are medium rare.

Grill *(or broil)* the marinated vegetables for 2 to 3 minutes, or until they are warmed through.

On each of 4 individual serving plates place two of the lamb chops and an attractive arrangement of the vegetables.

serves 4

"You can cook the lamb on the grill, or you can just sear it and then bake it in the oven with a little white wine. We like to serve it with the grill marks on top of the meat."

"This is a Mediterranean dish that is simple to make and very healthy. The marinade gives the lamb and the baby vegetables a wonderful flavor."

"I love people, and I get a real kick out of watching them mop up the last of the sauce on their plate with a piece of good bread. I know then that they enjoyed the meal with the innermost part of their being. This is my creative reward!"

Fresh Mango Sorbetto
with Coulis of Raspberries

*"This dessert is very
popular in Italy. It is a
creamy, flavored ice, and
it can be used as a palate
cleanser as well as a
dessert. You may use
fresh strawberries,
peaches, or any other
kind of fresh fruit that is
in season."*

*"I believe in keeping
cooking as simple as
possible. When I first
started cooking I read
some French cookbooks. I
remember thinking,
'Wow! This is ridiculous!'
I was overwhelmed by the
complexity of the recipes."*

*"A good cook must treat
the food with care and
kindness. He also must be
willing to experiment."*

*"I really and truly enjoy
what I am doing. I put in
long hours, but to me it is
not work.....it is a
pleasure!"*

4	mangoes, peeled and seeded
2/3	cup champagne
2/3	cup fresh mint, finely chopped *(reserve 6 leaves for the garnish)*
2	cups fresh raspberries
1/2	cup orange juice, freshly squeezed
2/3	cup fresh raspberries
6	Ladyfingers *(recipe on page 303)*

Place the mangoes in a blender and purée them.

Add the champagne and mint, and blend them in. Place the mixture in bowl and freeze it for 4 hours.

Place the 2 cups of raspberries and the orange juice in a blender, and liquefy them. Strain the mixture through a fine sieve so that the seeds are removed. Chill the coulis of raspberries in the refrigerator.

Remove the frozen mango sorbet and blend it again.

In each of 6 chilled bowls place the coulis of raspberries. Place the frozen mango sorbet on top. Sprinkle on part of the 2/3 cup of the fresh raspberries. Garnish the dessert with a mint leaf and a Ladyfinger.

serves 6

Building Façade Detail, Hermosa Beach

Chez Melange

Redondo Beach

The popular Chez Melange keeps the feeling of newness, freshness, and excitement alive by serving an imaginative, eclectic Continental cuisine.

Menu

Chez Melange Gazpacho

Cajun Tostada with Tomato Cumin Dressing

Turkey Jalapeño Sausage Reuben with Southwestern Slaw and Black Bean Relish

Shrimp and Sea Scallop Stir-Fry with Julienned Vegetables and Soba Noodles

Country Chicken Ragoût

Pesto Salmon and Sea Scallops with Lemon Roasted Garlic Beurre Blanc

Loin of Lamb en Croûte with Roasted Shallot Balsamic Vinegar Sauce

Chez Melange Dipping Sauce

Biscotti di Anise

Executive Chef Bill Donnelly says, *"I like to serve this soup in a big bowl with chips around it and some guacamole on the side. It's a wonderful, refreshing dish that is perfect on a hot summer day."*

Chez Melange Gazpacho

1	cucumber, peeled, seeded, and diced
2	tomatoes, diced
½	onion, diced
½	red bell pepper, seeded and diced
½	yellow bell pepper, seeded and diced
½	green bell pepper, seeded and diced
2	tablespoons fresh dill, chopped
2	tablespoons fresh cilantro, chopped
1	pint beef stock
1	tablespoon olive oil
1½	tablespoons red wine vinegar
1	teaspoon garlic, finely chopped
1	teaspoon tabasco sauce
2	teaspoons salt
½	teaspoon white pepper
1	pint tomato juice

Combine all of the ingredients and mix them together well. Chill the soup.

serves 8

Cajun Tostada with Tomato Cumin Dressing

Cajun Tostada

4	chicken breasts, skin and bones removed
½	cup Cajun blackening powder *(or as needed)*
3	tablespoons vegetable oil
¼	cup vegetable oil
4	flour tortillas
2	cups iceberg lettuce, shredded
6	ounces feta cheese, crumbled
	Tomato Cumin Dressing *(recipe on next page)*
⅔	cup spiced refried beans, heated
1	avocado, peeled, pitted, and sliced

Dredge the chicken breasts in the Cajun blackening powder so that they are well coated

In a large cast iron skillet place the 3 tablespoons of vegetable oil and heat it on high until it is very hot. Add the coated chicken breasts and fry them for 2 minutes on each side, or until they are done. Remove the chicken and slice it into diagonal strips. Set it aside.

In another large skillet place the ¼ cup of oil and heat it on medium high until it is hot. One at a time, fry each tortilla for 1 minute on each side, or until it is crisp. Drain the fried tortillas on paper towels and set them aside.

In a medium bowl place the lettuce and the feta cheese. Sprinkle on the Tomato Cumin Dressing and toss the ingredients together well.

Spread the refried beans on each of the fried tortillas. Place the tossed lettuce, sliced chicken, and cheese on top. Garnish the tostada with 2 avocado slices.

serves 4

"This dish used to be a special in the restaurant, but it proved to be so popular that we put it on the regular menu. It's one of the best tostadas you'll ever eat!"

"You can buy the blackening powder ready made in the store, although we make our own at the restaurant. The chicken will turn black on the outside when you fry it. It won't be burned, so don't be scared! This way of cooking the chicken will give it a great flavor and keep it moist on the inside."

Tomato Cumin Dressing

3	tomatoes, cored, halved, and grilled
1	egg yolk
1	jalapeño chile pepper, halved
⅓	bunch cilantro
3	tablespoons lime juice, freshly squeezed
4½	tablespoons Dijon mustard
2	teaspoons ground cumin
1½	cups salad oil
	salt *(to taste)*
	pepper *(to taste)*

In a food processor place the tomatoes and purée them.

Add the egg yolk, jalapeño chile pepper, cilantro, lime juice, mustard, and cumin. Blend the ingredients together until the mixture is smooth.

With the food processor running on low, very slowly dribble in the oil. Add the salt and the pepper.

makes 2½ cups

"In this recipe we do not remove the seeds from the jalapeño pepper, even though they are the hottest part. The dressing is not very spicy.....it just has a nice bite to it. You may use the roasted jalapeños that come in a can, if you want. Their flavor is delicious, but they are really fiery! So if you use these, be very cautious. Add just a tiny bit at a time and keep tasting the dressing until you get it right."

"I got into cooking because of my grandmother. Every summer I would visit her in Nova Scotia, and in the winter she lived with our family. She was always cooking and I was always watching her. I remember how I would stand and watch her kneading the dough for fresh bread, and she would slap me in the face with it!"

Turkey Jalapeño Sausage Reuben with Southwestern Slaw and Black Bean Relish

Turkey Jalapeño Sausage Reuben

1	tablespoon bacon fat
⅔	cup onions, finely diced
3	cloves garlic, finely minced
3	jalapeño chile peppers, seeded and finely diced
⅓	cup bread crumbs
⅓	cup milk
1¼	teaspoons salt
1	egg
1	egg white
⅓	cup heavy cream
1	tablespoon vegetable oil
1	pound ground turkey
¼	bunch cilantro, finely chopped
8	slices rye bread
8	slices Monterey Jack cheese
8	slices tomato
	Southwestern Slaw *(recipe on next page)*
	Black Bean Relish *(recipe on next page)*

In a medium skillet place the bacon fat and heat it on medium until it is hot. Add the onions and garlic, and sauté them for 4 to 5 minutes, or until the onions are tender. Let the vegetables cool and then purée them.

In a large bowl place the jalapeño chile peppers, bread crumbs, milk, salt, and puréed onions. Gently mix the ingredients together so that they are well blended.

In a medium bowl place the egg, egg white, and heavy cream. Whisk the ingredients together.

Add the oil and ground turkey, and mix them in with your hands. Add the cilantro and mix it in. Add the bread crumb mixture, and mix it in well with your hands. Shape the meat mixture into 8 patties that are the size of the bread slices.

Preheat the oven to 350°. Place the patties in a baking pan and bake them for 10 minutes on each side, or until they are firm.

(continued on next page)

"Once you get all of the ingredients gathered, this is very easy to put together. In the restaurant we stuff the sausage meat into casings, so this recipe is a simplified version because it calls for sausage patties instead. They taste just as good!"

"The raw sausage meat is quite sticky, so when you are ready to form the patties you should coat your hands with some oil."

"Turkey is wonderful to work with. It's inexpensive, tasty, and low in fat. People who live in Southern California and on the beach are really into their bodies and their health. And, as we all know, foods that are low in fat are good for you. So this is a great recipe, because it is both delicious and healthy."

On each slice of the bread place a slice of cheese and tomato. Place the bread slices under a preheated broiler until the cheese has melted.

Place one baked sausage patty on top of each grilled bread piece. Top it with the Southwestern Slaw. Serve the Black Bean Relish on the side.

serves 8

Southwestern Slaw

½   **head red cabbage, julienned**
½   **red onion, finely julienned**
½   **teaspoon salt**
2   **teaspoons ground cumin**
2   **tablespoons brown sugar**
¼   **cup red wine vinegar**
1   **teaspoon Colorado chile powder**

In a medium bowl place all of the ingredients. Toss them together well.

Let the mixture sit for 15 minutes.

Black Bean Relish

⅔   **cup black beans, cooked until tender and drained**
½   **bunch cilantro, chopped**
½   **cup corn**
⅓   **cup red bell peppers, seeded and diced the size of the beans**
2   **tablespoons olive oil**
1   **lime, juiced**
2   **dashes tabasco sauce** *(or to taste)*
     salt *(to taste)*
     pepper *(to taste)*

In a medium bowl place all of the ingredients and stir them together. Let the relish sit for 1 hour before serving it.

"The flavor of this coleslaw is really neat! It's sweet, sour, and hot, like the yin and the yang of the Orient. Yet, it definitely has a Southwestern taste to it."

"Although the recipe says to let the slaw sit for 15 minutes, that's just the minimum time. You can make it a day ahead, if you want."

"This relish makes a nice, colorful addition to your plate. The flavors from the lime and olive oil combine very well with the heat of the tabasco sauce. I love recipes like this where something so simple to make tastes so wonderful!"

74

Shrimp and Sea Scallop Stir-Fry with Julienned Vegetables and Soba Noodles

6	tablespoons vegetable oil
8	ounces shrimp, peeled and deveined
8	ounces sea scallops
3	carrots, julienned
4	stalks celery cut into 1" pieces *(at an angle)*
2	red bell peppers, seeded and julienned
2	yellow bell peppers, seeded and julienned
2	green bell peppers, seeded and julienned
12	mushrooms, sliced
3	teaspoons garlic, minced
1	bunch cilantro, chopped
1	bunch scallions, cut into 1" pieces *(at an angle)*
2	limes, juiced
1	teaspoon dried red pepper flakes *(or to taste)*
¼	cup dry sherry
⅓	cup soy sauce
1	pound soba noodles, cooked al dente

In a large, heated wok *(or sauté pan)* place the oil and heat it on high until it just begins to smoke. Add the shrimp and scallops, and stri-fry them for 3 minutes.

Add the carrots, celery, bell peppers, mushrooms, and garlic. Stir-fry them for 2 minutes.

Add the cilantro and scallions, and toss them in.

Add the lime juice, dried red pepper flakes, and sherry. Mix the ingredients together and cook them for 1 minute, or until the liquid is reduced by ½.

Add the soy sauce and mix it in.

Add the soba noodles and toss them in.

serves 4

"Here is another example of a dish that is easy to make, tasty, and healthy. Our restaurant caters to people who are very health and diet conscious. We get a lot of good looking people in here!"

"The soba noodle is a buckwheat noodle that has a very distinctive flavor all its own. You can substitute another kind of noodle, or even rice, if you want, but I think that the soba tastes the best."

"We have a free rein in the kitchen to be as creative as we dare. This freedom keeps the energy level extremely high! We like to be innovative, so that we are at the forefront of new trends."

Chez Melange

Country Chicken Ragoût

2	tablespoons vegetable oil
4	6-ounce chicken breasts, skin and bones removed
32	canned pearl onions, outer skins removed
8	large mushrooms, quartered
8	slices extra thick bacon, diced, cooked, and drained
2	cloves garlic, crushed
12	baby artichokes (fresh or frozen), cooked and halved
12	sun-dried tomatoes, julienned
4	teaspoons fresh tarragon, chopped
¼	cup pine nuts
¼	cup cream sherry
1	cup chicken stock (recipe on page 297)
1	cup heavy cream
	salt (to taste)
	pepper (to taste)

In a large skillet place the oil and heat it on medium high until it is hot. Add the chicken breasts and sauté them for 3 minutes on each side, or until they are lightly browned.

Add the pearl onions, mushrooms, bacon, and garlic. Sauté the ingredients for 3 minutes.

Add the baby artichokes, sun-dried tomatoes, tarragon, and pine nuts. Sauté the ingredients for 2 minutes.

Add the sherry and cook it for 1 minute, or until it is reduced by ¼.

Add the chicken stock and cook it for 3 to 4 minutes, or until it is reduced by ¾.

Add the heavy cream and cook it for 2 to 3 minutes, or until the sauce thickens.

Add the salt and the pepper.

serves 4

"This is an excellent recipe that is served a lot in the restaurant. There are many flavors in it, and they combine together in a most excellent way! It is based on a French regional country dish."

"Every Monday we offer specials that are based on the cuisine of one particular country. This forces us to keep experimenting so that we are always coming up with new ideas for recipes."

"I really recommend using chicken stock that you have made yourself. I know that it's a lot of trouble, but your dish will taste so much better, and it freezes well."

"If you can find fresh baby artichokes that would be great, because they really do add a lot of character to the dish."

Pesto Salmon and Sea Scallops with Lemon Roasted Garlic Beurre Blanc

Pesto Salmon and Sea Scallops

4	tablespoons Basic Pesto *(recipe follows)*
4	6-ounce salmon fillets
1	cup herbed bread crumbs
8	large sea scallops
	Lemon Roasted Garlic Beurre Blanc *(recipe on next page)*

Brush the Basic Pesto on top of each salmon fillet. Sprinkle the herbed bread crumbs on top.

Preheat the oven to 375°. In an oiled baking dish place the salmon and the scallops. Bake them for 12 to 15 minutes, or until they are just done. Turn them over once.

On each of 4 individual serving plates place the Lemon Roasted Garlic Beurre Blanc. Place a salmon fillet and two sea scallops on top of the sauce.

serves 4

Basic Pesto

1	cup fresh basil
¼	cup pine nuts
3	cloves garlic
½	cup olive oil *(or as needed)*
3	tablespoons heavy cream
¼	cup Parmesan cheese

In a blender place the basil, pine nuts, and garlic. Purée them so that they are smooth. With the blender running on low, slowly dribble in enough of the olive oil until a puréed consistency is achieved *(do not add too much oil)*. Add the heavy cream and Parmesan cheese, and stir them in.

"At Chez Melange we use a Norwegian salmon, but you could also use a halibut or Chilean sea bass. You need a firm-fleshed fish that can be baked."

"This dish makes a beautiful presentation because of all the nice colors in it. And the great thing is that it is so simple to make."

"There is a nice contrast of textures in this dish, with the crispiness of the crust, and then the tenderness of the fish. It's a wonderful thing to eat, from top to bottom!"

"The only warning that I have in making the pesto is not to add too much of the olive oil. If you do, then the purée will break. Add more Parmesan cheese if the pesto seems too thin."

Lemon Roasted Garlic Beurre Blanc

16	**cloves garlic**
1	**cup white wine**
2	**lemons, juiced**
1	**lemon, zested** *(outer yellow part grated off)*
2	**tablespoons heavy cream**
3	**shallots, finely diced**
2	**sticks butter, cut into small pieces**
	salt *(to taste)*
	pepper *(to taste)*

Preheat the oven to 375°. Place the garlic cloves on a baking sheet and roast them for 10 to 12 minutes, or until they are golden brown. Chop the roasted garlic.

In a small saucepan place the white wine, lemon juice, lemon zest, heavy cream, and shallots. Cook the ingredients on medium high for 8 to 10 minutes, or until the liquid is reduced to ¼ and is the consistency of a thin syrup.

Reduce the heat to low. While stirring constantly, slowly add the pieces of butter one at a time, and whisk each piece in so that it is well incorporated.

Add the roasted garlic, salt, and pepper.

"All of you garlic lovers should really love this sauce! Actually, the garlic flavor is not overwhelming because the cloves have been roasted. It provides a delicious complement to the lemon."

"We have a good time in the kitchen, and we really enjoy what we are doing. The job requires long hours, but it is fun! I think that people pick up on our energy level here, and they really do appreciate the fruits of our labor."

Chez Melange

Loin of Lamb en Croûte with Roasted Shallot Balsamic Vinegar Sauce

Loin of Lamb en Croûte

4	6-ounce lamb loins, cleaned
1	tablespoon olive oil
1	clove garlic
	salt
	pepper
2	tablespoons olive oil
4	sheets puff pastry
2	red bell peppers, roasted, peeled, seeded, and cut into ½" strips
8	ounces feta cheese, crumbled
1	cup cooked spinach, drained
1	egg, beaten with 1 tablespoon water
	Roasted Shallot Balsamic Vinegar Sauce *(recipe on next page)*

Rub the lamb loins with the 1 tablespoon of olive oil and the clove of garlic. Sprinkle them with the salt and the pepper.

In a heavy skillet place the 2 tablespoons of olive oil and heat it on medium until it is hot. Sear the lamb on both sides.

Cut each puff pastry sheet so that it is the length of the lamb loin and 2½ times as wide. Place the lamb in the center of the sheet. Top the lamb with the roasted peppers, feta cheese, and cooked spinach. Fold one end of the dough over the lamb. Brush the other side of the pastry with the egg wash and then fold it over on top of the other pastry end by 2". Cut off the extra dough and reserve it. Crimp the open ends together with your fingers.

Turn the wrapped lamb over. Make a braid the length of the lamb with the left-over pastry dough. Brush the top of the dough with the egg wash and place the braid on top.

Preheat the oven to 425°. Bake the wrapped lamb for 12 to 15 minutes, or until the dough is golden brown.

Serve the baked lamb with the Roasted Shallot Balsamic Vinegar Sauce.

serves 4

"This is a delicious, wonderful, elegant dish that looks like it took a lot of time and skill to prepare. But the truth is, it's easy!"

"Lamb is one of the healthiest red meats that you can eat. It has a wonderful flavor which most people love."

"You can buy the puff pastry already made in the supermarket. It comes frozen, in sheets."

"When I entertain, I don't like to be in the kitchen cooking. I want to be enjoying my guests. So this is a perfect recipe for me because everything can be prepared in advance and then cooked at the last minute."

Roasted Shallot Balsamic Vinegar Sauce

2	cups beef stock
1¼	cups balsamic vinegar
2	sticks butter, cut into small pieces
8	shallots, roasted and finely chopped
	salt *(to taste)*
	pepper *(to taste)*

In a medium saucepan place the beef stock and balsamic vinegar. Heat them on medium high for 10 to 15 minutes, or until the liquid is reduced to ¼.

While stirring constantly, add the butter pieces one at a time, and whisk them in so that they are well incorporated.

Add the roasted shallots, salt, and pepper.

Chez Melange Dipping Sauce

6	ounces anchovies
½	cup olive oil
1	pound carrots, coarsely chopped
1	onion, coarsely chopped
1	pound celery, coarsely chopped
1½	cups dry white wine
6	pounds whole tomatoes, finely chopped
12	ounces crushed tomatoes
½	cup tomato paste
1¼	quarts chicken stock *(recipe on page 297)*
1½	lemons, zested *(outer yellow skin grated off)* **and juiced**
⅓	cup Worcestershire sauce
4	beef bouillon cubes
1½	teaspoons salt
1¼	teaspoons black pepper
1¼	teaspoons granulated garlic
¾	teaspoon crushed red chiles
1¼	teaspoons ground basil
1½	teaspoons ground thyme
1½	cups light brown sugar

In a medium large saucepan place the anchovies and the olive oil. Simmer them on medium low for 12 to 15 minutes, or until the anchovies have dissolved.

In a large saucepan place the dissolved anchovies and the oil. Add the remainder of the ingredients and stir them together. Simmer the mixture for 1 hour.

"This is probably the most asked for item on the menu. It is served in a bowl with freshly baked bread, and it's fantastic!"

"There are so many wonderful ingredients in this sauce. Even though there are anchovies in it, you can't really taste them. Be sure that you don't eliminate them because they add a very important, subtle flavor."

"This sauce is very versatile. It is excellent with fish, and even pasta. Make it a day ahead of time and it will taste even better. Also, the sauce freezes very well."

Biscotti di Anise

2	sticks butter
2	cups sugar
6	eggs
4	tablespoons anise seeds
1	teaspoon vanilla
3	tablespoons anisette
5½	cups flour
1	tablespoon baking powder
2	cups blanched almonds, chopped

In a large bowl place the butter and sugar, and cream them together.

One at a time add the eggs and beat them in.

Add the anise seeds and mix them in.

Add the vanilla and anisette and beat them in.

In a medium bowl place the flour and baking powder, and mix them together. Add the flour to the butter mixture. Combine the ingredients together well.

Add the almonds and stir them in well.

Form the dough into a flat loaf. Cover it and place it in the refrigerator overnight.

Preheat the oven to 375°. Place the loaf on a cookie sheet and bake it for 20 minutes, or until it is firm.

Remove the loaf and let it cool. Slice it diagonally into ¾" thick slices.

Preheat the oven to 375°. Place the slices on a cookie sheet and bake them for 15 minutes, or until they are golden brown. Let them cool before serving.

serves 8

"This is a light and refreshing dessert. It is the perfect ending to a wonderful meal. People love it!"

"To be really decadent, you can serve this with some melted chocolate. Then people can dip their slices into it."

"You can make this 2 or 3 days ahead. It keeps very well."

Chez Melange

Lighthouse, Palos Verdes

Coral Cafe
Redondo Beach

Located in the Sheraton at Redondo Beach, the Coral Cafe serves an inspired contemporary California cuisine in a pleasant, garden-like setting.

Menu

Pinto Bean Soup

Temecula Salad with Lemon Basil Vinaigrette

Thai Chicken

Southwestern Marinated Beef with Spicy Salsa

Baked Grouper with Grapefruit Tequila Sauce

Veal Chops and Calla-Lees Sauce

Individual Apple Pies

Chocolate Chip Cookies

Executive Chef Julian Drummond says, *"This is a basic pinto bean soup that has a little more flair and excitement to it because of the Mexican spices. You can purée the soup, although I prefer the beans to be whole."*

Pinto Bean Soup

4	tablespoons butter
½	pound bacon, finely chopped
¼	cup onions, finely chopped
2	tablespoons green bell peppers, finely chopped
2	tomatoes, finely chopped
1	teaspoon garlic, finely chopped
1	teaspoon fresh cilantro, finely chopped
1	teaspoon red chile powder
1	pinch cayenne pepper
1	tablespoon tomato paste
10	ounces pinto beans, soaked overnight and drained
3	quarts chicken stock *(recipe on page 297)*
	salt *(to taste)*
	pepper *(to taste)*
4	teaspoons sour cream

In a large saucepan place the butter and heat it on medium until it has melted. Add the bacon, onions, green bell peppers, tomatoes, and garlic. Cover the pan with a lid and simmer the ingredients for 4 minutes.

Add the cilantro, red chile powder, cayenne pepper, and tomato paste. Stir the ingredients together and simmer them for 3 minutes.

Add the pinto beans, chicken stock, salt, and pepper. Bring the ingredients to a boil and cook them vigorously for 1½ to 2 hours, or until the beans are tender.

In each of 4 individual serving bowls place the soup. Garnish the soup with a dollop of sour cream.

serves 4

Temecula Salad with Lemon Basil Vinaigrette

Temecula Salad

½	head radicchio, washed, dried, and torn
½	head mache lettuce, washed, dried, and torn
½	head romaine, washed, dried, and torn
½	head iceberg lettuce, washed, dried, and torn
½	green bell pepper, seeds removed, and thinly sliced
½	red bell pepper, seeds removed, and thinly sliced
½	yellow bell pepper, seeds removed, and thinly sliced
¼	cup walnuts, chopped
4	slices Montrachet cheese, ¼" thick
	Lemon Basil Vinaigrette *(recipe follows)*

On each of 4 individual serving plates attractively arrange the four lettuces and the three bell peppers.

Sprinkle the walnuts on top. Add a slice of the cheese.

Serve the salad with the Lemon Basil Vinaigrette on the side.

serves 4

"Once I did a wine promotion with Callaway Vineyards, which is located in Temecula Valley, north of San Diego. I designed this salad to go with some of their wines. You can use any different kinds of lettuce that you like because it is the flavors of the Montrachet cheese, bell peppers, and Lemon Basil Vinaigrette that really make the salad."

Lemon Basil Vinaigrette

2	egg yolks
1	teaspoon sugar
2	teaspoons fresh basil, chopped
2	teaspoons lemon juice, freshly squeezed
	salt *(to taste)*
	pepper *(to taste)*
1	cup vegetable oil

In a small bowl place the egg yolks, sugar, basil, lemon juice, salt, and pepper. Whisk the ingredients together so that they are well blended.

While whisking constantly, slowly dribble in the vegetable oil so that it emulsifies with the egg yolks.

makes 1½ cups

"The egg yolks mix with the oil, and this is what gives the dressing its creamy texture. Be sure to dribble the oil in very slowly. If you add it too fast, then the dressing will separate."

Thai Chicken

4	tablespoons butter
1½	pounds chicken breasts, skin removed, boned, and cut into thin strips
2	cups carrots, peeled and thinly sliced
1	stalk celery, thinly sliced
1	cup bean sprouts
1	teaspoon garlic, chopped
2	tablespoons soy sauce
¾	cup heavy cream
½	cup peanut butter
	salt *(to taste)*
	pepper *(to taste)*
½	cup vegetable oil
4	ounces Mai Fun noodles *(or rice noodles)*
½	cup sliced almonds, roasted
2	scallions, thinly sliced

In a large frying pan place the butter and heat it on medium high until it has melted. Add the chicken and sauté it for 1 to 2 minutes, or until it turns white. Remove the chicken and set it aside.

Reduce the heat to medium low. Add the carrots, celery, bean sprouts, and garlic. Sauté the ingredients for 3 to 5 minutes, or until the vegetables are tender.

Add the soy sauce and cook it for 1 minute.

Add the heavy cream and bring it to a boil. Reduce the heat and simmer the ingredients for 2 minutes.

Reduce the heat further and add the sautéed chicken, peanut butter, salt, and pepper. Stir in the ingredients until the peanut butter has melted. Keep the mixture warm.

In a medium sauté pan place the vegetable oil and heat it on medium high until it is hot. Add the Mai Fun noodles and let them puff up. Stir them once and then remove them.

On each of 4 individual serving plates place the noodles. Ladle on the chicken with the sauce. Sprinkle on the toasted almonds and the sliced scallions.

serves 4

"I came up with this recipe because I was working on the pasta section of the menu, and I wanted something that was really different. Since it has been on our menu it has skyrocketed in popularity. In fact, it now is the top selling dish. I was completely shocked!"

"This is so simple to make, and people absolutely love it. Once you get the ingredients ready you can put it together in 5 or 6 minutes, so it's a great thing for a working person to make."

"The peanut butter is the essential flavor, with just a hint of soy. All of the other ingredients are mild, and they are centered around these two flavors. But the nice thing is that you still can taste every other item in the dish, because the peanut butter flavor is not overpowering. The heavy cream smooths out the sauce and softens the taste."

"You could serve this with rice or with a soft noodle, although I prefer the rice noodles because they are deep-fried. They give the dish a good crunchy texture and a great flavor."

Southwestern Marinated Beef with Spicy Salsa

Southwestern Marinated Beef

2   cups olive oil
½   cup malt vinegar
½   cup red wine
1   tablespoon fresh rosemary, chopped
1½   teaspoons fresh thyme, chopped
1   teaspoon fresh oregano, chopped
1   tablespoon crushed red pepper
1½   teaspoons garlic, chopped
¼   cup country Dijon mustard
4   10-ounce New York steaks, cut in half vertically
1   eggplant, sliced into ¼" thick pieces
2   zucchinis, sliced into ¼" thick pieces
2   yellow squashes, sliced into ¼" thick pieces
1   red bell pepper, seeds removed, and sliced into ¼" thick
        pieces
        Spicy Salsa *(recipe on next page)*

In a large bowl place the olive oil, malt vinegar, red wine, rosemary, thyme, oregano, crushed red pepper, garlic, and Dijon mustard. Whisk the ingredients together so that they are well blended.

Add the steaks and place them in the refrigerator. Let them marinate overnight.

Grill the steaks for 3 to 4 minutes on each side, or until the desired doneness is achieved.

Brush the vegetables with the marinade, and quickly grill them until they are tender.

On each of 4 individual serving plates place 2 steak halves. Place the grilled vegetables in between the 2 pieces of meat. Ladle the Spicy Salsa on top.

serves 4

"Here is a wonderfully flavored beef that would be a big hit at any outdoor barbecue party. The marinade is spicy, but the beef itself has a more subtle spiciness when you eat it. It's just great with the grilled vegetables and the salsa. You could use chicken instead of beef, and it would be just as good."

"When you grill the vegetables put the eggplant on first, because it will take longer to cook than the other vegetables."

Spicy Salsa

2	tablespoons butter
1	teaspoon garlic, chopped
1	medium onion, chopped
2	scallions, chopped
1	jalapeño chile pepper, minced
1	teaspoon fresh basil, chopped
6	tomatoes, chopped
½	cup country Dijon mustard
2	quarts chicken stock *(recipe on page 297)*

In a medium large saucepan place the butter and heat it on medium until it has melted. Add the garlic, onions, scallions, jalapeño chile peppers, basil, and tomatoes. Cover the pan with a lid and cook the ingredients for 5 minutes.

Add the country Dijon mustard and stir it in. Cook the ingredients for 3 minutes.

Add the chicken stock and bring the mixture to a boil. Reduce the heat to low and simmer the ingredients for 1 to 1½ hours, or until a thick but pourable sauce consistency is achieved.

makes 2 cups

"This is a great recipe for salsa! The country Dijon mustard gives it a unique taste. You can serve this salsa with chips, but not if you are serving it with the marinated beef as well, because that would be overkill."

"When I was 11 years old I went to boarding school, and the food there was not very good. When I would come home for vacations I loved to help my mother in the kitchen. She was an excellent cook and I wanted to help her fix good meals. So, I attribute my love of cooking both to my mother and to the horrible food that I used to eat at the boarding school!"

Baked Grouper with Grapefruit Tequila Sauce

Baked Grouper

4	8-ounce grouper fillets
1	pink grapefruit, cut horizontally into 4 slices
¼	cup dry white wine
	Grapefruit Tequila Sauce *(recipe follows)*
1	grapefruit, zested *(outer yellow part grated off)*, and segments removed from membranes

Preheat the oven to 350°. In a buttered baking pan place the grouper fillets. Place a slice of grapefruit on top of each fillet. Pour on the white wine. Bake the fish for 15 to 20 minutes, or until it is just done.

Remove the grapefruit from the fish.

On each of 4 individual serving plates place a grouper fillet. Ladle the Grapefruit Tequila Sauce on top. Garnish the dish with the grapefruit zest and the grapefruit sections.

serves 4

Grapefruit Tequila Sauce

½	cup grapefruit juice
½	cup tequila
1	cup heavy cream
3	ounces butter *(room temperature)*, cut into small pieces
	salt *(to taste)*
	pepper *(to taste)*

In a small saucepan place the grapefruit juice and the tequila. Cook them on medium heat for 8 to 10 minutes, or until the liquid is reduced by ½.

Add the heavy cream and cook it on medium low for 15 to 20 minutes, or until the liquid is reduced by ½.

Remove the saucepan from the heat. While whisking constantly, add the pieces of butter one at a time. Season the sauce with the salt and the pepper.

"Believe it or not, I created this dish for a Hawaiian luau, although I think it might have been more appropriate for a Mexican fiesta because of the tequila. In any case, the dish is outstanding! It is our most popular seafood item."

"The grapefruit flavor seeps into the fish when you bake it, which gives it a slightly sweet and sour taste. It is fantastic with the sauce. I hope that you try this recipe, because it really is something!"

"Each customer that we have is completely different, and I try to please each one, which is extremely difficult to do! The wait staff helps by asking the right questions, and I will go out in the dining room and meet the guests when I have time. I know that a lot of chefs are very shy, but I am outgoing and I love doing this. I believe that a chef should be visible."

Veal Chops and Calla-Lees Sauce

1   **cup flour**
1   **teaspoon thyme**
¼   **teaspoon nutmeg**
¼   **teaspoon salt**
¼   **teaspoon pepper**
4   **10-ounce veal chops**
1   **Washington apple, quartered, cored, and sliced**
¼   **cup salad oil**
½   **teaspoon garlic, chopped**
2   **whole cloves**
½   **teaspoon nutmeg**
½   **cup dry white wine**
1   **cup heavy cream**
4   **tablespoons butter** (room temperature)**, cut into small pieces**

In a medium bowl place the flour, thyme, the ¼ teaspoon of nutmeg, salt, and pepper. Mix the ingredients together. Dust the veal chops and the apple slices in the flour mixture.

In a large, heavy frying pan place the salad oil and heat it on medium high until it is hot. Add the veal chops and sauté them for 6 to 8 minutes on each side, or until the desired doneness is achieved. Remove the veal from the pan and keep it warm.

Add the apple slices and sauté them for 2 minutes on each side, or until they are tender. Remove the slices from the pan and keep them warm.

Add the garlic, whole cloves, the ½ teaspoon of nutmeg, and the white wine to the pan. Cook the ingredients on medium heat for 8 to 10 minutes, or until the liquid is reduced by ½.

Add the heavy cream and cook it on medium low heat for 15 to 20 minutes, or until it is reduced by ½.

Remove the pan from the stove. While whisking constantly, add the pieces of butter one at a time so that they are well incorporated. Remove the cloves.

On each of 4 individual serving plates place a veal chop. Arrange the apple slices on top. Spoon on the sauce.

serves 4

"I got the idea for this recipe because I wanted to do a regional dish from the future, so to speak. By the future, I mean that the dish is based on the cuisine from the northwest (Oregon and Washington). I believe that this cuisine is destined to be the new trend in cooking. The dishes are simple, with nothing complicated or bizarre, and they are made with the local fresh fruits, vegetables, and herbs."

"The sauce is flavored with nutmeg and cloves, which is a nice accent to the apples and the veal."

Individual Apple Pies

1	**egg**
¼	**cup sugar**
5	**ounces butter**
1	**cup flour**
1	**pinch salt**
1	**pound Granny Smith apples, peeled, cored, and sliced**
1	**tablespoon sugar**
	water *(as needed)*
1	**pinch cinnamon**
1	**lemon, zested** *(outer yellow part grated off)*
¼	**cup raisins**
¼	**cup milk**
2	**tablespoons sugar**
4	**scoops vanilla ice cream**

In a medium bowl place the egg and the ¼ cup of sugar, and beat them together. Add the butter and whisk it in well.

Sift the flour and salt together. While stirring constantly, slowly add the flour to the egg-butter mixture. Mix the dough until it is smooth. Cover and refrigerate the dough so that it is chilled.

In a medium saucepan place the apples, the 1 tablespoon of sugar, and enough water to fill the pan up to ⅛". Cook the ingredients on medium heat for 6 to 8 minutes, or until the apples are halfway cooked. Add the cinnamon, lemon zest, and raisins. Mix the ingredients together and cook them for 6 to 8 minutes, or until the apples are tender. Let the mixture cool.

Roll out the chilled dough on a floured board so that it is ⅛" thick. Cut out four rounds that are large enough to line 3" pie pans. Cut out four more rounds for the tops.

In each of four lightly greased 3" pie pans place the larger round of pie dough. Press it in and prick the bottom with a fork. Place the apple filling inside. Lay the other pastry round on top. Crimp the edges together. Brush the top with the milk and sprinkle on some of the 2 tablespoons of sugar.

Preheat the oven to 375°. Place the pies on a baking sheet and bake them for 25 to 30 minutes, or until they are nicely browned. Serve each pie with a scoop of vanilla ice cream.

serves 4

"This recipe is an old favorite that my mother used to make in England. You may think that apple pie is an American dish, which it is, but it also is an English dish. It is just as popular there as it is here."

"My mother would make one large pie, but I wanted to make individual pies because I think that they make a nicer presentation than just serving a slice of pie. I decorate the top with some dough that is cut into the shape of a leaf and a flower."

"Be sure to use a firm apple, like the Granny Smith. If you use a Red Delicious, then the apples will turn to mush when you cook them."

Chocolate Chip Cookies

½   cup butter, softened
½   cup sugar
5   tablespoons brown sugar
2   drops vanilla extract
1   egg
¾   cup flour
⅛   teaspoon baking soda
1   pinch salt
1   cup chocolate chips
¼   cup pecans, chopped

In a medium bowl place the butter, sugar, and brown sugar. Cream the ingredients together so that they are well mixed.

Add the vanilla extract and egg, and mix them in.

Sift together the flour, baking soda, and salt. Add small amounts of the flour mixture to the butter mixture, and mix it in well.

Add the chocolate chips and pecans, and mix them in well.

Form the dough into balls that are 1" in diameter. Refrigerate them for ½ hour.

Preheat the oven to 325°. Cover a baking sheet with baker's paper. Place the dough balls on the sheet so that they are 1½" apart. Bake the cookies for 12 to 15 minutes, or until they are brown around the edges and light brown in the center.

Let the cookies sit for 15 minutes before serving them.

makes 20 to 24 cookies

"Chocolate chip cookies are very American, and they are just delicious! I am a real chocolate lover and I eat about 4 or 5 of these a day, to get my fix. The pastry chef knows how to keep me happy!"

"I love everything about my job, and I wouldn't trade it for anything, except maybe to be a professional soccer player. That was my secret ambition in my younger days, and it still is, even though my body is old and decrepit!"

Entry Stairway, El Porto

Eats

El Segundo

Popular for its consistently good food, Eats serves a classic American fare to an enthusiastic crowd in an open, modern, award-winning dining room.

Menu

Eats' Black Bean Soup

Cream of Broccoli and Cheddar Cheese Soup

Baked Mushroom Mozzarella

Basic White Sauce

Ratatouille

Eats' Lasagna with Italian Meat Sauce

Eats' California Chicken

Chicken Florentine

Owner Ray Marney says, *"This soup is so good that even Fidel Castro would fall in love with it!"*

Eats' Black Bean Soup

2	cups black beans, soaked for 2 hours and drained
4	quarts water
3	whole cloves
1	whole onion, peeled
½	pound lean beef, diced
¼	pound salt pork, rinsed and rind cut several times
⅛	teaspoon cayenne pepper
½	cup sherry
	salt *(to taste)*
	pepper *(to taste)*

In a large saucepan place the black beans and the water.

Stick the whole cloves into the whole onion and add it to the beans.

Add the diced beef, salt pork, and cayenne pepper. Bring the liquid to a boil. Cover the saucepan, reduce the heat to low, and simmer the ingredients for 3 hours, or until the beans are tender. Skim off any foam that appears.

Add the sherry, salt, and pepper.

serves 8

Cream of Broccoli and Cheddar Cheese Soup

2	pounds broccoli, cut into florets
3	cups chicken stock *(recipe on page 297)*
3	cups milk
1½	teaspoons salt
¼	teaspoon pepper
1	cup half and half
2	cups cheddar cheese, grated
¼	cup butter

In a medium large saucepan place the broccoli and ½ of the chicken stock. Bring the liquid to a boil, cover the pan, and then reduce the heat to low. Simmer the broccoli for 10 minutes, or until it is tender. Remove the broccoli with a slotted spoon and coarsely chop it. Set the broccoli aside.

Add the remainder of the chicken stock to the saucepan. Add the milk, salt, and pepper. Bring the liquid to a boil, while stirring it occasionally.

Add the half and half, cheddar cheese, butter, and the cooked, chopped broccoli. Cook the soup on medium heat until the cheese has completely melted.

serves 8

"Here is a great recipe! It is easy to follow and it tastes outstanding. The cheese flavor comes through, yet it doesn't overpower the taste of the broccoli."

"Cheese and broccoli complement each other so well. There's an ad on TV where a little kid has a plate of broccoli. He's poking at it with his fork with a frown on his face, and not eating a bite. Then, in the next scene his mother gives him a plate of broccoli with some cheese sauce on top. His face lights up and he digs right in! Of course, I know that this is just a plug for the cheese manufacturers, but it is true that cheese definitely spruces up broccoli."

Baked Mushroom Mozzarella

*"This dish makes a
wonderful appetizer, and
it also is great as a
vegetarian main dish. It
is one of those dishes that
everyone loves. And, like
all of our recipes, it is so
simple to make."*

2	tablespoons clarified butter
24	medium white mushrooms, quartered
1½	cups lightly cooked spinach, drained
½	cup **Basic White Sauce** *(recipe on next page)*
¼	cup Monterey Jack cheese, grated
¼	cup mozzarella cheese, grated
	salt *(to taste)*
	pepper *(to taste)*

*"When my wife, Pat, and
I were negotiating for the
purchase of this
restaurant, some of our
close friends came and
tried it out so that they
could give us their
impression of it. The
Baked Mushroom
Mozzarella was one dish
that they had, and they
raved to us about it. So
my wife and I came and
tried it, and we agreed
that it was pretty
fantastic and definitely
should stay on the menu."*

In a medium skillet place the clarified butter and heat it on medium high until it is hot. Add the mushrooms and sauté them for 4 to 6 minutes, or until they are tender and lightly browned. Set them aside.

In the bottom of a small casserole dish place the spinach. Place the sautéed mushrooms on top.

Add the white sauce.

Sprinkle on the two cheeses, the salt, and the pepper.

Preheat the oven to 350°. Cook the dish for 20 to 25 minutes, or until the cheese is hot and bubbly.

serves 4

*"If you want to
experiment, try making
this with some exotic
mushrooms."*

Basic White Sauce

3	tablespoons butter
3	tablespoons flour
2	cups milk
¾	teaspoon salt
¼	teaspoon pepper

In the top of a simmering double boiler place the butter and melt it. Add the flour and stir it in for 1 to 2 minutes, or until it is smooth.

While stirring constantly, gradually add the milk. Continue to stir and cook the sauce for 8 to 10 minutes, or until it is thick.

Add the salt and pepper, and stir them in.

Strain the sauce through a fine sieve.

makes 2 cups

"This is a very simple, basic white sauce. We top almost all of our casseroles with this sauce, including our crêpes. It is very mild and lets the food items speak out for themselves. Yet, at the same time it helps to keep the dish moist. In our kitchen it is a staple..... we can't do without it!"

"The only trick here is not to overcook the sauce. You need to keep it smooth and pliable. Any leftover sauce will keep very well in the refrigerator."

Ratatouille

2	medium eggplants, cut into ½" slices and then cubed
1	tablespoon salt
⅓	cup olive oil
1	medium onion, finely chopped
1	bell pepper, seeded and coarsely chopped
3	small zucchinis, thinly sliced
2	cloves garlic, finely chopped
1	teaspoon sweet basil
4	medium tomatoes, blanched, peeled, seeded, and coarsely chopped
1	teaspoon sugar
1½	teaspoons salt
¼	teaspoon black pepper, freshly ground

In a medium bowl place the eggplant cubes. Sprinkle on the salt and cover them with water. Weigh them down with a plate and let them soak for 30 minutes. Drain the eggplant pieces and pat them dry.

In a large saucepan place the oil and heat it on medium high until it is hot. Add the onions, bell peppers, and zucchini. Cover the pot and cook the vegetables for 5 minutes. Stir them occasionally.

Add the garlic and basil, and stir them in.

Add the drained eggplant cubes and stir them in. Cover the pot and cook the mixture for 5 minutes while stirring it occasionally.

Add the tomatoes, sugar, salt, and pepper. Stir the ingredients together thoroughly.

Cover the pot and cook the mixture for 10 minutes, or until the eggplant is tender and the flavors are well blended.

serves 4

"It's a little embarrassing to admit this, but I used to think that ratatouille was some kind of pasta. I was not familiar with it at all! As it turns out, this is one of our most popular items, particularly with vegetarians."

"Be careful not to over-cook the individual ingredients. Each one must be identifiable when the dish is done."

"Ratatouille is a very versatile dish. We use it in crêpes and also in omelettes. Another really neat thing is to put it in the bottom of a casserole dish, add some boneless sautéed chicken breasts, some white sauce, grated Jack cheese, and some paprika. Bake it all until it is hot and bubbly. It's fantastic!"

Eats' Lasagna
with Italian Meat Sauce

Eats' Lasagna

1 pound lasagna noodles, cooked al dente
1 pound mozzarella cheese, sliced
   Italian Meat Sauce *(recipe on next page)*
1 8-ounce can tomato purée
½ cup Parmesan cheese, freshly grated

In a large casserole dish place a layer of the lasagna noodles. Add a layer of the mozzarella cheese. Add a layer of the Italian Meat Sauce.

Repeat the process until the casserole dish is full, ending with a layer of the meat sauce.

Evenly spread on the tomato purée.

Sprinkle on the Parmesan cheese.

Preheat the oven to 375°. Bake the lasagna for 30 to 40 minutes, or until it is bubbly and heated through.

serves 6 to 8

"This recipe is very straightforward and easy to follow. There are thousands of lasagna recipes in existence, and this is one that the restaurant has been serving for many years."

"A lot of players from the L.A. Raiders football team eat here, and this is one of their favorite dishes."

Italian Meat Sauce

¼	cup butter
½	cup olive oil
1½	cups onions, finely chopped
½	cup celery, finely chopped
2½	cups mushrooms, finely chopped
2	teaspoons parsley, finely chopped
2	pounds lean ground sirloin
2	tablespoons flour
2	tablespoons tomato purée
1	cup red wine
3½	cups beef broth
	salt *(to taste)*
	pepper *(to taste)*

In a large saucepan place the butter and oil, and heat them on medium high until the butter has melted and the oil is hot. Add the onions and sauté them for 1 minute.

Add the celery, mushrooms, and parsley. Sauté the vegetables for 1 minute.

Add the ground beef. Cook and stir it until it is lightly browned.

Sprinkle the flour over the mixture and stir it in so that it is well blended.

Add the tomato purée and stir it in.

While stirring constantly, gradually add the red wine and the beef broth. Season the sauce with the salt and the pepper.

Simmer the sauce for 1 hour, or until it is thick. Stir it occasionally.

makes 5 cups

"All of the ingredients are easily obtained at your local supermarket. Just make sure to get the leanest meat that you can, and be sure that the vegetables are fresh."

"This meat sauce is delicious! It's so simple to make, and I guarantee that you will be happy with the end product."

Eats' California Chicken

2	tablespoons clarified butter
4	chicken breasts, skinned, boned, and sliced into ½" pieces
	salt
	pepper
2	avocados, peeled, pitted, and thinly sliced
2	medium tomatoes, thinly wedged
½	cup Basic White Sauce *(recipe on page 96)*
½	cup Monterey Jack cheese, grated

In a large skillet place the clarified butter and heat it on medium high until it is hot. Add the chicken slices and sauté them for 3 to 5 minutes, or until they start to turn brown.

Season the chicken with the salt and the pepper.

In a medium casserole dish place the chicken. Place the avocado and tomato pieces on top of the chicken, in an alternating pattern.

Evenly pour on the white sauce.

Sprinkle on the cheese.

Preheat the oven to 350°. Cook the casserole for 30 minutes.

serves 4

"One evening our chef, Estefan Gonzales, prepared a sample of this dish for my wife and me. We both just fell in love with it and immediately included it in our specials. It has really taken off with our customers. A lot of people come to the restaurant for this dish only."

"One time my wife was eating this for her dinner in the restaurant. But then we got busy so she left it on the counter top for an hour or so. When she came back to it later and took a bite, she found that it was still delicious, even though it was cold."

Chicken Florentine

1½   cups cooked spinach, drained
4   chicken breasts, skinned, boned, and pounded until thin
½   cup Basic White Sauce (recipe on page 96)
½   cup Monterey Jack cheese, grated
      salt (to taste)
      pepper (to taste)

In a medium casserole dish place the spinach. Place the flattened chicken on top.

Evenly pour on the white sauce.

Sprinkle on the cheese.

Sprinkle on the salt and pepper.

Preheat the oven to 350°. Bake the chicken for 30 minutes, or until it is done and the cheese is hot and bubbly.

serves 4

"Here's another simple, delicious recipe. It only takes a few minutes to put it together, and then you just pop it into the oven until it gets hot and bubbly and yummy!"

"We like Eats to be a place that people look forward to coming to. Our clientele, as well as our employees, are very loyal. And, our food is consistently good."

Fisherman, Hermosa Beach

Erika's
Pacific Palisades

Serving an international cuisine in a historic Pacific Palisades building, Erika's absolutely sparkles with an old Hollywood elegance that caters to an enthusiastic crowd.

Menu

Salmon Mariposa

Potage of Roasted Eggplant with Garlic-Beet Purée

Neptune Flan

Grilled Duck Breast Clea with Cider-Mint Sauce and Potato Pie

Marscapone Stuffed Pear with Brown Sugar Glaze

Owners Richard Christian and Jeff Holden attribute much of their restaurant's success to the talent of Executive Chef Michael Rodak and Sous Chef Tim Boyd. Richard says, *"These recipes were designed to compose an elegant, full course gourmet meal that anyone can successfully make at home."*

Salmon Mariposa

¼	cup sour cream
½	cup half and half
1	pinch salt
1	teaspoon lemon juice *(or to taste)*, freshly squeezed
1	English muffin, sliced in half
8	ounces smoked salmon, sliced paper thin and cut into 16 pieces
2	ounces orange salmon roe
2	ounces whitefish caviar *(or sturgeon)*
1	bunch chives, the top 2" cut off and the remainder finely chopped

(Note: This recipe explains how to form a butterfly sculpture using the above ingredients.)

In a small bowl place the sour cream and the half and half. Whisk them together until the mixture is smooth, thick, and pourable. Add the salt and lemon juice, and whisk them in. Set the sauce aside.

Cut the 2 English muffin slices in half. Trim each piece so that it forms an oval shape. Toast the ovals.

On each of 4 individual serving plates evenly spread on the sauce. Place 1 English muffin oval, toasted side up, in the center of each plate *(this forms the "body" of the butterfly)*.

For each plate roll up 4 pieces of the salmon to form 4 cones. Place 2 cones on each side of the ovals, so that the pointed ends meet at the middle of the oval *(this forms the "wings" of the butterfly)*.

(continued on next page)

In an alternating pattern, carefully spoon on thin rows of the orange salmon roe and the whitefish caviar across the oval (like the stripes of a bumblebee).

Place 2 of the chive tops at the top of each oval (this forms the "antennas" of the butterfly). Sprinkle the chopped chives on the sauce surrounding the butterfly.

serves 4

Potage of Roasted Eggplant with Garlic-Beet Purée

10	small Japanese eggplants
2	tablespoons mild olive oil (or as needed)
	salt (to taste)
	pepper (to taste)
12	cloves garlic
1	cup olive oil
1	medium beet, peeled and thinly sliced
1	cup water (or as needed)
½	cup heavy cream (or as needed)
¼	cup fresh basil, chopped
1	tablespoon fresh thyme, chopped
2	tablespoons white vinegar
1	cup chicken stock (recipe on page 297)
2	tablespoons fresh parsley, chopped
¼	cup Parmesan cheese, freshly grated

Preheat the oven to 350°. Place the eggplants on a baking sheet. Lightly brush them with the 2 tablespoons of olive oil and season them with the salt and the pepper. Stab each eggplant with a fork 3 or 4 times. Bake them for 30 to 40 minutes, or until they are soft and pulpy. Set them aside and let them cool.

In a small baking pan place the garlic and the 1 cup of olive oil. Roast the garlic in the oven at 350° for 10 to 15 minutes, or until the garlic is lightly browned on the edges (do not let it get darker than a potato chip). Remove the pan from the oven and let the garlic cool in the oil.

(continued on next page)

"The success of this recipe is dependent upon the taste of the salmon, so make certain that you buy the absolute best quality that you can find. And try to find an English muffin that has been baked that same day at a bakery, rather than buying the pre-packaged ones."

"One of the keys to this recipe is to use fresh herbs instead of the dried ones. Dried herbs often will affect a food in a negative way, especially if they are stored in a warm place. A lot of people keep their jars of herbs on their stove, and this is not good. Herbs should be kept in a cool (not refrigerated) place."

"Eggplant is a very temperamental vegetable. It can easily become mushy or rubbery, and the flavor can change so that it doesn't taste good. You must treat eggplant with kindness! And remember, eggplant is like a sponge in that it absorbs everything. So, be very careful about the ingredients that you cook with it, because those flavors will definitely be there."

"Buy your garlic the same day you are going to make this dish. Most people keep their garlic too long. Buy less, but buy more often."

"Vinegars add sparkle to cooking! This is one of the great secrets that good chefs know. Each type of vinegar has its own particular flavor and use. Many times just a few drops are needed to really perk up a sauce. But use it sparingly, because the strength of the vinegar flavor will increase in compounding, large jumps. In other words, you can ruin a beautiful sauce VERY QUICKLY!"

"You may use chicken stock in place of the cream if you want less calories, or you may use all cream and no chicken stock if you want a richer soup."

In a small saucepan place the beet slices and enough of the water so that they are just covered. Simmer the beets for 5 to 7 minutes, or until they are very tender. Set the saucepan aside and let the beets cool in the liquid.

Remove the roasted garlic cloves from the oil *(reserve the oil)* and place them in a food processor. Remove the beet slices from the liquid *(reserve the liquid)* and add them to the food processor. Purée the garlic and beet pulp, adding the reserved beet liquid as necessary so that the mixture is of a smooth consistency. Add the heavy cream and purée the mixture further so that it is of a pourable consistency. Season the purée with the salt and the pepper. Remove it from the food processor and set it aside.

Cut the roasted eggplants in half, lengthwise. Scrape out the flesh from the skin and place it in the food processor. Add the basil, thyme, and white vinegar. Purée the ingredients together. Add enough of the chicken stock so that a smooth, pourable consistency is achieved. Season the soup with the salt and the pepper.

Heat the garlic purée and the eggplant soup in 2 separate double boilers.

Pour the roasted eggplant soup into individual serving bowls. Swirl in some of the garlic beet purée. Drizzle on some of the reserved olive oil. Sprinkle on some of the parsley and the Parmesan cheese.

serves 4

Neptune Flan

¼	cup olive oil
1	small yellow onion, minced
4	large cloves garlic, minced
4	medium tomatoes, seeded and finely diced
⅓	cup white wine
3	tablespoons fresh basil, chopped
	salt *(to taste)*
	pepper *(to taste)*
2	quarts water
1	teaspoon salt
4	baby zucchinis, sliced into ⅛" thick round pieces
2	large yellow squash, sliced in half, lengthwise
2	teaspoons olive oil
1	tablespoon Parmesan cheese, freshly grated
3	**Spanish olives** *(stuffed with pimientos)*, **sliced into 12 pieces**
½	cup vinaigrette *(your favorite recipe)*

(Note: In this recipe a "fish" is sculpted using the above ingredients.)

In a medium large skillet place the ¼ cup of olive oil and heat it on medium until it is hot. Add the onions and garlic and sauté them for 3 to 4 minutes, or until the onions are clear and tender.

Increase the heat to medium high. Add the tomatoes and sauté them for 3 to 4 minutes, or until the pan begins to sizzle. Add the wine. Cook the ingredients for 2 to 3 minutes, or until the tomatoes soften but do not lose their shape.

Add the basil, salt, and pepper. Stir the ingredients together. Place the mixture in a bowl and let it cool to room temperature. Strain off any excess liquid.

In a large pot place the water and bring it to a boil on high heat. Add the salt. Add the zucchini slices and blanch them for 10 to 15 seconds. Remove them and immediately plunge them into ice water. Let them remain there until they are cold. Drain the zucchini slices and pat them dry. Repeat the same process for the yellow squash, only blanch it for 1 to 2 minutes, or until it is tender.

(continued on next page)

"This is a wonderful and attractive dish that can be served hot as a main course, or at room temperature for an unusual first course."

"The squash must be chosen carefully for the proper size and firmness. The yellow squash should be no larger than the well of the plates you intend to use. Assembly of the dish takes time and care, but it can be done a day ahead of time. Be careful not to over-blanch the squash."

"A key thing about cooking at home with a gourmet quality is to create a rhythm. Most great chefs instinctively cook rhythmically.....like so many shakes of salt, and so many pinches of pepper, or whatever. You home cooks should practice this. Take a bowl and shake some salt into it (always use the same shaker), counting your shakes. Then measure how much it is. Shake, shake, shake.....like a dance! Get used to your rhythm."

On a baking sheet place the 4 pieces of yellow squash, with the flat side down *(these form the "bodies" of the fish)*. Spread the tomato filling evenly over the fish bodies.

Starting 1" down from the large, round end of the squash *(this uncovered portion forms the "head" of the fish)*, overlap the zucchini slices *(to form the "scales" of the fish)*. Cut the slices into smaller pieces where necessary. Cut 4 of the slices into 8 half-moon shaped pieces and reserve them *(these will form the "tail fins")*.

Sprinkle on the 2 teaspoons of olive oil. Season the "fish" with the salt and the pepper.

Preheat the oven to 350°. Bake them for 10 to 15 minutes, or until they are heated through, but not browned.

On each of 4 individual serving plates place 1 "fish". Sprinkle on the Parmesan cheese. Press on the zucchini "tail fins". Press on the olive slices to form the eyes and the mouth. Serve a small bowl of vinaigrette dressing on the side.

serves 4

Grilled Duck Breast Clea with Cider-Mint Sauce and Potato Pie

Grilled Duck Breast Clea

2	whole Muscovy duck breasts, halved, with the fat and excess skin trimmed off
2	teaspoons vegetable oil
	salt
	pepper
	Cider-Mint Sauce *(recipe follows)*
2	tablespoons fresh mint, julienned
	Potato Pie *(recipe on next page)*

Score the skin of the duck breasts in several places with a sharp knife. Rub on the oil. Sprinkle on the salt and the pepper.

Grill *(or broil)* the duck breasts for 3 to 4 minutes on each side, or until they are just done. Place them on a warmed platter *(reserve the juices that accumulate for use in the Cider-Mint Sauce)*. Remove the bones and skin. Slice the breasts into thin pieces.

On each of 4 individual serving plates place one portion of the sliced breasts. Spoon on the Cider-Mint Sauce and sprinkle on the mint. Add a serving of the Potato Pie.

serves 4

Cider-Mint Sauce

¾	cup butter, softened
4	tablespoons honey, warmed to room temperature
¾	cup white wine
1	cup chicken stock *(recipe on page 297)*
2	tablespoons cider vinegar *(or as needed)*
½	cup apple cider
	duck juices *(saved from the preparation of the Grilled Duck Breast Clea)*
¼	cup golden raisins

(continued on next page)

"When you trim the fat and excess skin off the duck make sure that your knife is very sharp. You want the duck to look pretty, so you don't want to mess it up by gouging it with a dull knife. So, be careful!"

"If you have to buy your duck frozen, which I would rather you didn't, then thaw it out by placing it in a sink filled with cold water. Or else leave it in your refrigerator and let it defrost there. Never, ever defrost a bird in the microwave! If you do, then the fat seeps into the bird and the meat will be very greasy.....it's disgusting!"

"Muscovy duck is recommended in this recipe because you will get a better end result with it. You may have to special order it from your butcher. If you can't get it, don't worry.....just use another kind."

"A great investment for the home gourmet cook is a simple, inexpensive warmer. This way you can keep the temperature up for the dishes you have finished, so they won't get cold and congeal."

In a small bowl place the butter and honey, and whisk them together. Set the honey-butter aside.

In a small saucepan place the white wine and cook it on medium high heat for 3 to 4 minutes, or until it is reduced by ½.

Add the chicken stock, vinegar, apple cider, and the duck juices. Cook the ingredients for 4 to 6 minutes, or until the liquid is reduced to ⅔ cup. Add more vinegar if the taste is not distinctly sour.

Bring the liquid to a boil. Add ¾ of the honey-butter and the golden raisins. Bring the sauce to a boil and cook it for 20 seconds, or until it thickens. Add the remainder of the honey-butter and stir it in.

Potato Pie

1	pint half and half
3	cloves garlic, minced
	salt *(to taste)*
	pepper *(to taste)*
6	tablespoons fresh marjoram, chopped
4	tablespoons fresh thyme, chopped
8	large russet potatoes, peeled, thinly sliced, and covered with cold water
1	cup Parmesan cheese, freshly grated

In a medium bowl place the half and half, garlic, salt, pepper, marjoram, and thyme. Mix the ingredients together. Set the bowl aside.

In a greased baking dish place a layer of the potato slices and sprinkle on some of the Parmesan cheese. Repeat the process until the dish is full.

Pour on the half and half mixture so that the potatoes are just covered with the liquid when you press them down with your finger. Sprinkle on some more of the Parmesan cheese.

Preheat the oven to 375°. Cover the dish with foil and bake the potatoes for 25 to 30 minutes, or until they are tender when you pierce them with a knife. Remove the foil and bake them for 5 to 10 minutes more, or until the Parmesan cheese is golden brown. Let the pie cool. Cut the pie into triangles and reheat the pieces before you are ready to serve them.

serves 6

"When you use wine in cooking don't use one that is too sweet. Blue Nun and Cold Duck are definite NO–NO's! A nice California chardonnay is good, but don't use one that is too cheap. A bottle that costs under $4.50 will not be of the quality you want. You should be paying at least $7.95 for a cooking wine. The difference in the taste can be incredible. Only a very great chef can make a cheap wine work!"

"The only time a microwave should be used in gourmet cooking is for softening butter, for reheating, and for doing certain kinds of defrosting. I know that microwave companies have spent millions of dollars in advertising saying that you can do all sorts of things in them, but the bottom line is, bread or meat cooked in a microwave is still rubber.....I don't care what they say!"

"A fabulously sinful, high cholesterol thing to do with left-over potato pie is to fry the pieces in butter and then serve them with scrambled eggs. Delicious!"

Erika's

Marscapone Stuffed Pear with Brown Sugar Glaze

6	whole cloves
7	tablespoons clover honey
7	tablespoons brown sugar
2	cups Marscapone (or cream cheese), **softened to room temperature**
1	tablespoon lemon juice, freshly squeezed
3	tablespoons powdered sugar, sifted
1	teaspoon cinnamon
¼	cup toasted hazelnuts, chopped
¼	cup hazelnut oil
3	tablespoons bittersweet chocolate, shaved
1	cup burgundy wine
2	quarts water
5	whole cloves
1	whole vanilla bean, halved, with seeds scraped out
6	bay leaves
2	large rose d'anjou (red pears), **halved lengthwise and cored** (leave the stems on)
1	cup heavy cream
4	sprigs mint

"There are many simple little tricks to make your food come out better. For instance, make sure that the plates you use are the proper temperature for the item you are serving on them. Serve your cold salad on chilled plates, and serve your hot items on warmed plates."

In a small saucepan place the 6 whole cloves and toast them on low heat for 1 minute.

Add the honey and brown sugar. Raise the heat to medium and cook the ingredients until the sugar is melted and the honey is thin. Remove the whole cloves. Stir the glaze and set it aside.

In a large bowl place the Marscapone. Add the lemon juice and fold it in with a rubber spatula. One at a time, add and fold in the powdered sugar, cinnamon, chopped hazelnuts, hazelnut oil, and shaved chocolate. Gently mix the ingredients together just enough so that they are combined. Cover the bowl and refrigerate the mixture.

In another small saucepan place the burgundy wine, water, the 5 whole cloves, vanilla bean halves, and bay leaves. Bring the liquid to a boil and then reduce it to a simmer. Add the pear halves and gently simmer them for 15 minutes, or until they are tender.

"A lot of people make loud, smacking noises when they eat, so if you are having an elegant dinner, don't serve a lot of choppy or chewy food. Save that kind of food for more casual dinners."

(continued on next page)

"Don't use flowers on your dinner table that have a scent, because the odor will interfere with the aroma and taste of the food."

"I would recommend to you home gourmet cooks that you first make a new recipe for yourself, before making it for guests, just to make sure that you get it right. Then take a color polaroid of it and save the picture. Do this for all of your dishes, so that you have a collection of pictures. Then, when you are ready to plan a dinner party, you can get all of your pictures out, and pick the ones that you want to serve. You can see what each dish looks like, which will help you to pick a nice contrast of colors. And then, because you will know what the entire meal will look like, you can decide on the color of your centerpiece, your tablecloth, and other accessories. It's a great system!"

"A gourmet dinner begins the instant the guests enter your home. Have some bread baking or a soup simmering so that there will be some delicious aromas to stimulate their appetites."

Preheat the oven to 400°. Remove the poached pears from the liquid *(reserve the liquid)* and place them in a baking dish. Warm the honey glaze and brush part of it evenly on the pears. Set the pears aside.

Heat the poaching liquid on medium high and cook it for 1 to 2 minutes, or until it is reduced to ⅓ cup. Add enough of the remaining honey glaze to make a thick sauce *(the consistency of maple syrup)*. Keep the sauce warm.

In a small saucepan place the heavy cream and heat it on low until it is warm *(do not boil)*. Set it aside and keep it warm.

Place the pears in the preheated oven for 3 to 4 minutes, or until they are warm.

On each of 4 individual serving plates make 1" thick stripes of the honey sauce. Fill in the warm cream between the stripes. Place ¼ of the Marscapone filling in the center of the plate. Place 1 pear half, cut side down, on top of the cold cheese filling. Garnish the half pear with a mint sprig.

serves 4

Fountain Detail, J. Paul Getty Museum, Malibu

Fennel
Santa Monica

Located on the lofty cliffs above Santa Monica Beach, Fennel serves wonderful French food in a pleasant setting that is bright, modern, and cool.

Chef Jean-Pierre Bosc says, *"This is a fresh, light dish that is wonderful as an appetizer in the summertime."*

Tomato, Mozzarella, and Eggplant Terrine

2	eggplants, peeled and sliced into ¼" thick rounds
	salt
1½	teaspoons unflavored gelatin
5	medium tomatoes, peeled, seeded *(reserve the seeds and juice)*, cut into wedges, and drained on paper towels
	pepper
½	pound buffalo mozzarella, cut into ¼" thick slices

Preheat the oven to 450°. Place the eggplant slices on a lightly oiled baking sheet. Lightly salt the eggplant and bake it for 5 minutes. Remove the eggplant and set it on paper towels to drain.

In a small saucepan place the gelatin. Add 1 cup of the reserved tomato seeds and juice *(add some water if necessary)*. While stirring constantly, bring the liquid to a boil. Reduce the heat to low and simmer the mixture for 1 minute. Season the mixture with the salt and the pepper. Set it aside.

Line the bottom and sides of a baking dish with the eggplant slices *(reserve some slices for the top)*. Layer on ½ of the tomato wedges. Ladle on half of the gelatin mixture. Layer on the cheese. Add the remainder of the tomato pieces. Ladle on the rest of the gelatin mixture. Place the remainder of the eggplant slices on top. Fold over the slices around the sides.

Cover the terrine with plastic wrap. Place a heavy weight on top to press the ingredients down. Refrigerate it for 3 hours.

serves 8

Carrot and Zucchini Vichyssoise

¼   **cup olive oil**
2   **pounds carrots, chopped medium small**
2   **large onions, chopped medium small**
      water *(as needed)*
¼   **cup olive oil**
1½   **pounds zucchini, peeled** *(reserve the skins)* **and chopped medium small**
1   **large leek, well washed and chopped medium small**

In a large skillet place the first ¼ cup of the olive oil and heat it on medium high until it is hot. Add the carrots and onions, and sauté them for 4 to 5 minutes, or until the onions are clear. Add enough water to cover the vegetables. Simmer them for 30 to 40 minutes, or until the liquid is absorbed. Place the vegetables in a blender and purée them until they are smooth. Set the purée aside and let it cool.

In another large skillet place the second ¼ cup of olive oil and heat it on medium high until it is hot. Add the peeled zucchini and leeks, and sauté them for 4 to 5 minutes, or until they are just tender. Add enough water to cover the vegetables. Simmer them for 25 to 30 minutes, or until the liquid is absorbed. Place the vegetables in a blender and purée them until they are smooth. Set the purée aside and let it cool.

Place the zucchini skins in a pot of boiling water and blanch them for 3 minutes. Drain the skins and place them in a blender. Add a small amount of cold water and purée the skins so that a thick, smooth consistency is achieved *(the same consistency as the other 2 purées)*. Set the purée aside and let it cool.

Refrigerate the 3 soups until they are cold.

In each of 8 individual serving bowls place a portion of the 3 soups. Swirl them together with a knife to form a design.

serves 8

"Vichyssoise is a cold soup. There are only five ingredients in this recipe and so it is very easy to prepare. You actually are making three different soups.....one with carrots and onions, one with the peeled zucchini and leeks, and one with the zucchini skins."

"You can play with the three colors of the soups, which are orange, white, and dark green. Try to make a pretty design when you swirl them around."

"This soup is gorgeous to look at, and it is very healthy. The only trick to making it is to get all three soups to be of the same consistency."

Lobster Tabbouleh with Basil

¾ **cup chicken stock** *(recipe on page 297)*
1 **tablespoon butter**
¼ **teaspoon salt**
¾ **cup couscous**
½ **cup fresh basil leaves, minced**
1 **medium garlic clove, minced**
¾ **cup olive oil**
¼ **teaspoon salt**
2 **1¼-pound lobsters**
1 **medium tomato, peeled, seeded, and diced medium**
1 **medium cucumber, peeled, seeded, and diced medium**
2 **tablespoons lemon juice, freshly squeezed**

"This dish has always been very popular with our customers. There is nothing complicated in making it, and it tastes just delicious."

"Couscous is like rice, only it is easier and faster to cook. There is practically no way that you can ruin it, like you can with rice."

"We use Maine lobster that is flown in live from the east coast. In France we use Maine lobster as well."

In a medium saucepan place the chicken stock, butter, and the first ¼ teaspoon of salt. Bring the liquid to a boil and then remove the pan from the heat. Add the couscous, cover the pan, and let it sit for 5 minutes. Transfer the couscous to a glass bowl and let it cool.

In a small bowl place the basil, garlic, olive oil, and the second ¼ teaspoon of salt. Mix the ingredients together and set the sauce aside.

In a large saucepot place 4" of water and bring it to a boil over high heat. Add the lobsters, cover the pot, and steam the lobsters for 12 minutes. Remove the lobsters and let them cool.

Remove the lobster meat from the tails and claws. Remove and discard the intestinal tract from each tail. Cut the lobster meat into ½" pieces.

In a medium bowl place the lobster pieces and 6 tablespoons of the basil-oil mixture. Toss the ingredients together so that the lobster is well coated. Set it aside.

In another medium bowl place the cooled couscous, tomatoes, cucumbers, lemon juice, and the remainder of the basil-oil mixture. Toss the ingredients together well to make the tabbouleh.

In the center of each of 4 individual serving plates place a mound of the tabbouleh. Arrange the lobster pieces around the edge.

serves 4

Bourride of Mahi Mahi and Garlic Mayonnaise

Bourride of Mahi Mahi

2   tablespoons dry white wine
1   teaspoon saffron
2   tablespoons Pernod
4   6-ounce mahi mahi fillets
2   tablespoons olive oil
3   fennel bulbs, stems removed *(reserve the stems)*, **cores removed, and julienned**
1   sprig fresh thyme
1   tomato, diced
     salt *(to taste)*
     pepper *(to taste)*
1   cup vegetable oil
     Garlic Mayonnaise *(recipe on next page)*

In a small saucepan place the white wine and bring it to a boil. Add the saffron and stir it in so that it is dissolved. Remove the pan from the heat and let it cool. Add the Pernod and stir it in.

In a medium bowl pour the wine mixture. Add the mahi mahi and coat it with the sauce. Let the fish marinate for 2 hours.

In a small skillet place the olive oil and heat it on medium high until it is hot. Add the julienned fennel, thyme, tomatoes, salt, and pepper. Sauté the ingredients for 2 to 3 minutes, or until the fennel is tender. Set the mixture aside and keep it warm.

In a large saucepan place the vegetable oil and heat it on high until it is hot. Add the reserved fennel stems and deep-fry them for 1 to 2 minutes, or until they are crisp. Drain them on paper towels, set them aside, and keep them warm.

Grill the mahi mahi for 3 to 4 minutes on each side, or until it is just done.

In the center of each individual serving plate place a fish fillet. Place the sautéed fennel mixture next to the fish. Spoon the Garlic Mayonnaise between the fish and the fennel mixture. Place the deep-fried fennel on top of the fish for a garnish.

serves 4

"This is a version of an old French recipe from the south of France. Originally it was done with monkfish that was poached in a fish stock. Here we use mahi mahi and we grill it."

"We named the restaurant Fennel because fennel is a very popular vegetable in France. We wanted to call it the French pronunciation, but it was much too hard for Americans to pronounce."

"Serve this as a lunch or dinner entrée. It is very light and fresh tasting, with just a hint of a licorice flavor."

Fennel

Garlic Mayonnaise

1	**bulb garlic, cloves peeled and finely chopped**
1	**egg yolk**
1	**tablespoon Dijon mustard**
	salt *(to taste)*
	pepper *(to taste)*
1	**cup olive oil**
1	**tablespoon boiling water**

In a small bowl place the garlic, egg yolk, mustard, salt, and pepper. Whisk the ingredients together so that they are well blended.

While whisking constantly, slowly add the olive oil so that a mayonnaise consistency is achieved.

Add the boiling water to the mayonnaise, and stir it in well.

Strain the garlic mayonnaise and keep it warm until it is served.

"You had better like garlic if you make this recipe, because that is the primary flavor! It goes really well with the fish. The taste of the garlic helps to balance out the sweet licorice flavor of the Pernod and the fennel."

"To be a good chef you must be very generous, because cooking good food takes a lot of work, and you are making it for others. You also must have a deep love for good food."

Grilled Meli Melo of Seafood with Soy Beurre Blanc

Grilled Meli Melo of Seafood

3   cups vegetable oil
4   large leeks *(white parts only)*, **finely julienned**
2   5-ounce salmon fillets
2   5-ounce swordfish steaks
2   5-ounce sea bass fillets
12   medium shrimp, peeled and deveined
12   medium scallops
¼   cup olive oil
      Soy Beurre Blanc *(recipe on next page)*

In a large saucepan place the vegetable oil and heat it on medium high until it is hot *(350°)*. Add the leeks and fry them for 3 minutes, or until they are golden brown. Drain the leeks on paper towels. Set them aside and keep them warm.

Brush the seafood pieces with the olive oil. Grill *(or broil)* the salmon, swordfish, and sea bass for 2 to 3 minutes on each side, or until they are just done. Cut each piece of fish crosswise into 3 pieces.

Grill the shrimp and scallops for 1 to 2 minutes on each side, or until they are just done.

On each of six individual serving plates place the fried leeks. Place 1 piece of each kind of fish on top. Add 2 of the shrimps and 2 of the scallops. Drizzle on the Soy Beurre Blanc.

serves 6

"The word 'meli melo' is a French term, and it means 'mixed'. There are five different kinds of fish in this dish. You can substitute any kind of fish that you want, but the ones called for in this recipe work well because they have a nice contrast of flavors and textures."

"Deep-fried leeks are really, really good. They aren't common in the United States, but they are very popular in France."

"I love it when a customer doesn't order any specific thing, but instead tells me to create what I want and to surprise him. This is when I am at my best!"

Soy Beurre Blanc

2	tablespoons butter
1	medium onion, coarsely chopped
1	large carrot, coarsely chopped
3	stalks of celery, coarsely chopped
2	cups white wine
½	pound butter, cut into small pieces
1	tablespoon soy sauce

In a medium saucepan place the 2 tablespoons of butter and heat it on medium until it has melted. Add the onions, carrots, and celery. Sauté the vegetables for 4 to 5 minutes, or until they are tender.

Add the white wine. Reduce the heat to low and simmer the ingredients for 45 to 60 minutes, or until the liquid is reduced to 1 cup.

Place the mixture in a food processor and purée it. Return the purée to the saucepan. While whisking constantly over low heat, add the pieces of butter one at a time. Add the soy sauce and stir it in.

Gribiche Sauce

2	tablespoons Dijon mustard
½	cup red wine vinegar
2	cups salad oil
2	tablespoons shallots, finely chopped
2	tablespoons chives, finely chopped
2	tablespoons parsley, finely chopped
4	cornichons, finely chopped
2	tablespoons capers
2	hard boiled eggs, peeled and finely chopped

In a medium bowl place the Dijon mustard and the red wine vinegar. Whisk them together so that they are well blended.

While whisking constantly, slowly dribble in the oil. Add the remainder of the ingredients and whisk them in.

makes 3 cups

"I would describe our food as French Provençal with a California twist. People think that French food means cream and butter everywhere, but that is not true. Provençal food uses a lot of olive oil, anchovies, fresh herbs, olives, and garlic. It is much lighter than the food from northern France, which does use a lot of butter and cream."

"Gribiche Sauce is very tangy and flavorful. It goes well with a lot of different things.....it is especially wonderful with cold asparagus!"

"A lot of the recipes at Fennel have been developed and changed from what we did in France in order to respond to what people of Southern California like and want. The food tends to be lighter and healthier, with less cream."

Grilled *pot-au-feu* of Beef with Gribiche Sauce

Grilled *pot-au-feu* of Beef

1	whole beef shank
	water *(as needed)*
1	onion
1	carrot
1	bouquet garni *(1 leek, parsley, thyme, bay leaves, and celery tied in a cheesecloth)*
1	teaspoon salt
½	teaspoon pepper
¼	cup olive oil
8	baby leeks, steamed
	Gribiche Sauce *(recipe on previous page)*

In a large, heavy saucepot place the beef shank. Add enough water to cover it completely. Bring the water to a boil over high heat. Skim off any foam that rises to the top.

Add the onion, carrot, bouquet garni, salt, and pepper. Reduce the heat to low and simmer the beef for 6 to 8 hours, or until it is very tender.

Remove the bone from the beef shank and discard it. Return the meat to the liquid and let it cool.

Slice the beef into eight ⅜" thick medallions. Brush the medallions with the olive oil. Grill them for 2 to 3 minutes on each side, or until they are nicely browned and heated through.

On each of 4 individual serving plates place 2 of the medallions and 2 of the steamed baby leeks. Place the Gribiche Sauce next to them.

serves 4

"This is a very old and classic recipe from France. We have changed it slightly by grilling the meat at the end. Serve it with some mashed potatoes.....it is simply delicious!"

"I grew up with gourmet cooking because my grandmother and aunt both owned restaurants, and my father loved to cook as well. At the age of sixteen I attended a French cooking school and later worked with some excellent, famous chefs."

"This restaurant is owned by four French chefs. Each one owns a restaurant in France. Every month a different chef will come here for one week to show us what he is doing in France, and to see what we are doing here. We get ideas and recipes from each other. This system works great for all of us because it keeps us creative and stimulated. Also, we love to fax recipes to each other!"

Orange and Grand Marnier Parfait

½   cup Grand Marnier
4   ounces sponge cake, diced
⅓   cup water
3   oranges, zested *(outer orange part grated off)*, **and sectioned
       with the membranes removed**
½   cup sugar
8   egg yolks
1   cup Grand Marnier
8   egg whites
½   cup sugar
1¼   cups heavy cream, whipped

In a small bowl place the ½ cup of Grand Marnier and the pieces of the sponge cake. Let the cake sit for 10 minutes, or until all of the liquid is absorbed.

In a small saucepan place the water and bring it to a boil. Add the orange zest and blanch it for 3 minutes. Drain off the water and add the orange zest to the soaked cake. Mix it together well and set it aside.

In a medium bowl place the first ½ cup of sugar, egg yolks, and the 1 cup of Grand Marnier. Whip the ingredients together for 4 to 6 minutes, or until the mixture becomes light and creamy.

In another medium bowl place the egg whites and the second ½ cup of sugar. Whip the ingredients together for 4 to 6 minutes, or until stiff peaks are formed.

Gently fold the egg white mixture into the egg yolk mixture.

Gently fold in the soaked sponge cake with the orange zest.

Gently fold in the whipped cream.

Pour the mixture into a large serving bowl and freeze it for 1 hour.

Garnish the parfait with the orange sections.

serves 8

"You can make this in small, individual ramekins or you can put it in a large bowl and then slice it. The nice thing about this dessert is that you can make it in advance and then freeze it. Also, oranges are available all year around so it is not dependent upon a fruit that is really a seasonal one."

"People go to a particular restaurant for a lot of different reasons..... because of the ambiance, because it's trendy, or whatever. But people come to Fennel just for the food."

Small Park, Redondo Beach

Five Crowns
Corona Del Mar

This well known Lawry's restaurant serves a wonderful Continental cuisine in a setting that is elegant yet friendly.....just like a fine English country inn!

Executive chef Dennis Brask says, *"The most difficult thing about this recipe is shucking the oysters, or coaxing them out of their shells. How do you do that? Very carefully!"*

Warmed Oysters Mignonette

16 Pacific oysters, on the half shell
16 basil leaves
    black pepper *(as needed)*, freshly ground
1   tablespoon shallots, finely chopped
2   tablespoons balsamic vinegar

On a baking sheet place the oysters on the half shell. Place 1 basil leaf underneath each oyster, between the oyster and the shell.

Grind on the black pepper.

In a preheated oven broil the oysters 4" from the flame for 3 minutes.

Remove the oysters on the half shell and place them on 4 individual serving plates.

In a small bowl place the shallots and balsamic vinegar, and mix them together.

Dribble the shallot-vinegar mixture on top of the oysters.

serves 4

Mushroom Bisque

2	tablespoons butter
1	pound mushrooms, very finely chopped
3	tablespoons onions, very finely chopped
2	tablespoons flour
4	cups chicken stock *(recipe on page 297)*
¾	cup white wine
1	bay leaf
1	pinch nutmeg, freshly grated
3	tablespoons cornstarch dissolved in 3 tablespoons water
1	cup heavy cream, warmed
	salt *(to taste)*
	white pepper *(to taste)*
1	tablespoon fresh parsley, chopped

In a medium large saucepan place the butter and heat it on medium until it has melted. Add the mushrooms and onions, and sauté them for 3 to 5 minutes, or until they are tender.

Sprinkle in the flour and stir it for 2 to 3 minutes, making certain that no lumps are formed.

Add the chicken stock, white wine, bay leaf, and nutmeg. Bring the mixture to a boil and then simmer it for 15 minutes. Remove the bay leaf.

Add the cornstarch-water mixture and stir it in well. Simmer the soup for another 10 minutes.

Add the warmed heavy cream and stir it in.

Season the soup with the salt and the white pepper.

Garnish the soup with the chopped parsley.

serves 8

"This is one of the most requested dishes that we serve at the restaurant. The consistency is unusual in that the mushrooms are chopped up rather than puréed or sliced, as you will find in most other mushroom soups. If you want to use a food processor rather than finely chopping them up by hand, be sure that you don't get them too fine. A couple of pulses should do it."

"When you purchase the mushrooms for this recipe, forget everything you've heard about looking for snow-white, tight caps. You want mushrooms that are dark, old, and with the caps open so that the underneath part is exposed. They will have a much stronger fungus taste and this will really heighten the flavor of the soup."

"Have fun with this recipe! You can use a mixture of different kinds of mushrooms, and experiment with different kinds of fresh herbs."

"A good, homemade chicken stock is much preferable to canned, if you have time to make it."

Pride of the Crown's Salad with Lawry's Vinaigrette

Pride of the Crown's Salad

2	heads Bibb lettuce, washed, dried, and torn into bite-size pieces
¾	cup walnut quarters
¼	pound thick sliced bacon, diced medium, fried, and drained of grease
½	cup Gruyère cheese, coarsely grated
1½	cups croutons
	Lawry's Vinaigrette *(recipe follows)*

In a medium large salad bowl place the Bibb lettuce, walnut quarters, fried bacon pieces, Gruyère cheese, and croutons. Toss the ingredients together.

Dribble on the Lawry's Vinaigrette dressing and toss it together so that the pieces of lettuce are well coated.

serves 8

Lawry's Vinaigrette

1	teaspoon dry mustard
1	teaspoon Lawry's Seasoned Salt
1	teaspoon Lawry's Seasoned Pepper
1	teaspoon Lawry's Pinch of Herbs
¼	teaspoon Lawry's Garlic Powder with Parsley
⅓	cup red wine vinegar
1	cup Bertolli olive oil

In a tight-sealing container place the dry seasonings and the red wine vinegar. Shake them together well.

Add the olive oil and shake the container for another 30 seconds.

Refrigerate the dressing for 2 hours.

Hearts of Romaine
with Stilton Cheese Dressing

1   package Lawry's Caesar Dressing Mix
2   teaspoons Lawry's Seasoned Salt
2   teaspoons sugar
3   tablespoons apple cider vinegar
1   tablespoon lemon juice, freshly squeezed
16   ounces sour cream
¾   cup buttermilk
½   cup salad oil
⅔   cup Stilton cheese, crumbled
4   hearts of romaine lettuce

In a medium bowl place the Lawry's Caesar Dressing Mix, Lawry's Seasoned Salt, and the sugar. Mix the ingredients together.

Add the vinegar and lemon juice, and stir them in so that they are well combined.

Add the sour cream and stir it in.

Add the buttermilk and stir it in.

Add the oil and stir it in.

Add the Stilton cheese and fold it in.

On each of 4 individual serving plates place 1 heart of romaine lettuce. Dribble the dressing on top.

serves 4

"The salad dressing would be great to use as a dip for raw vegetables, or even with chips or crackers. You might want to use a little less of the buttermilk so that the consistency is thicker."

"Stilton cheese is a type of blue cheese that doesn't have the bite of Danish, or quite the saltiness of Roquefort."

"The Five Crowns is one of five Lawry restaurants owned by the Frank family. Over 50 years ago Lawrence Frank opened a restaurant where he served only prime rib of beef. In order that his customers could properly season the beef after it was sliced and served to them, he developed a seasoned salt which he put into shakers and left on the tables. This salt was so popular that people would constantly steal it and take it home with them. Finally, he decided to market it, and so Lawry's Seasoned Salt was born! Since then many other Lawry products have been developed, and they are extremely popular."

Creamed Spinach à la Lawry's

2	slices bacon, finely chopped
½	cup onions, finely chopped
1	clove garlic, minced
2	tablespoons flour
1	teaspoon Lawry's Seasoned Salt
¼	teaspoon Lawry's Seasoned Pepper
1	cup milk
1	10-ounce package frozen, chopped spinach, cooked and well-drained

In a medium skillet place the bacon, onions, and garlic. Sauté the ingredients over medium high heat for 7 to 10 minutes, or until the bacon is browned and the onions are tender. Remove the skillet from the heat.

Add the flour, Lawry's Seasoned Salt, Lawry's Seasoned Pepper, and garlic. Blend the ingredients together thoroughly.

Return the skillet to medium heat. While stirring constantly, slowly add the milk. Continue to stir and cook the sauce for 5 to 7 minutes, or until it thickens.

Add the cooked spinach to the sauce and stir it in.

serves 4

"It's a funny thing, but I get phone calls from housewives all over the country who want to know how to make this creamed spinach. Or, more frequently, who want to know how to correctly cook an expensive prime rib of roast that they just bought. They are so apprehensive about how to prepare it correctly, and I have to calm them down and tell them to use a meat thermometer. A lot of them will say, 'Oh, I already have a meat thermometer, but I don't trust it!' I say, 'So what are you going to do..... guess? Please, trust it!' The closer to the holidays we get, the more calls I get, and the more panicky they sound. Usually they are planning a big holiday dinner, and they want it to be as perfect as the meal they had at our restaurant. I feel like an air traffic controller who is trying to guide a terrified passenger into successfully landing a plane because the pilot has just keeled over from a heart attack!"

Five Crowns Spinach Fusilli

1 **pound pancetta** (*Italian bacon*), **thinly sliced and diced into** ¼" **pieces**
¼ **cup shallots, chopped**
4 **tablespoons fresh sage, chopped**
3 **cups heavy cream**
 salt (*to taste*)
 white pepper (*to taste*)
1 **pound spinach fusilli pasta, cooked al dente**
¼ **cup aged Parmesan cheese, freshly grated**

In an extra large skillet place the pancetta and fry it on medium high heat until it is crisp. Drain off all of the fat and reduce the heat.

Add the shallots and sauté them for 4 to 6 minutes, or until they are tender.

Add the sage and stir it in.

Add the heavy cream and cook it for 7 to 10 minutes, or until the liquid is reduced by ½ and is of a nice, light sauce consistency. Add the salt and the white pepper, and stir them in.

Add the cooked pasta and toss it with the sauce so that it is well coated.

Sprinkle the Parmesan cheese on top.

serves 8

"You don't have to use fusilli pasta.....you can use rigatoni or rotelli, or any other kind of pasta that is thick. Because of the strength of the sauce you want a pasta that is heavy, not delicate like angel hair."

"Pancetta is like bacon, except that it is not smoked. You can find it in an Italian specialty shop. It comes in a casing like salami, and the butcher can slice it off in any amount and in any thickness that you want."

"Try to buy a really good quality, aged Parmesan cheese. This shouldn't be too difficult to find in most places."

"The fresh sage gives the dish a beautiful, aromatic flavor which combines very well with the taste of the pancetta and the Parmesan cheese."

"Make this dish and then serve and eat it immediately."

"Yes, this is as good as it sounds! The colors are beautiful and it tastes wonderful."

"The length of time that you poach the salmon depends upon the thickness of the fillets. The liquid should cover the fish completely."

"Use some red salmon caviar as a garnish. The best grade of salmon caviar is used in sushi bars, so try to talk your local sushi chef into selling you a small amount."

"You can make the pesto way ahead of time.....it keeps forever. You may try using other kinds of nuts, if you prefer. There are no hard and fast rules."

"I find that the fresh parsley and cilantro give a really nice green color to the sauce without overpowering the flavor of the salmon."

Poached Salmon with Cilantro Pesto Cream

Poached Salmon

4 cups water
½ cup white wine
3 tablespoons shallots, chopped
1 teaspoon salt
4 6-ounce salmon fillets
Cilantro Pesto Cream *(recipe follows)*

In a wide, shallow pan place the water, white wine, shallots, and salt. Bring the liquid to a boil and then reduce it to a simmer.

Carefully place the salmon fillets into the simmering liquid and cook them for 3 to 5 minutes, or until they are just done.

On each of 4 individual serving plates spoon on some of the Cilantro Pesto Cream. Place a poached salmon fillet on top.

serves 4

Cilantro Pesto Cream

½ bunch parsley, coarsely chopped
1 bunch cilantro, coarsely chopped
2 tablespoons pine nuts
2 teaspoons garlic, coarsely chopped
¼ teaspoon salt
¼ teaspoon pepper
¼ cup olive oil
1 cup heavy cream

In a food processor place all of the ingredients except for the heavy cream. Purée them so that a coarse pesto is formed.

In a small saucepan place the heavy cream and heat it on medium for 4 to 6 minutes, or until it is reduced by ½.

Add ¼ cup of the cilantro pesto and stir it in *(refrigerate any leftover pesto for future use)*.

English Beef Chop
with Choron Sauce

English Beef Chop

1   **3-pound loin end rib roast, small end** *(Note: Ask your butcher to prepare the roast with the 11th rib attached to the rib eye and to remove the fat cover, silverskin, and bone)*
    Lawry's Seasoned Salt *(to taste)*
    pepper *(to taste)*
    Choron Sauce *(recipe on next page)*

Using the flat side of a cleaver, flatten the beef chop out so that it is 1½" thick.

Place the beef chop over hot charcoal briquettes and cook it for 10 to 12 minutes on each side, or until the desired doneness is achieved.

Sprinkle the meat with the seasoned salt and the pepper. Place it on a serving platter and let it rest for 10 minutes before carving.

Serve the beef with the Choron Sauce

serves 4

"This is a very festive dish that we are well known for."

"The only problem is in getting your butcher to prepare the chop correctly. It would be nice if you had a picture of what the chop should look like. Then you could show it to him and he would know just what to do. But since you don't have one, copy down the description that is listed in the ingredients and show it to him. Now, if you don't want to go to the trouble of having your butcher prepare the chop to these exact specifications, then you should go out to dinner instead!"

Choron Sauce

2	tablespoons dry white wine
2	tablespoons white wine vinegar
1	tablespoon shallots, finely minced
2	tablespoons fresh tarragon, finely chopped
1	teaspoon dry chervil
1	pinch thyme
¼	teaspoon black pepper, freshly ground
1	tablespoon tomato paste
¼	teaspoon Kitchen Bouquet
1	cup **Simple Hollandaise Sauce** *(recipe follows)*, **room temperature**

In a small skillet place the white wine, vinegar, shallots, tarragon, chervil, thyme, and pepper. Stir the ingredients together and simmer them on low heat for 3 to 4 minutes, or until most of the liquid has evaporated.

Add the tomato paste and Kitchen Bouquet, and stir them in. Let the sauce cool to lukewarm.

Carefully fold the sauce into the Simple Hollandaise Sauce.

Simple Hollandaise Sauce

4	egg yolks
½	lemon, juiced
2	tablespoons water
2	sticks butter

In a simmering double boiler place all of the ingredients and whisk them together for 8 to 10 minutes, or until a mayonnaise consistency is achieved.

"Choron Sauce is a classical sauce. It's excellent with broiled or grilled meats, as well as with fish. Essentially it is a béarnaise sauce with a tomato product."

"The decor in this restaurant around the holidays is just incredible. We have carolers dressed in Charles Dickens period costumes who stroll around singing."

"This is one of the easiest recipes for a hollandaise sauce that you will ever find. It will work for you at home without your having to go through all of the steps that most recipes call for. In the restaurant we use a much more complicated recipe, but at home this is the one that I use, and it works great!"

"Be sure that you use a double boiler. The top part should not be touching the water.....it must be above the water."

English Trifle

1	4½-ounce package vanilla pudding mix
2	cups light cream
2	tablespoons dark Puerto Rican rum
2¼	cups heavy cream
3	tablespoons sugar
2	tablespoons raspberry preserves
1	10" round sponge cake
¼	cup brandy
¼	cup sherry
30	whole strawberries, washed and stems removed

In a medium saucepan place the pudding mix and the light cream. While stirring constantly, cook the mixture on medium heat until it comes to a boil and begins to thicken. Add the rum and stir it in. Pour the pudding into a bowl. Let it cool and then chill it in the refrigerator.

In another medium bowl place the heavy cream and sugar. Whip them until the cream is stiff. Measure out 1 cup of the whipped cream and reserve it for later use. Fold the remaining 1¼ cups of whipped cream into the chilled pudding.

Coat the inside of a deep 10" bowl with the raspberry preserves to within 1" of the top.

Cut the sponge cake, horizontally, into 4 slices. Place the top slice, crust side up, in the bottom of the bowl, curving the edges of the cake upward. Sprinkle 1 tablespoon of both the brandy and the sherry over the cake. Spread on ⅓ of the chilled pudding. Repeat the process two additional times.

Arrange 15 strawberries on the third layer of the pudding. Place the remaining cake layer, crust side down, on top. Sprinkle on the remaining brandy and sherry.

Place the reserved 1 cup of whipped cream in a pastry bag with a fluted tip. Make 12 mounds around the edge of the bowl and 3 mounds across the diameter. Top each mound with a strawberry.

Chill the cake for 6 to 8 hours before serving.

serves 12

"This recipe was developed by the home economist of Lawry's Foods. It's a much requested recipe in the restaurant."

"My roots are in classical Continental cooking, although I really do enjoy authentic, regional cuisines that utilize fresh, local ingredients."

"All cooking is like building a skyscraper. The better your foundation, the higher you can go with the end result. So a cook is like an architect creating a beautiful, tall building. The basic quality of the ingredients used will determine the final outcome."

Flourless Chocolate Mousse Cake

6	eggs
½	cup sugar
1	pound semi-sweet chocolate, melted
¼	cup strong coffee
1	cup heavy cream
1	teaspoon vanilla extract

In a medium bowl place the eggs and sugar, and beat them together for 3 to 4 minutes, or until the eggs are light in color.

Add the melted chocolate and coffee, and stir them in until the mixture is smooth.

In another medium bowl place the heavy cream and whip it until it is stiff. Add the vanilla and stir it in.

Gently fold the whipped cream into the chocolate mixture.

Preheat the oven to 350°.

Pour the mixture into a buttered 9" springform pan. Place the pan in a baking dish that is half filled with hot water. Bake the mousse cake in the water bath for 1 hour.

Turn off the heat and let the cake sit in the oven for another 15 minutes.

Remove the cake from the oven and let it cool for 30 minutes.

serves 8

"This is a wonderful, dense, almost brownie-like cake. Sprinkle on some powdered sugar and serve it with vanilla ice cream. YUMMY is the word!"

"If you like chocolate, you will love this cake. It's rich, delicious, and very decadent!"

"We live in a phenomenal day and age where you can get fresh ingredients from all over the world. I know that there is always somewhere on the planet where fresh asparagus is sprouting at any time of the year, and if I'm willing to pay the price I know that I can get it."

Fishing Boat Detail, King Harbor, Redondo Beach

The Golden Truffle
Costa Mesa

Like a warm, friendly neighborhood bistro, The Golden Truffle exudes a genuine hospitality while offering an imaginative, eclectic California cuisine.

Alan Greely says, *"This will just melt in your mouth! Eating raw fish gives a lot of people the heebie-jeebies, but when the salmon is pounded this thin you can't tell that it is raw."*

Salmon Carpaccio with Golden Relish

4   tablespoons Dijon mustard
2   tablespoons fresh basil, minced
4   tablespoons sugar
  white pepper, freshly ground *(to taste)*
4   2-ounce pieces fresh salmon, pounded until paper thin
  salt *(to taste)*
  pepper *(to taste)*
½   cup fennel, blanched and finely diced
1   ear sweet corn, cooked and kernels removed
¼   cup kumquats, peeled and finely diced
1   lemon, freshly squeezed

In a small bowl place the Dijon mustard, basil, and sugar. Mix the ingredients together so that they are well blended. Add the white pepper and stir it in.

Season the salmon with the salt and pepper. Spread the mustard mixture on top.

On each of 4 individual serving plates place the salmon.

Sprinkle on the fennel, corn, and kumquats.

Sprinkle on the lemon juice.

serves 4

Lobster Gazpacho

12	ounces lobster meat, cooked, chilled, and minced
1	cucumber, peeled, seeded, and diced
1	yellow bell pepper, diced
1	red bell pepper, diced
½	red onion, diced
3	ripe tomatoes, diced
1	jalapeño chile pepper, seeded and finely minced
2	avocados, peeled, pitted, and diced
8	artichoke hearts, diced
1	bunch cilantro, chopped
3	tablespoons balsamic vinegar
6	tablespoons olive oil
1	lemon, juiced
1	teaspoon salt
½	teaspoon black pepper
⅛	teaspoon sugar

In a large bowl place all of the ingredients. Gently mix them together.

Let the soup sit for 4 hours. Correct the seasoning if it is necessary.

Serve the soup cool, in chilled bowls.

serves 8

"Sometimes people will purée their gazpacho, and that is a major, serious crime! The key to a good gazpacho is that you can taste the individual flavors of all the different ingredients. If you purée it, the whole thing will taste like bell peppers."

"I like to serve this soup cool, rather than cold, because the colder a dish is the less flavor it has. Also, you should be sure to eat the soup within 12 hours after you make it, because otherwise the vegetables will start to wilt."

"The balsamic vinegar is important to the flavor of the soup because it adds a nice tang that is also sweet. Under no circumstances use cider vinegar."

"A good meal should be filled with adventure! Maybe that's why I love to use strong and gutsy flavors."

"This is kind of a tropical dish that is similar to gazpacho. Be sure to serve it in an elegant glass.....don't put it into an ordinary bowl."

"It is important to get a mango that is not too ripe, because then it will be too sweet. This dish has a pickle-y quality to it and a sweet taste will throw off the clarity of the flavor. The mango should be green on the outside, with no red on the skin."

"Alan Greely's Gourmet Sauce is made in the Caribbean. It is like a supercharged A1 Sauce. You can substitute A1 if necessary, but there is no comparison to the taste."

"The abalone is already cooked, so this is not like a ceviche. You can use clams, shrimp, or even octopus. I think that octopus is fabulous, even though most people are reluctant to eat it because they think that it is too weird. But really, octopus is one of the most delectable seafoods that exists. The key to good octopus is to cook it long enough so that it is tender. Boil it in salted water for 1½ hours."

Chilled Abalone Cocktail with Green Mango

1	pound abalone, lightly poached and thinly sliced
1	Haas avocado, peeled, pitted, and diced
1	small red onion, finely diced
2	stalks celery, finely diced
½	jalapeño chile pepper, seeded and minced
2	Roma tomatoes, diced
¼	bunch cilantro, minced
2	lemons, juiced
1	green mango, peeled and diced
½	cup clam juice
1	cup catsup
1	dash tabasco sauce *(or to taste)*
½	cup Alan Greely's Gourmet Sauce
1	Haas avocado, peeled, pitted, and sliced
1	lemon, cut into 4 wedges

In a large bowl place all of the ingredients, except for the second avocado that is sliced and the lemon wedges. Gently mix the ingredients together so that they are well blended.

Place the bowl in the refrigerator and chill the mixture for 1 hour.

In each of 4 tall wine glasses place the chilled abalone mixture. Garnish the dish with the sliced avocado and the lemon wedges.

serves 4

Fresh Fish Carnival

1	cup clam juice
1	cup catsup
1	lemon, juiced
1	lime, juiced
1	bunch cilantro, chopped
1	jalapeño chile pepper, seeded and minced
½	cup cucumber, peeled, seeded, and diced
½	cup red onions, minced
½	cup celery, minced
½	cup tomatoes, diced
2	tablespoons Papaya Pepper Sauce
	salt *(to taste)*
	pepper *(to taste)*
¼	cup olive oil
4	6-ounce fillets of fresh dorado
2	cups red cabbage, shredded

In a large bowl place the clam juice, catsup, lemon juice, lime juice, cilantro, jalapeño chile pepper, cucumber, red onions, celery, tomatoes, Papaya Pepper Sauce, salt, and pepper. Mix the ingredients together well.

Let the sauce sit at room temperature for ½ hour.

Place the sauce in the refrigerator for 1 hour.

In a large skillet place the olive oil and heat it until it is hot. Add the fish fillets and sauté them for 3 to 4 minutes on each side, or until they are crispy brown and just done.

On each of 4 individual serving plates place a bed of the shredded red cabbage. Place a fish fillet on top. Spoon on the sauce.

serves 4

"This calls for fresh dorado fillets, preferably just caught. You can use other kinds of firm-fleshed fish, like sea bass or halibut (not sword-fish). The main thing is that the fish should be as fresh as possible."

"The inspiration for this dish comes from Rio de Janeiro. It is very colorful and festive, just like a celebration or festival. We like to play Latin music really loud when we make it. It's light, refreshing, and has a real zing to it."

"The sauce is more of a relish than anything else. Don't make it too far in advance because you want all of the colors to be really vibrant. You put the cold sauce on top of the hot fish and the cool juices run down the sides onto the dish. Have this with a nice crisp glass of Muscadet.....and you're off to the races!"

"The Papaya Pepper Sauce might be hard to find. Try, but if you can't get it, then don't worry."

Sautéed Lobster Scallopini and Turner Bay Scallops with Kumquats

½	cup flour
½	teaspoon salt
¼	teaspoon black pepper, freshly ground
1	lobster tail, meat removed, cut into ½" pieces, and beaten flat
8	ounces Turner Bay scallops
¼	cup extra virgin olive oil
¼	pound kumquats, sliced
1	bunch chives, finely sliced
1	lemon, juiced
¼	pound kumquats, juiced

In a medium bowl place the flour, salt, and pepper. Mix the ingredients together.

Dredge the lobster and scallops in the seasoned flour.

In a large skillet place the olive oil and heat it on medium high until it is hot. Add the lobster medallions and sauté them for 1 to 2 minutes on each side, or until they are golden brown. Remove them and set them aside.

Add the scallops and sauté them for 2 to 3 minutes, or until they are golden brown.

On each of 4 individual serving plates place the lobster and the scallops. Place the sliced kumquats on top. Sprinkle on the chives. Squeeze on the lemon juice and the kumquat juice. Season the dish with some freshly ground black pepper.

serves 4

"Turner Bay scallops are from New Zealand and they are the preferred kind to use if you can find them. They are much sweeter than other scallops."

"Kumquats are like little oranges. If you can't find them, then you can substitute tangerines or tangelos."

"I like to have complexity in my dishes. The easiest thing in the world is to serve lobster with butter, and I admit that it is delicious that way, because lobster and butter are both rich. But I would rather contrast the richness with a tart citrus taste, like in this recipe. Lobster served with pineapple chutney is out of sight!"

"This dish is perfect for a nice luncheon. It's different, elegant, and you don't have to spend a fortune to make it."

"I used to cook in the Caribbean and a lot of my recipes reflect that influence. When I was there I cooked for a lot of famous rock stars like Elton John, Alice Cooper, and the Rolling Stones."

Cajun Napoleon of Lobster, Swordfish, and Shrimp Ettoûffe

1½ cups clam juice
1   leek, washed and chopped
1   cup fish stock
1   large clove garlic, sliced in half
1   jalapeño chile pepper, seeded and finely diced
1   small lemon, juiced
1½ tablespoons gumbo filé powder
1   stick butter, cut in half
    salt (to taste)
    pepper (to taste)
1   lobster tail, shelled and thinly sliced
8   large shrimp, peeled and deveined
8   ounces swordfish, thinly sliced
½   cup flour (or as needed)
1   tablespoon Cajun Seasoning
2   tablespoons fresh Italian parsley, chopped

In a small saucepan place the clam juice and the leeks. Bring the liquid to a boil on medium high heat and cook the leeks for 6 to 8 minutes, or until the liquid is reduced to 1 cup. Strain the liquid.

In a medium saucepan place the strained clam juice, fish stock, garlic, jalapeño chile pepper, lemon juice, and filé powder. Cook the ingredients on medium high heat for 5 to 7 minutes, or until the liquid is reduced by ½. Reduce the heat to low.

Cut the first half of the stick of butter into small pieces. While whisking constantly, add the pieces of butter one at a time. Add the salt and pepper, and stir them in. Keep the sauce warm.

Dust the lobster, shrimp, and swordfish with the flour. Sprinkle on the Cajun Seasoning.

In a large, heavy skillet place the second half of the butter and heat it on medium high until it has melted. Quickly sauté the lobster, shrimp, and swordfish so that they are just done.

On each of 4 individual serving plates stack the seafood so that they are layered. Pour the warmed sauce over the top. Sprinkle on the Italian parsley.

serves 4

"The word 'Napoleon' does not mean that this is a pastry dish. But rather, it refers to the layering of the different kinds of seafood. It looks really beautiful on the plate."

"This is not a namby-pamby kind of a dish. It is quite boldly seasoned and it has a real punch to it. I would serve this dish in the wintertime because of the heat from the spices. If you don't like hot food, don't make this recipe!"

"Serve this with a mound of white rice and a Dixie beer.....and you're in great shape!"

"We have a lot of regular customers here and so we get to know their likes and dislikes. We will custom make a dish for their own particular tastes. The waitress will come back to the kitchen and tell us that Susie is at table 4, and we know that Susie wants olive oil instead of butter, she can't have tomatoes but she loves capers, and so on."

Kahlua and Passion Fruit Grilled Shrimp

6	fresh passion fruits, halved and pulp scooped out *(reserve the shells)*
⅓	cup Kahlua
2	tablespoons fresh herbs *(basil, rosemary, thyme)*, chopped
1	tablespoon frozen orange juice concentrate
1	tablespoon chipotle peppers, chopped
½	pound large shrimp, peeled and deveined seasoning salt *(to taste)*
1	lemon, freshly squeezed
½	bunch cilantro, chopped

In a medium bowl place the passion fruit pulp, Kahlua, herbs, orange juice concentrate, and chipotle peppers. Mix the ingredients together well.

Add the shrimp and cover them with the mixture. Marinate the shrimp for 1 to 2 hours at room temperature.

Remove the shrimp and sprinkle on the seasoning salt.

Grill the shrimp over hot coals for 1 to 2 minutes on each side, or until they are barely done. On each of 4 individual serving plates place the marinade. Place the shrimp in each of the reserved passion fruit shells. Set them on top of the marinade.

Sprinkle on the lemon juice. Garnish the shrimp with the chopped cilantro.

serves 4

"This is a great appetizer that has a lot of flavor to it. A first course should not be bland.....it should be bold and exciting, because you usually have just a few bites, and those bites should be very impressive."

"The passion fruit has a very perfumy, exotic essence to it.....it's almost like Chanel No. 5. The combination of this flavor with the sweet Kahlua and the smoky spice of the chipotle makes for a wonderful, unusual dish. Try serving this with champagne. It's out-standing!"

"We design the day's menu according to the weather. If the weather is warm we will make light, refreshing dishes like the gazpacho. If the weather is cold, then we make something heartier, like a hot dill soup. Of course, this gets us into trouble a lot of times because in the morning it might be cold and foggy and by noon the sun is out and it's 80 degrees outside. So then we have to put the hot soup in the freezer and serve it cold!"

Steamed Prawns and Pike with Yucca Root Hashbrowns and Pomegranate Blood Orange Butter

Steamed Prawns and Pike

2	carrots, peeled and cut in half
2	medium turnips, peeled and quartered
2	parsnips, peeled and cut in half
1	quart court bouillon *(recipe on page 55)*
2	ounces star anise
1	cup orange peels
8	fresh prawns, peeled and deveined
4	5-ounce pike fillets
	Yucca Root Hashbrowns *(recipe follows)*
	Pomegranate Blood Orange Butter *(recipe on next page)*
⅓	bunch cilantro, chopped

In a large pot of salted, boiling water place the carrots, turnips, and parsnips. Cook them for 4 to 6 minutes, or until they are tender. Remove the vegetables and cut them into small balls with a melon cutter. Set them aside and keep them warm.

In the bottom of a saucepan with a steamer on top place the court bouillon, star anise, and orange peels. Place the prawns and pike fillets in the top of the steamer. Steam them for 8 to 10 minutes, or until they are just done.

On each of 4 warmed, individual serving plates place the Yucca Root Hashbrowns. Place the prawns and pike on top. Place the vegetable balls around the fish. Pour on the Pomegranate Blood Orange Butter. Sprinkle on the cilantro.

serves 4

Yucca Root Hashbrowns

¾	pound yucca root, peeled
¼	cup butter
	salt *(to taste)*
	pepper *(to taste)*

(continued on next page)

"This recipe was developed for a national seafood competition which I won at the state level in California. But when I entered at the national level I lost. The recipe sounds really wild, and when the judges from the east coast saw it they thought I was from Mars! The California judges really liked it.....but of course, we all know that California is an innovative state."

"There are a lot of steps involved in preparing this recipe, but none of them are difficult. You will feel like a hero if you make it because the end result is completely unique. If a person thinks he has invented a recipe, quite often it turns out that other people have come up with the same thing. However, I don't think you will find that to be the case with this dish."

"If you can't find yucca root, then just substitute regular potatoes."

Place the yucca root in a pot of boiling water, and parboil it for 15 minutes. Remove the root and let it cool.

Grate the yucca root.

In a large sauté pan place the butter and heat it on medium high until it has melted. Add the grated yucca root and sauté it for 3 to 5 minutes, or until it is slightly tender.

Add the salt and the pepper, and toss them in well.

Preheat the oven to 375°. Place the sautéed yucca root in a lightly buttered baking dish and bake it for 25 to 30 minutes, or until it is crisp and golden brown.

Pomegranate Blood Orange Butter

2	**tablespoons butter**
1	**bunch shallots, minced**
1½	**teaspoons fresh basil, chopped**
1½	**teaspoons fresh cilantro, chopped**
½	**cup fish stock**
½	**cup red wine** *(good quality)*
½	**cup pomegranate juice**
½	**cup blood orange juice, freshly squeezed**
	salt *(to taste)*
	pepper *(to taste)*
2	**sticks butter, cut into small pieces**

In a medium saucepan place the 2 tablespoons of butter and heat it on medium high until it has melted. Add the shallots, basil and cilantro. Sauté them for 2 to 3 minutes, or until they are tender.

Add the fish stock, red wine, pomegranate juice, and blood orange juice. Cook the ingredients for 5 to 7 minutes, or until the liquid is reduced to ½ cup.

Add the salt and the pepper, and stir them in.

While whipping constantly, add the pieces of butter one at a time so that each one is well incorporated.

"There are a lot of factors involved in enjoying food.....it is more than just eating and tasting it. You can eat a plain ol' cheese sandwich that you share with a good friend on a beautiful day while out on a sailboat, and it can be one of the most memorable meals in your life. Or, you can have a beautifully prepared meal with someone that you can barely stand and the weather is awful, and you will think that it is the worst meal you have ever eaten."

"The colors are very important to this dish. The sauce is like pouring crimson onto your plate.....it almost glows in the dark!"

"You can buy the pomegranate juice at a health food store. If not, use cranberry juice. If you have a fresh pomegranate you can squeeze the juice out yourself. Put the seeds in an old tee-shirt (wash it first!) and squish out the liquid. Or else simmer the seeds in some red wine and then strain it."

Window and Light Detail, Malibu

La Rive Gauche
Palos Verdes

Capturing the quaint elegance of a French country chateâu, La Rive Gauche serves a classic French and Continental cuisine, flavored with a hint of California.

Menu

Marinated Cucumber Salad

Smoked Chicken and
Marinated Goat Cheese

Papoutsakia with Meatballs

Shrimp and Scallops in
Puff Pastry with Red Wine
Butter Sauce

Sautéed Halibut with
Kiwi Chardonnay Sauce

Veal Stock

Roasted Stuffed Quail with
Pear Herb Sauce

Sautéed Pork Medallions
with Red Wine Shallot
Cream Sauce

Stuffed Filet Mignon
with Red Wine Sauce

Angel Hair Pesto Primavera

Strawberries Romanoff

Executive Chef Steve
Dukes says, *"This salad
has a wonderful, zesty
flavor that most people
seem to love."*

Marinated Cucumber Salad

2	cucumbers, thinly sliced
2	tomatoes, wedged
½	red onion, thinly sliced
2	large avocados, peeled, pitted, and cubed
4	ounces feta cheese, crumbled
16	Calamata olives
8	fresh basil leaves, julienned
¾	cup extra virgin olive oil
1	lemon, juiced

In a medium large bowl place all of the ingredients except for the lemon juice. Toss everything together well. Let the salad sit for 2 hours.

Add the lemon juice and toss it in.

serves 4

Smoked Chicken and Marinated Goat Cheese

1	bunch fresh basil, julienned
2	shallots, sliced
3	cups extra virgin olive oil
1	cup white wine
1	bay leaf
6	peppercorns
12	ounces goat cheese, sliced into 8 pieces
1	small chicken, smoked, skinned, boned, and sliced
½	cup pine nuts, toasted
6	tablespoons butter, softened
1	French baguette, sliced into 2" thick pieces
4	leaves romaine lettuce

In a medium bowl place the basil, shallots, olive oil, white wine, bay leaf, and peppercorns. Mix the ingredients together.

Add the slices of goat cheese. Cover the bowl and refrigerate the cheese for 2 days.

Remove the cheese from the marinade and pat it dry. Place it in a large bowl. Add the sliced chicken and toasted pine nuts. Toss the ingredients together.

Spread the butter on the pieces of bread. Place the bread slices under a preheated broiler for 1 minute, or until they are toasted.

On each of 4 individual serving plates place a leaf of the romaine lettuce. Place the chicken and goat cheese mixture on top. Serve the salad with the toasted bread.

serves 4

"You can buy chicken that is already smoked. It usually can be found in specialty stores. Otherwise you can smoke your own. If you don't own a smoker then you can buy a small smoking box that you place in a barbecue. Leave the skin on while you smoke it."

"The combination of the marinated goat cheese and the smoked chicken is excellent! And, the toasted pine nuts add another dimension with their crispness and delicate flavor."

"It's very easy to toast the pine nuts. Put them in a pan and heat them in the oven for about 5 minutes at 400˚. Keep an eye on them because they burn very easily. They should be just a golden color."

Papoutsakia with Meatballs

½	pound ground beef
2	teaspoons fresh oregano, chopped
1	clove garlic, finely minced
	salt *(to taste)*
¼	cup olive oil
1	large onion, diced medium
8	small zucchini, cut into ½" long pieces
5	cloves garlic, finely diced
1½	tablespoons fresh oregano, chopped
12	ounces tomato paste
12	ounces tomato sauce
2	quarts water
1	cup rice, cooked

In a medium bowl place the ground beef, the 2 teaspoons of oregano, the 1 clove of minced garlic, and the salt. Mix the ingredients together with your hands so that they are well combined. Roll the meat into 1" round meatballs.

Preheat the oven to 400°. Place the meatballs on a flat sheet and bake them for 8 minutes, or until they are pink in the middle. Set the meatballs aside.

In a large stockpot place the olive oil and heat it on medium high until it is hot. Add the onions and zucchini, and sauté them for 2 to 3 minutes, or until the onions are clear.

Add the 5 cloves of diced garlic and the 1½ tablespoons of oregano, and sauté them for 2 minutes.

Add the tomato paste and tomato sauce. Stir the ingredients together and cook the ingredients for 2 minutes.

Add the water. Bring the liquid to a boil and then reduce the heat to low. Simmer the soup for 45 to 60 minutes, or until the desired consistency is achieved.

Add the meatballs and the cooked rice.

Add more salt if necessary.

serves 8

148

Shrimp and Scallops in Puff Pastry with Red Wine Butter Sauce

Shrimp and Scallops in Puff Pastry

4   sheets puff pastry, cut into eight 3" x 6" pieces
1   egg, beaten
2   tablespoons butter
8   large scallops
8   large shrimp, peeled and deveined
3   cloves garlic, minced
1   leek, julienned
2   shallots, diced
1   carrot, julienned
½   cup white wine
      Red Wine Butter Sauce *(recipe on next page)*

On a surface that is dusted with flour place 4 of the puff pastry pieces. Brush a ½" strip around the edges with the beaten egg. Lay the other 4 pieces of pastry on top. Score the dough around the edges, ½" in *(make sure that the scores go halfway through the top pieces of dough, like a perforation).* Lightly score the center part of the dough at a diagonal, for decoration.

Preheat the oven to 350°. Place the pastry pieces on a buttered cookie sheet and bake them for 25 to 30 minutes, or until they are raised and golden brown.

Very carefully cut out the top center piece of each pastry, where it was scored around the edges. Set the lids and the bottom sections aside.

In a large skillet place the butter and heat it on medium high until it has melted. Add the scallops and shrimp, and sauté them for 2 minutes.

Add the garlic, leeks, shallots, and carrots. Sauté the ingredients for 2 to 3 minutes, or until the seafood is done and the vegetables are tender. Deglaze the pan with the white wine.

On each of 4 individual serving plates place the bottom piece of the pastry. Spoon in the seafood and vegetables, so that some of it falls out on the side. Spoon on the Red Wine Butter Sauce. Place the pastry lid on top.

serves 4

"Pepperidge Farms makes a good puff pastry that you can buy in the market. We make our own at the restaurant and it is very time consuming. It takes us about five hours to make a batch. If you are ambitious enough to make your own there are many cookbooks that provide the recipe."

"When you read this recipe it may sound very confusing. This is because it is so difficult to explain what to do with scoring the pastry, without being able to show you in person, or with pictures. But, in reality it is a very simple thing to do. Basically, what you are making is a hollow pocket inside the pastry that has a lid on it. Read the instructions over until you can visualize what to do. Once you figure it out the rest is a snap."

"This dish is very elegant and it looks beautiful on the plate. Serve it as an appetizer."

Red Wine Butter Sauce

¾	**cup Burgundy wine**
3	**shallots, finely diced**
¾	**pound cold sweet butter, cut into small pieces**
1	**lemon, juiced**
1	**pinch salt**

In a medium saucepan place the Burgundy wine and shallots. Cook them on medium high heat for 4 to 6 minutes, or until the liquid is reduced to 2 tablespoons. Reduce the heat.

While whisking constantly, add the butter pieces one at a time.

Remove the sauce from the heat. Add the lemon juice and salt, and stir them in.

Keep the sauce warm until you are ready to use it.

"The color of this sauce is purple when you are finished, because of the red wine. It looks quite beautiful on the plate."

"The service that a restaurant provides is very important. The waiters should be professional, the food must be prepared correctly, and it must be served hot. Even a three year old kid can tell if his food is cold!"

"I love the creativity of cooking. It is very satisfying to me on a deep level. I also am an artist, and I find that there is not a lot of difference between creating art and cooking."

Sautéed Halibut with Kiwi Chardonnay Sauce

Sautéed Halibut

4	8-ounce halibut fillets
	salt
¼	cup flour *(or as needed)*
4	tablespoons clarified butter
	Kiwi Chardonnay Sauce *(recipe follows)*
1	kiwi, peeled and sliced into 8 pieces

Sprinkle the halibut with the salt. Lightly dust the fish with the flour.

In a large skillet place the clarified butter and heat it on medium until it is hot. Sauté the floured halibut fillets for 3 to 4 minutes on each side, or until they are golden brown and just done.

On each of 4 individual serving plates place one of the sautéed halibut fillets. Pour on the Kiwi Chardonnay Sauce. Garnish each dish with 2 of the kiwi slices.

serves 4

"Definitely buy fresh fish for this recipe. However, you have to be careful because a lot of markets will buy fish that is frozen and then sell it thawed out so that it looks like it is fresh. Quiz the fishman before you buy! If you can't find fresh fish, don't worry. The Kiwi Chardonnay Sauce is so tasty that it will make up for any loss of flavor that may occur because the fish was frozen."

Kiwi Chardonnay Sauce

3	kiwis, peeled
3	shallots, diced
¾	cup Chardonnay wine
½	pound cold sweet butter, cut into small cubes
	salt *(to taste)*

Place the kiwis in a blender and purée them.

In a small saucepan place the puréed kiwi, shallots, and Chardonnay. Heat the ingredients on high heat and cook them for 4 to 6 minutes, or until the liquid is reduced to 3 tablespoons. Reduce the heat to medium.

While whisking constantly, add the butter cubes one at a time. Add the salt and stir it in. Remove the sauce from the heat and keep it warm until you are ready to serve it.

"I came up with this recipe. It seemed to me that the kiwi would go very well with the Chardonnay and the fish. Actually, the sauce ended up coming out a lot better than I had imagined it would. The flavor is wonderful! The sweet tang of the wine complements the tartness of the kiwi. Also, the color is very pretty.....it's a nice, light green."

Veal Stock

16	**veal bones** *(knuckles and joints)*
3	**carrots, coarsely chopped**
3	**onions, coarsely chopped**
3	**leeks, coarsely chopped**
6	**stalks celery, coarsely chopped**
1	**bunch parsley**
6	**bay leaves**
1	**bunch thyme**
2	**bulbs garlic, cut in half crosswise**
2	**6-ounce cans tomato paste**
	water *(as needed)*

Preheat the oven to 400°. On a flat baking sheet place the veal bones, carrots, onions, leeks, celery, parsley, bay leaves, thyme, and garlic. Roast them for 30 to 45 minutes, or until they are dark brown on all sides. Remove the veal bones and set them aside.

Spread the tomato paste on top of the browned vegetables. Roast them for 30 minutes more, or until the tomato paste has turned very dark brown.

In a large stockpot place the roasted veal bones and vegetables. Cover them with water.

Bring the liquid to a boil. Skim off any foam that appears on top. Reduce the heat to low and simmer the ingredients for 12 to 16 hours, or until the liquid is reduced by ½.

Strain the liquid.

"Some people may already know how to make a good stock, but others may not. It is a rather lengthy process, but it is worth the trouble if you want to prepare a really nice meal. You can freeze the stock so you don't have to make it too often."

"Be sure that you buy the bones that have the knuckles and joints in them. They have a lot of bone marrow and that is where the flavor comes from."

Roasted Stuffed Quail
with Pear Herb Sauce

Roasted Stuffed Quail

2	cups wild rice
3	cups water
2	tablespoons butter
½	small onion, diced
2	pears, peeled, cored, and thinly wedged
1	teaspoon fresh basil, chopped
1	teaspoon fresh thyme, chopped
8	quails, spines and rib cages removed
	Pear Herb Sauce *(recipe on next page)*

In a medium large saucepan place the wild rice. Cover it with water that is kept warm *(100°)* for 30 minutes, or until the grains puff. Strain off the excess water.

Add the 3 cups of water and bring it to boil. Cover the saucepan with a lid and reduce the heat to low. Simmer the rice for 15 to 20 minutes, or until all of the water is absorbed and the rice is tender.

In a small skillet place the butter and heat it on medium high until it has melted. Add the onions and sauté them for 2 to 3 minutes, or until they are translucent. Add the pears, basil and thyme. Sauté the ingredients for 2 to 3 minutes.

In a medium bowl place the cooked rice and the sautéed pear-herb mixture.

Mix the ingredients together well. Stuff the quails with the wild rice.

Preheat the oven to 400°. Place the stuffed quails on a baking sheet. Roast them for 10 to 15 minutes, or until they are done.

Top the roasted quails with the Pear Herb Sauce.

serves 4

"You can find quail in your better markets. If not, ask your butcher to order some. If he can't, then use cornish hens, although the quail will have a much better flavor. They are more gamy tasting, whereas cornish hens taste a lot like chicken."

"Be sure not to overcook the quail, or any other wild game that you may use, because it can easily become tough. You can tell if the quail is done by using a meat thermometer. Or, you can poke it with a knife to see if the juice is clear. If you use cornish hens, they will take about 30 minutes to cook, because they are larger."

"Wild rice is not really a rice, but rather it is a water grass that mainly grows in the Wisconsin and Minnesota area. The Indians gather it by rowing through the reeds in the lakes. One man sits in the back of the boat and paddles. The other man sits in front and beats the reeds with 2 sticks so that the wild rice falls into the boat. Then the women go through a long process of drying it out. So this is why a quality wild rice is so expensive to buy"

"I used to hunt quail when I lived in Illinois, and there were a lot of pear trees that grew there. So quail and pears seem like the perfect match because they came from the same area"

"This is a wonderful dish! Serve the quail and the sauce with a fresh vegetable, and you will have yourself an elegant, delicious, and healthy meal."

"I like to cook simple, even though my recipes may not seem like it! I don't like to try to turn a food into something it is not. California and Italian cuisines are two of my favorites, because they essentially just enhance the flavor of the food that is already there."

Pear Herb Sauce

2	tablespoons butter
2	pears, peeled, cored, and wedged
1	teaspoon fresh basil, chopped
1	teaspoon fresh thyme, chopped
2	tablespoons red wine vinegar
2	tablespoons honey
1	pinch salt

In a medium saucepan place the butter and heat it on high until it has melted. Add the pears, basil, and thyme. Sauté the ingredients for 2 to 3 minutes.

Add the red wine vinegar, honey, and salt. Simmer the sauce until it is heated.

154

Sautéed Pork Medallions with Red Wine Shallot Cream Sauce

Sautéed Pork Medallions

3   pounds pork loin, sliced into 8 pieces
1   cup flour, seasoned with salt and pepper
4   tablespoons butter
    Red Wine Shallot Cream Sauce *(recipe follows)*

Place the pork medallions between 2 sheets of wax paper. Pound them with a meat mallet so that they are twice as big around *(and half as thick)*.

Dredge the pork slices in the seasoned flour.

In a large skillet place the butter and heat it on medium high until it has melted. Sauté the floured pork medallions for 3 to 4 minutes on each side, or until they are nicely browned and the meat is done.

Serve the sautéed pork with the Red Wine Shallot Cream Sauce poured on top.

serves 4

Red Wine Shallot Cream Sauce

½   cup dry red wine
8   shallots, sliced
1   cup heavy cream
    salt *(to taste)*

In a small saucepan place the red wine and the shallots. Cook them on medium high heat for 3 to 4 minutes, or until almost all of the liquid has evaporated.

Add the heavy cream and cook it for 3 to 4 minutes, or until it has reduced by ¼.

Add the salt and stir it in.

"Here is one of my favorite recipes. It's easy as pie to make and the flavor is outstanding!"

"I started cooking when I was in college. I used to work in a German delicatessen and that is where I first realized how incredibly much work there is in running a restaurant. I was in pre-law but decided that I would rather be a chef than a lawyer. I've never regretted my decision."

"I've always been interested in wine sauces. The red wine gives it a deeper, richer flavor. You can tell by looking at the recipe how simple this is to put together."

"My grandfather is one of my most beloved relatives. I remember watching him cook when I was a little boy and it was from him that I got my love of cooking. He was a very generous man who was always happy to see me. Every time I would visit him he would give me a small gift. Once I remember him taking off his shoes and giving them to a poor person on the street."

Stuffed Filet Mignon with Red Wine Sauce

Stuffed Filet Mignon

4	10-ounce filet mignons
12	ounces Roquefort cheese, crumbled
12	shiitake mushrooms, thinly sliced
½	cup clarified butter, melted
	Red Wine Sauce *(recipe follows)*

In the side of each filet mignon make a slit 1" long. Stick a paring knife through the slit and cut out a pocket inside the filet.

Stuff the filets with alternating layers of the cheese and the mushrooms. End the top layer with the mushrooms. Press the slit together so that it closes.

In a large skillet place the butter and heat it on medium high until it is hot. Add the stuffed filet mignons and sauté them for 4 to 6 minutes on each side, or until the desired doneness is achieved.

Pour the Red Wine Sauce over the top of the filets.

serves 4

Red Wine Sauce

½	cup red wine
6	shallots, diced
2	cups veal stock *(recipe on page 151)*
¼	stick sweet butter, cut into small pieces
	salt *(to taste)*

In a small saucepan place the red wine and the shallots. Cook them on medium high for 4 to 6 minutes, or until the liquid is reduced to 3 tablespoons.

Add the veal stock and cook the sauce for 15 minutes, or until it is reduced by ¼.

While whisking constantly, add the pieces of butter one at a time.

Add the salt and stir it in.

Angel Hair Pesto Primavera

8	tablespoons olive oil
1	bunch fresh basil
¼	cup pine nuts
4	cloves garlic
	salt *(to taste)*
	white pepper *(to taste)*
3	tablespoons butter
2	shallots, chopped
1	tablespoon fresh basil, chopped
1½	cups broccoli, cut into tiny florets
1½	cups carrots, julienned
1½	cups zucchini, julienned
1½	cups snow peas
2	cups heavy cream
32	ounces angel hair pasta, cooked al dente
½	cup Parmesan cheese, freshly grated

In a food processor place the olive oil, the bunch of basil, pine nuts, and garlic. Blend the ingredients together until a paste is formed. Add the salt and white pepper, and stir them in. Set the pesto aside.

In a large skillet place the butter and heat it on medium high until it has melted. Add the shallots, the 1 tablespoon of basil, broccoli, carrots, zucchini, and snow peas. Sauté the vegetables for 3 to 4 minutes, or until they are cooked al dente.

Add the heavy cream and stir it in. Bring the ingredients to a boil.

Add the cooked pasta and stir it in.

Add the pesto to the angel hair pasta and stir it in well. Season the dish with the salt and the white pepper.

On each of 4 individual serving plates place the pasta.

Sprinkle the Parmesan cheese on top.

serves 4

"This is a wonderful dish that is very popular with vegetarians. You can use many different kinds of vegetables.....whatever is fresh and in season."

"Capellini pasta is the same as angel hair. So when you go to the store you can look for either name."

"There is a big controversy over what is better to use.....fresh or dried pasta. My personal opinion is that some kinds of pasta are better fresh, and some kinds are better dried. It all depends on the kind of sauce that you use. Fresh pasta absorbs sauces and dried pasta leaves the sauce to itself. So a thick, red marinara sauce would be better with the dried, and a creamed sauce would be better with the fresh."

Strawberries Romanoff

32	strawberries, cored and sliced
½	cup Grand Marnier
1	quart heavy cream, whipped
4	cups vanilla ice cream

In a medium bowl place the strawberries and the Grand Marnier. Let them sit for 10 minutes.

In a large bowl gently fold the strawberries *(with the juice)*, whipped cream, and ice cream together.

Place the ice cream mixture in champagne glasses.

serves 4

"This is a classic dessert that is easy to make and tastes wonderful. It is fairly light and is good after a large meal."

"Have all of your ingredients ready and then put them together at the last minute. You can't make this in advance, because otherwise the Grand Marnier may melt the whipped cream and the ice cream."

"In the classic recipe vodka is used, because this is a Russian recipe. But I prefer Grand Marnier because of the sweeter taste."

"The worst thing that you can do is to stuff someone with too much food. You don't want them to feel so full and fat and miserable that they don't remember the great meal they just had."

Plant Life, Laguna Beach

Mangiamo
Manhattan Beach

If you want to enjoy exquisitely prepared contemporary, Northern Italian cuisine with a fresh, California flair, then Mangiamo is the place to be!

Menu

Puréed Black Bean Soup

Salmon Napoleon in White Dill Cream Sauce

Blackened Shrimp Salad

New Zealand Green Lip Mussels with Linguini

Charbroiled Scallops with Buttered Angel Hair Pasta and Santa Fe Red Bell Pepper Purée

Mangiamo's Ahi with Fettucini

Caramel Rice Pudding

Ronald Guidone, owner and Executive Chef, says, *"This recipe is tasty, healthy, and economical to make. The cilantro and sour cream garnish makes it nice and colorful."*

Puréed Black Bean Soup

3	cups black beans, soaked overnight and drained
2	gallons chicken stock *(recipe on page 297)*
6	bay leaves
½	onion, diced
4	cloves garlic, diced
2	carrots, grated
½	cup heavy cream
	salt *(to taste)*
	pepper *(to taste)*
	sour cream *(as needed)*
2	tablespoons fresh cilantro, chopped
2	tablespoons tomatoes, diced

In an extra large saucepan place the black beans, chicken stock, bay leaves, onions, garlic, and carrots. Simmer the ingredients for 2 to 3 hours, or until the beans are tender. Remove the bay leaves. Add more chicken stock or water if needed.

Strain the beans *(reserve the liquid)* and place them in a food processor. Blend the beans, adding enough of the reserved liquid so that a thick, puréed consistency is achieved.

Add the heavy cream, salt, and pepper. Stir them in so that they are well blended.

Garnish the soup servings with a dollop of sour cream. Sprinkle on the cilantro and the tomatoes.

serves 8 to 10

Salmon Napoleon in
White Dill Cream Sauce

Salmon Napoleon

8   3" squares puff pastry
3   tablespoons butter
8   ounces salmon, thinly sliced
1   cup blanched spinach *(see chef's comments on this page)*,
    chopped
    White Dill Cream Sauce *(recipe on next page)*

Preheat the oven to 350°. Place the puff pastry squares on a buttered cookie sheet and bake them for 15 to 20 minutes, or until they are golden brown and puffed up. Cut them in half horizontally, so that the top is separate from the bottom.

In a large skillet place the butter and heat it on medium high until it has melted. Add the salmon slices and sauté them for 1 to 2 minutes, or until they are heated through. Set them aside.

On each of 4 individual serving plates place a bottom piece of the pastry. In this order, layer on the spinach, salmon, and White Dill Cream Sauce. Repeat this process 3 times, ending with a top layer of the pastry. Pour some of the sauce on top.

serves 4

"Not only is this dish wonderful tasting, it looks absolutely gorgeous on the plate. The combination of colors is very striking. There is the pink salmon, the green spinach, the golden pastry, and the white sauce. We serve this on a black plate that is set on a larger white plate. Beautiful!"

"To blanch the spinach you should place it in boiling, salted water for 1 minute. Remove it and then plunge it into ice water."

"I like to combine contrasting tastes and textures together, much like the Orientals do. People these days are a lot more sophisticated in their eating habits than they used to be. They are well aware of the different flavors that are in a dish."

White Dill Cream Sauce

2½ **tablespoons butter**
1 **teaspoon dried dill**
¼ **cup dry white wine**
1 **cup heavy cream**
   salt *(to taste)*
   pepper *(to taste)*
½ **tablespoon butter**
½ **tablespoon sifted flour**

In a small saucepan place the 2½ tablespoons of butter and heat it on medium high until it has melted. Add the dill and white wine, and cook the ingredients for 3 to 4 minutes, or until the liquid is reduced by ¼.

Add the heavy cream, salt, and pepper. Bring the liquid to a boil and then reduce it to a simmer.

In another small saucepan place the ½ tablespoon of butter and heat it on medium until it has melted. Add the flour and stir it in to make a roux. Cook the roux for 2 to 3 minutes.

Very slowly add the roux to the simmering sauce and stir it in until the sauce thickens.

makes 1 cup

Blackened Shrimp Salad

16	medium shrimp, peeled, deveined, and split lengthwise down to the tail
4	tablespoons blackening powder *(or as needed)*
2	tablespoons margarine
6	tablespoons olive oil
1	tablespoon balsamic vinegar
	salt *(to taste)*
	pepper *(to taste)*
4	cups mixed salad greens *(romaine, red leaf, and radicchio)*, torn
1	scallion, thinly sliced
1	tomato, cut into thin wedges
1	green apple, peeled, cored, and sliced

Coat the shrimp with the blackening powder.

In a small, cast iron skillet place the margarine and heat it on high until it is very hot. Add the shrimp and stir them constantly for 3 minutes, or until they are just done. Set them aside and keep them warm.

In a small bowl place the olive oil, balsamic vinegar, salt, and pepper. Whisk the ingredients together to make a vinaigrette.

In a medium bowl place the salad greens, scallions, tomatoes, and apples. Toss the ingredients with the vinaigrette so that they are well coated.

In the center of each of 4 individual serving plates place the tossed salad. Place the blackened shrimp, standing up, around the salad.

serves 4

"You can buy the blackening mix in the supermarket. It comes in a little box. If the shrimp are dry when you are ready to coat them in the mix, then you should first moisten them with some water or olive oil so that the powder will stick."

"I love dishes like this, ones that have a lot of different flavors. You have the hot, spicy, salty shrimp, the sour apple, and the pungent, bitter taste of the radicchio. You can use another vinaigrette dressing if you prefer. All of the flavors combine together to make a really interesting, tasty salad! Also, the warm shrimp is a delightful contrast to the cold, crisp salad."

"It's important not to overcook the shrimp. Otherwise, they will get tough and start to shrivel up. Keep stirring them. Also, when you split the shrimp, be sure that you don't cut them in half. They should be cut almost clear through, but not quite."

New Zealand Green Lip Mussels with Linguini

"Green Lip mussels are the preferred choice, if you can find them. Otherwise, use another kind."

"When you cook the mussels, if any of the shells don't open, then you should discard them."

"These mussels are just excellent! You can serve them without the linguini, and have them be an appetizer. I like to eat a good, sourdough bread with them so that I can sop up the sauce."

"The sauce should be thick and creamy. If it doesn't seem to be thick enough, then you can add a little roux."

"This dish has the most magnificent flavor! I can't describe the taste to you, but take my word for it.....it's exquisite! Don't substitute clams or oysters. You must use mussels for this recipe to work."

1	stick butter
4	cloves garlic, minced
24	New Zealand Green Lip mussels, scoured under running water, and beards removed
1	cup dry white wine
2	teaspoons dry mustard
2	teaspoons dried thyme
1/4	teaspoon salt *(or to taste)*
1/8	teaspoon white pepper *(or to taste)*
1/2	cup heavy cream
1½	pounds linguini, cooked al dente
1/2	cup Parmesan cheese, freshly grated

In a large skillet place the butter and heat it on medium high until it has melted. Add the garlic and sauté it for 1 minute.

Add the mussels and white wine. Cover the skillet and poach the mussels for 2 to 3 minutes. Add the dry mustard, thyme, salt, and white pepper. Continue to poach the mussels with the lid on for another 1 to 2 minutes, or until the shells open. Remove the mussels and set them aside.

Add the heavy cream. While stirring constantly, bring the liquid to a boil. Reduce the heat and cook the sauce for 3 to 4 minutes, or until it becomes creamy. Add more salt and pepper if necessary.

Add the cooked linguini and toss it so that is well coated with the sauce.

On a large, warmed platter place the linguini. Sprinkle on the Parmesan cheese. Place the mussels around the linguini.

serves 4

Charbroiled Scallops with Buttered Angel Hair Pasta and Santa Fe Red Bell Pepper Purée

Charbroiled Scallops

24	**very large scallops**
½	**cup olive oil**
4	**servings Buttered Angel Hair Pasta** *(recipe follows)*
1	**cup Santa Fe Red Bell Pepper Purée** *(recipe on next page)*

In a medium bowl place the scallops and toss them with the olive oil. Place them in a colander to drain.

Charbroil the scallops over charcoal briquettes for 4 minutes. Rotate the scallops around so that they cook evenly.

On each of 4 serving plates place 6 of the scallops. Add a serving of the Buttered Angel Hair Pasta and the Santa Fe Red Bell Pepper Purée.

serves 4

Buttered Angel Hair Pasta

¾	**pound angel hair pasta, cooked al dente**
½	**cup butter, melted**
¼	**cup parsley, chopped**
	salt *(to taste)*
	pepper *(to taste)*
¼	**cup Parmesan cheese, freshly grated**

In a warmed, medium bowl place the pasta, butter, parsley, salt, and pepper. Toss the ingredients together so that the pasta is well coated with the other ingredients.

Using a fork, twist the pasta into 4 equal ball shapes. Sprinkle the Parmesan cheese on top.

serves 4

"I'm a big advocate of charbroiling. It can really improve the flavor of a lot of things. For instance, instead of steaming or boiling your fresh vegetables, try slicing them, brushing on some olive oil, sprinkling on some lemon juice and pepper, and then charbroiling them. The flavor will be completely different.....they will taste great!"

"Before you charbroil your scallops be sure that the grill is nice and clean. You should brush it with a little oil so that the scallops won't stick. The fire should be medium..... if it is too hot they are liable to catch on fire."

"You can put charbroiled scallops on top of a green salad. Their juice seeps down into the lettuce and it tastes wonderful!"

"This makes for a beautiful looking presentation. The angel hair pasta looks like a baseball sitting in the middle of the plate and it looks so pretty next to the scallops and the red pepper purée."

Santa Fe Red Bell Pepper Purée

2	**cups chicken stock** *(recipe on page 297)*
4	**red bell peppers, seeded and chopped**
½	**onion, diced**
1	**carrot, chopped**
½	**dried Santa Fe chile** *(or dried red pepper flakes to taste)*, **seeded, crumbled, boiled until soft, and drained**
4	**cloves garlic**
1	**bay leaf**
1	**bunch parsley, tied with a string**
	salt *(to taste)*
	white pepper *(to taste)*

In a medium saucepan place all of the ingredients. Cover the pan and bring them to a boil. Cook the mixture for 45 minutes.

Strain the liquid into a bowl.

Remove the bunch of parsley and the bay leaf.

Place the remainder of the ingredients in a food processor and blend them together. Add enough of the liquid to thin the mixture out so that it is of a purée consistency. Add the salt and white pepper, and stir them in.

"This is an extremely versatile recipe because you can use it for so many different things. For instance, you can make it into a soup by adding cream and some roux to thicken it, and then serving it with a dollop of sour cream and some cilantro on top. Or, you can take tortillas and layer them with mashed black beans, fried eggs, the red pepper purée, sour cream, cilantro, and avocado. Great! It also goes very well with mild vegetables."

"This purée is very sweet and rich tasting, with just a hint of spiciness. Naturally, you can vary the amount of the dried red chile that you use, depending on how hot you want it."

"Ideas for new recipes just pop into my head at odd times, especially when I'm doing something relaxing, like gardening. A favorite time of mine to get a good idea is when I am golfing. The idea will come at the precise moment that I am in the middle of an important putt.....and so of course I miss the shot!"

Mangiamo's Ahi with Fettucini

¾   **stick margarine**
½   **onion, finely diced**
4   **cloves garlic, diced**
½   **cup cream sherry**
8   **Roma tomatoes, diced**
4   **8-ounce ahi fillets**
2   **bunches fresh basil, chopped** *(reserve 8 of the leaves for
        the garnish)*
     salt *(to taste)*
     pepper *(to taste)*
1½   **pounds fettucini, cooked al dente**
½   **cup Parmesan cheese, freshly grated**

In a large skillet place the margarine and heat it on medium high until it has melted. Add the onions and garlic, and sauté them for 2 to 3 minutes, or until the onions are clear.

Add the cream sherry and the tomatoes. Raise the heat to high and cook the ingredients for 2 minutes. Flambé the sherry. Cook the sauce for 1 minute more.

Add the ahi, basil, salt, and pepper. Reduce the heat, cover the skillet, and cook the fish for 10 minutes, or until it is just done.

Remove the ahi and keep it warm.

Add the cooked fettucini to the skillet and toss it thoroughly so that is is well coated with the sauce.

On each of 4 warmed individual serving plates place the fettucini. Sprinkle on the Parmesan cheese. Place the ahi on top. Garnish the dish with the basil leaves.

serves 4

"For this recipe to really work you must use ahi, or tuna. Don't substitute sea bass or halibut because the flavor won't be correct if you do."

"My father is from Italy, and he was always cooking and fooling around in the kitchen. He was in the grocery business, and as a very young boy I used to enjoy seeing all of the fresh vegetables and meats that he dealt with. I was further influenced by my aunt, who had a deli in New York City. At the time, we were living in Indiana, and she would send us cases of what I thought was the weirdest, most fascinating stuff..... like live snails, lobsters wrapped in seaweed, and live scungilli, which is an Italian conch."

Caramel Rice Pudding

2	quarts whole milk
1	cup raisins
2	cups water
⅔	cup short grain rice
½	cup super fine sugar
4	pinches cinnamon
1	dash vanilla

In a double boiler place the milk and bring it to a boil. Let the milk cool to room temperature.

In a small saucepan place the water and the raisins. Bring the water to a boil and remove it from the heat. Let the raisins soak for 30 minutes and then strain them.

In a large baking dish place the rice, sugar, and cinnamon. Stir them together.

Add the cooled milk, soaked raisins, and vanilla. Gently stir everything together.

Preheat the oven to 175°. Place the baking dish in the oven and bake the pudding for 6 hours, undisturbed. The pudding is done when the rice is covered with a thick, shiny brown skin.

serves 6

"What makes this recipe so good is that when you leave the pudding in the oven for a long time, you get this delicious, dark crust on it. A great variation is to add some chopped, roasted hazelnuts and some Frangelico on top of the pudding before you bake it."

"Once the caramel crust forms, then it seals in the moisture, so be sure that you don't poke it or else all of the steam will come out."

"This is a very soothing, secure feeling dessert. It reminds people of their childhoods because it's probably similar to something their mothers made."

"All throughout college I was very involved in organized athletics, and so I have a team sports concept which carries over to my restaurant. All of us who work here together are part of a team, with each individual role being as important as the next. The dishwasher is just as important to the smooth running of the team as is the head chef, and he is treated with just as much respect."

Child on Beach, Hermosa Beach

Papadakis Taverna
San Pedro

The wonderful Greek food, the entertaining waiters, and the festive ambiance of Papadakis Taverna make dining here a truly special experience.

Menu

Spanahorizo

Greek Patates

Makaronia

Papadakis Stuffed Grape Leaves

Marinated Lemon Chicken

Sea Bass Greek Style

Karithopita Spiced Walnut Cake

Baklava

Tom Papadakis says, *"This is a wonderful, uniquely Greek dish that tastes even better the next day. Serve it with bread, some Greek cheese, olives, a glass of wine.....you will have a feast!"*

Spanahorizo

½	cup olive oil
1	bunch parsley, finely chopped
1	large yellow onion, finely chopped
1	tablespoon garlic, finely chopped
3	cups water
2	tablespoons tomato paste
1	cup tomatoes, chopped
⅛	teaspoon salt
⅛	teaspoon pepper
2	bunches spinach, stems removed, and chopped
1	cup white rice, uncooked

In a large saucepan place the oil and heat it on medium high until it is hot. Add the parsley, onions, and garlic. Sauté the ingredients for 3 to 4 minutes, or until the onions are translucent.

Add the water and bring it to a boil.

Add the tomato paste, chopped tomatoes, salt, and pepper. Mix the ingredients together thoroughly so that everything is well combined.

Add the spinach and rice. Simmer the ingredients for 30 minutes on low heat, or until the rice is done.

serves 4

Greek Patates

3	pounds white potatoes, peeled and quartered
½	cup yellow onions, chopped
¼	cup garlic, finely minced
½	teaspoon salt
½	teaspoon pepper
½	teaspoon dry oregano
½	teaspoon basil
1	cup lemon juice, freshly squeezed
½	cup vegetable oil
	water *(as needed)*

Preheat the oven to 400°.

In a large baking pan place the potatoes *(add enough potatoes so that they fill the pan up, ¾" from the top)*. Sprinkle on the onions, garlic, salt, pepper, oregano, basil, lemon juice, and vegetable oil. Add enough water so that the potatoes are just covered. Stir the ingredients together very thoroughly so that everything is well mixed.

Bake the potato mixture for 45 minutes. Carefully stir the ingredients together so that they are re-mixed. Bake the potatoes for another 45 minutes, or until they are tender. Remove the potatoes with a slotted spoon.

serves 6 to 8

Makaronia

½	pound sweet butter
¼	pound Mouzithra Greek cheese *(or feta cheese)*, **grated**
1½	pounds spaghetti, cooked al dente
16	jumbo Calamata olives, meat shaved from the pits

In a large saucepan place the butter and heat it on medium until it has melted. Add the cheese and stir it in.

Add the pasta and toss it in so that it is well coated with the butter and cheese. Add the shaved olives and toss them in well.

serves 4

"People really, really love these potatoes! We are always getting requests for the recipe, more so than for any other dish that we serve. They are simple to make, they have a wonderful flavor, and they are unique."

"My brother used to play football at USC, and he had a friend on the team named John. John would come over to our house for dinner and my mother would make about ten pounds of this pasta. He would shovel it in as fast as he could, and my mother would say, 'John, slow down and taste the food!' And he would say, 'It's pasta, and I KNOW what pasta tastes like!' "

"To me pasta is like ice cream. It's the perfect thing to eat when you're in front of the tube or you're reading a good book, and there's no one else around to watch you.....there is practically nothing more satisfying in the world!"

Papadakis Taverna

"You must be ambitious to make this recipe because it takes some time to roll all the grape leaves. It is a very traditional Greek dish that has a lot of great flavors in it. A variation is to use cabbage instead of the grape leaves."

"Cooking is passionate..... you have to love it, whether it means creating something new or doing something the same way for the thousandth time. It requires discipline and hard work, as well as creativity. Just like in a relationship with a woman, you must constantly strive to renew yourself, so that the relationship does not become stagnant."

"The Greeks don't believe in harboring any bitterness or bad feelings inside. They get their emotions out at the moment, and then they go on to the next moment. A tangible expression of this belief is to throw a glass or break a plate, and that is why you see the waiters doing this in the restaurant. Get it out! Let it go! Let it happen! It's just a glass! It's just a plate! Let your spirit open and give yourself a chance to live!"

Papadakis Stuffed Grape Leaves

1½	pounds ground lamb
1	large yellow onion, finely chopped
1	bunch parsley, chopped
1	bunch fresh mint, chopped
1	cup pine nuts
½	cup lemon juice, freshly squeezed
½	cup olive oil
½	teaspoon oregano
½	teaspoon salt
½	teaspoon pepper
1	jar grape leaves, washed and stems removed
	water (as needed)

In a large bowl place the lamb, onions, parsley, mint, pine nuts, lemon juice, olive oil, oregano, salt, and pepper. Mix the ingredients together with your hands so that they are well combined.

Lay a grape leaf out flat. Place approximately 3 ounces of the lamb mixture in the center of the grape leaf. Fold over the stem end. Fold over the two sides. Roll up the grape leaf so that the mixture is completely encased. Repeat this process until all of the meat mixture is used.

Preheat the oven to 350°. Line the bottom of a large baking dish with approximately 10 grape leaves. Place the stuffed grape leaves in the dish so that they are tightly packed. Cover the stuffed grape leaves with water and bake them for 1 hour.

serves 8

Papadakis Taverna

172

Marinated Lemon Chicken

2   cups Greek virgin olive oil
8   large chicken breasts, skin and bones removed
6   cloves garlic, crushed
2   lemons, juiced
2   tablespoons fresh oregano, chopped
⅛   teaspoon white pepper
4   ounces feta cheese, cut into 8 slices

In a large pan place the olive oil. Add the chicken breasts and coat them well with the oil.

Spread the garlic on both sides of the chicken

Sprinkle the lemon juice over the chicken.

Sprinkle on the oregano and white pepper.

Cover the pan and place it in the refrigerator. Marinate the chicken for 24 hours.

Charbroil the chicken for 5 to 6 minutes on each side, or until it is done. Brush the chicken with the marinade the entire time that you are cooking it.

Place the broiled chicken on a large serving platter. Put a piece of feta cheese on top of each chicken breast.

serves 8

"This is a great dish to serve at an outdoor barbecue. You marinate the chicken overnight, put it on the grill.....and then have a lot of fun eating it!"

"It's very easy to overcook chicken, especially on a barbecue. You can see that the coals are hot, but you don't really know exactly how hot they are, and before you know it your chicken has caught on fire! That's why barbecuing is so exciting. You get all of this smoke in your eyes and you think you are dying so you get another drink and then you forget what you are doing on the grill. The hardest part is trying not to fall in the pool. It's a real adventure and that's why Americans love it!"

"My brothers and I believe in serving large portions because we really love to eat. You can tell this by looking at me. You might not say that I am overweight, but I am definitely THICK!"

Papadakis Taverna

Sea Bass Greek Style

"This is a wonderful dish to prepare at home because you can make it up to a day in advance. This way if you have guests over for dinner you can sit with them, have a few cocktails, and then 30 minutes before you are ready to eat you just pop it in the oven. It comes out all gorgeous looking and they will think you have been slaving away in the kitchen all day."

"I used to make this for my girlfriends in college to impress them. I would whip it out of the oven and they would be bowled over. I'd say, 'You're with a Greek, sweetheart! We're going to EAT!'"

"I learned this recipe from my grandmother. I had always loved it, and so I had her show me how to make it at her house. I first served it in the restaurant to an old and dear friend, Ben Binder, who used to encourage us to expand our menu. He came in with a party of eight and I made it for the whole table. He gave me the seal of approval, and believe me, if it wasn't any good he would have told me!"

8	8-ounce sea bass fillets
½	cup flour *(or as needed)*
2	tablespoons light olive oil
1	lemon, juiced
3	tablespoons vegetable oil
2	large yellow onions, finely chopped
6	cloves fresh garlic, crushed
1	bunch parsley, chopped
1	pinch pepper
3½	cups canned tomatoes
1	tomato, chopped
3	bay leaves
½	teaspoon rosemary
½	cup dry white wine
1	lemon, cut into 8 wedges

Dust the sea bass fillets with the flour.

In a large skillet place the 2 tablespoons of olive oil and heat it on medium high until it is hot. Quickly sear the fillets on both sides so that they are sealed. Place the fish in a large baking pan and sprinkle on the lemon juice. Set the fish aside.

In a medium skillet place the 3 tablespoons of vegetable oil and heat it on medium high until it is hot. Add the onions, garlic, and parsley. Sauté the ingredients for 3 to 4 minutes, or until the onions are translucent. Add the pepper and stir it in.

In a medium large saucepan place the sautéed onion mixture, canned tomatoes, chopped tomatoes, bay leaves, rosemary, and white wine. Stir the ingredients together and simmer them on low heat for 40 minutes.

Preheat the oven to 350°. Pour the sauce over the fish and bake it for 20 minutes, or until it is just done.

Garnish the dish with the lemon wedges.

serves 8

Karithopita Spiced Walnut Cake

6	eggs
2½	cups Bisquick
½	teaspoon cinnamon
1	teaspoon salt
½	teaspoon ground cloves
¾	teaspoon baking powder
2	cups sugar
2½	cups walnuts, chopped
1½	cups milk
1½	cups vegetable oil
¾	cup sugar
½	cup water
1	2" strip orange peel
1	2" strip lemon peel
½	cinnamon stick
¼	cup honey
½	lemon, juiced
¼	cup walnuts
1	teaspoon ground cinnamon

In a large mixing bowl place the eggs, Bisquick, cinnamon, salt, cloves, baking powder, the 2 cups of sugar, the 2½ cups of chopped walnuts, milk, and oil. Blend them together with an electric mixer for 5 minutes.

Turn the mixer on high and beat the batter for 15 seconds.

Preheat the oven to 375°. Pour the batter into a baking pan that is 10" x 14", and 2½" deep. Bake the cake for 45 minutes, or until a toothpick inserted comes out clean. Remove the cake and let it sit for 2 hours.

In a medium saucepan place the ¾ cup of sugar, water, orange peel, lemon peel, and cinnamon stick. Bring the ingredients to a boil and then simmer them for 5 minutes.

Add the honey and bring the mixture to a boil. Remove the pan from the heat and add the lemon juice. Stir the ingredients together and let the syrup cool. Remove the orange and lemon peels, and the cinnamon stick.

Spread the syrup over the cake. Sprinkle on the ¼ cup of chopped walnuts and the ground cinnamon.

serves 8

Papadakis Taverna

"Years ago my grandmother insisted that we serve her Karithopita in the restaurant. Finally we said, 'Fine. You make it.' And she said, 'Fine. You pay me.' So three or four times a week she would come over to the restaurant to get the ingredients and then she would take them back to her house and bake the cakes for us. After a year or more of her doing this my brothers and I decided that payday had arrived, so we sent her and our grandfather on a trip to Greece. She was a wonderful woman who was witty, sharp tongued, spunky, and full of energy! She had a great influence on all of us and we loved her very much."

"Where do Greek grandmothers come up with their recipes? When they are born all of the information is passed on through the umbilical cord. It's osmosis!"

Baklava

5	teaspoons cinnamon
3	cups walnuts, coarsely chopped
1	pound sweet butter, clarified and melted
1	pound phyllo pastry sheets
40	whole cloves
1½	cups sugar
1	cup water
1	2" strip orange peel
1	2" strip lemon peel
1	cinnamon stick
⅓	cup honey
½	lemon, juiced

In a medium bowl place the cinnamon and walnuts, and mix them together.

Brush the bottom of a 14" x 20" baking dish with the butter. Place one pastry sheet in the dish and brush it with the butter. Repeat this process so that 6 pastry sheets line the bottom of the dish.

Sprinkle ⅓ of the nut mixture over the top of the pastry sheets. Repeat this process so that there are 3 layers of the nut mixture and 4 layers of 6 buttered pastry sheets, ending with 6 pastry sheets.

Cut the baklava into 40 diamond shaped pieces. Place a whole clove in the center of each piece.

Preheat the oven to 350°. Bake the baklava for 40 minutes, or until it is golden brown.

In a medium saucepan place the sugar, water, orange peel, lemon peel, and cinnamon stick. Bring the ingredients to a boil and then simmer them for 5 minutes.

Add the honey and bring the mixture to a boil. Remove the pan from the heat and add the lemon juice. Stir the ingredients together and then let the syrup cool. Remove the orange and lemon peels, and the cinnamon stick.

Spread the cool syrup over the hot baklava. Cover the dish with a towel and let it sit for 1 hour before serving.

serves 8 to 12

"Baklava is served in every Greek restaurant in the country, and each Greek chef has his own particular recipe that he thinks is the very best in the world. Here at Papadakis we serve baklava the way mama made it."

"Everybody loves baklava. It's the kind of thing that people know they are going to order for dessert when they come to the restaurant, and they look forward to it all day."

"Our philosophy here at the restaurant is twofold: be natural, and take a nap in the afternoon!"

Papadakis Taverna

Fishing Boat Portholes, San Pedro Harbor

Papa Garo's
Redondo Beach

If you are in the mood for some delicious ethnic Mid-Eastern food, then come to Papa Garo's.....it's like stepping into an airy Mediterranean bistro!

Menu

Humus Tahini Dip

Lebanese Herb Salad

Tabouli Herb Salad

Falafel Golden Domes with Tahini Sauce

Armenian Pizza

Pizza Dough

Stuffed Grape Leaves Yalanchi Sarma

Cheese and Spinach Borag

Owner Raffi Dilsizian says, *"This is tasty, healthy, easy to do, and inexpensive to make. You can prepare a big batch and then freeze it. When you purée the chickpeas they should have a buttery quality to them. If you are getting little chunks and pieces, then you have not cooked them long enough. So maybe you should test a few in the blender first."*

Humus Tahini Dip

¾ **cup chickpeas, soaked overnight and drained**
2 **cloves garlic, minced**
1 **teaspoon salt**
¼ **teaspoon pepper**
6 **tablespoons tahini** *(sesame paste)*
2 **lemons, juiced**
1 **tablespoon corn oil** *(or as needed)*
1 **tablespoon olive oil**
¼ **teaspoon paprika**
1 **tablespoon fresh parsley, chopped**

In a medium saucepan place the soaked chickpeas and cover them with water. Bring the water to a boil over high heat and vigorously cook the chickpeas for 10 minutes. Reduce the heat to low and simmer the chickpeas for 1½ hours, or until they are tender *(add more water if necessary)*.

Drain the water from the chickpeas. Place them in a food processor *(reserve 8 chickpeas for the garnish)* and purée them until they are very smooth. Add some water if necessary.

In a medium bowl place the puréed chickpeas. Add the garlic, salt, pepper, tahini, and lemon juice. Mix the ingredients together so that they are well blended.

Add the corn oil and mix it in well so that a smooth paste is formed.

In a small serving bowl place the humus. Smooth it down evenly with a knife. Pour the olive oil in the center. Sprinkle on the paprika and parsley. Garnish the dish with the reserved chickpeas.

makes 1¼ cups

Lebanese Herb Salad

1	**pita bread**
½	**head leaf lettuce, washed, dried, and chopped**
½	**red bell pepper, seeded and finely chopped**
1	**bunch cilantro, chopped**
1	**bunch scallions, thinly sliced**
3	**tomatoes, diced**
2	**tablespoons fresh parsley, chopped**
1	**tablespoon fresh mint, chopped**
1	**tablespoon sumac**
¼	**cup olive oil**
2	**lemons, juiced**
½	**teaspoon cinnamon**
	salt (to taste)
	pepper (to taste)

Bake the pita bread so that it is dry. Break the bread up into small pieces and set them aside.

In a medium bowl place the lettuce, red bell peppers, cilantro, scallions, tomatoes, parsley, mint, and sumac. Toss the ingredients together.

Add the olive oil and toss it in well.

Add the lemon juice, cinnamon, salt, and pepper. Toss the ingredients together well.

Add the pita bread pieces and toss them in.

serves 4

"This is a traditional Lebanese salad that is served before the main entrée. It has more body than a regular tossed green salad because of the toasted pita bread pieces. They add a nice, additional texture."

"You can bake or broil the pita bread. We deep-fry it at the restaurant, which gives it a richer flavor. Make certain that you add the bread pieces right before you are ready to serve the salad. You want them to be nice and crisp, and if you add them too soon they will get soggy."

"Our family is of Armenian descent, but we come from Lebanon. We came to America 18 years ago, and started Papa Garo's restaurant. In Armenian families both the males and females cook, and so both of my parents were excellent in the kitchen."

Tabouli Herb Salad

4	tablespoons olive oil
3	lemons, juiced
	salt *(to taste)*
	pepper *(to taste)*
⅔	cup #1 bulgur *(the finest grain possible)*
1½	bunches parsley, finely chopped
2	tablespoons fresh mint, chopped
2	cloves garlic, minced
2	tomatoes, finely chopped
1	bunch scallions, minced
½	onion, grated
1	green bell pepper, seeded and finely chopped
½	head romaine lettuce, washed, dried, and leaves separated

In a small bowl place the olive oil, lemon juice, salt, and pepper. Whisk the ingredients together. Set the dressing aside.

Place the bulgur in a strainer and rinse it with cold water. Squeeze out the excess water.

In a medium bowl place the bulgur, parsley, mint, garlic, tomatoes, scallions, onions, and green bell peppers. Toss the ingredients together well.

Add the dressing and toss it in well.

On each of 4 individual serving plates arrange the romaine lettuce. Place the bulgur salad on top.

serves 4

"There is a lot of parsley in this salad, which is good for your diet. Parsley has a lot of zinc in it and it is good for the digestion. The parsley flavor will not be too strong because there are the other flavors of the garlic, olive oil, and lemon juice to blend in with it."

"One of the tricks to making a good tabouli lies in the preparation of the parsley. You should wash it and then let it drain so that it is completely dry. If any water remains, then it will bleed when you chop it, and this will make it taste bitter. Chop it fine with a very sharp knife. Never put it in a blender!"

"Another little trick that you can do is to let the bulgur soak in some fresh tomato juice and lemon juice. Do this instead of rinsing it in cold water."

Falafel Golden Domes
with Tahini Sauce

Falafel Golden Domes

1	pound chickpeas, soaked overnight, cooked, and drained
3	cloves garlic, minced
½	teaspoon baking powder
2	teaspoons ground coriander
2	teaspoons ground cumin
1	bunch parsley, minced
1	medium onion, grated
4	scallions, minced
2	tablespoons fresh cilantro, chopped
3	cups vegetable oil
4	pita breads, warmed
1	tomato, finely chopped
2	lemons, juiced
	Tahini Sauce *(recipe on next page)*

Remove the skins from the cooked chickpeas by rubbing them with a dish towel.

Place the chickpeas in a food processor and purée them.

Add the garlic, baking powder, coriander, cumin, parsley, onions, scallions, and cilantro. Blend the ingredients together so that a smooth paste is formed. Add some water if necessary. Let the mixture rest for 30 minutes.

Form the paste into patties that are 2" in diameter and ½" thick.

In a medium large saucepan place the vegetable oil and heat it on medium high until it is hot. Add the patties and deep-fry them for 2 to 3 minutes, or until they are golden brown. Drain them on paper towels.

In each of the pita breads place some of the falafel, tomatoes, lemon juice, and Tahini Sauce.

serves 4

"Falafel is popular all over the Middle East. It is known as a poor man's meal because it is inexpensive to make, and yet it is very filling and nutritious. If you eat this for lunch, then you probably won't want anything for dinner. You should be used to eating chickpeas, or else it might be somewhat hard on your digestion."

"Another way to serve the falafel is to put it on a plate with some humus, tabouli, tahini sauce, and some pita bread on the side. This way you can make your own little sandwiches, and it won't be quite so messy to eat."

"The oil for the deep-frying should be fresh. Almond oil would be best, if you can find it. Add enough to a saucepan so that it covers the falafel. Serve them as soon as they are cooked because they must be very crisp, and not soggy."

Tahini Sauce

⅔	**cup tahini** *(sesame paste)*
3	**tablespoons water** *(or as needed)*
2	**lemons, juiced**
2	**cloves garlic, minced**
1	**tablespoon fresh parsley, finely chopped**
	black pepper

In a small bowl place the tahini, water, and lemon juice. Mix the ingredients together so that a smooth sauce is formed *(add more water if necessary)*.

Add the garlic, parsley, and black pepper. Mix them in so that they are well blended.

makes 1 cup

"The Tahini Sauce really livens up the flavor of the falafel. You have to be careful to get it the right consistency.....it should not be too thick or too thin. Make it the consistency of a ranch dressing."

"My mother has been making this almost every day for many, many years, and nobody can make it better! She doesn't even measure the ingredients, she just eyes them."

"You can serve this sauce with fish, or as a dip for raw vegetables. It's really delicious."

"The restaurant business is difficult because you are open to the public. You must be very strong both physically and emotionally. If nothing else, your crew will drive you nuts!"

Armenian Pizza

½	pound ground lamb
1	onion, minced
1	clove garlic, minced
1	green bell pepper, seeded and finely chopped
1	tablespoon fresh parsley, chopped
1	cup canned tomatoes, drained and chopped
1	tablespoon tomato paste
½	teaspoon allspice
½	teaspoon salt
¼	teaspoon pepper
2	tablespoons olive oil
1	onion, chopped
1	cup spinach, chopped
½	cup mushrooms, sliced
2	tablespoons fresh basil, chopped
¼	cup chives, minced
1	tomato, peeled, seeded, and chopped
4	8" rounds pizza dough (recipe on next page), unbaked
½	cup mozzarella cheese, grated
½	cup Monterey Jack cheese, grated

"In America we call this an Armenian pizza, but the real title for it is an Arabic word that means meat-dough. You can make it with either beef or lamb, although the classic recipe calls for lamb. In Lebanon the quality of lamb is outstanding."

In a medium bowl place the ground lamb, minced onions, garlic, green bell peppers, parsley, canned tomatoes, tomato paste, allspice, salt, and pepper. Mix the ingredients together with your hands so that they are well combined. Set the mixture aside.

In a large skillet place the olive oil and heat it on medium high until it is hot. Add the chopped onions, spinach, mushrooms, and basil. Sauté the ingredients for 3 to 4 minutes, or until the onions are clear. Add the chives and the fresh tomatoes, and sauté them for 1 minute.

"Another way to make this, which is how we do it in Lebanon, is to cook some eggplant slices and squeeze on some fresh lemon juice. Place the eggplant on top of the pizza and then roll it up and eat it. It tastes really good!"

Spread the lamb mixture on top of the 4 pizza rounds. Spread on the sautéed vegetables. Sprinkle on the 2 cheeses.

Preheat the oven to 450°. Place the pizzas on a well-greased flat sheet. Bake them for 15 to 20 minutes, or until the lamb is cooked and the cheese is bubbly.

serves 4

"This is very popular at lunch time, especially with the secretaries. It is a nice size and you will not feel stuffed after eating it. If I were eating this for dinner, I probably would eat two of them, along with a salad."

"Roll the pizza dough out so that it is very thin. When it is baked it still should be thin."

"In Lebanon if you were making this pizza you would make up your topping and then take it to the bakery. They have the dough there and they will bake it for you. So you pay them for both the service and the dough."

"I believe that eating is a spiritual experience, and that one should be both conscious of and grateful for each bite. Many people have a prayer or a moment of silence before they eat, to help remind them of this spiritual quality. This also helps to calm down their minds so that the food can be better digested. I believe that when you eat it is best not to think, and you should talk as little as possible."

"We try to use fresh, organic products that have no preservatives or chemicals. In a way, I am a health fanatic. I think that when one lives close to water, like the ocean, there are certain vibrations that emanate which cause people to be more conscious of their health."

Pizza Dough

1	package active dry yeast
1	teaspoon sugar
⅔	cup warm water
2	cups white bread flour
½	teaspoon salt

In a small bowl place the yeast, sugar, and warm water. Stir the ingredients together. Set the mixture aside in a warm place for 5 to 10 minutes, or until it bubbles.

In a medium bowl sift together the flour and the salt. Add part of the yeast liquid and mix it in. Continue to add the yeast liquid and mix it in until a dough is formed.

Knead the dough for 10 minutes. Cover it with an oiled, plastic wrap, and set it aside in a warm place for 1 hour, or until it has doubled in size.

Divide the dough into 4 equal portions and roll them into balls. Cover the dough balls with the same oiled plastic wrap and let them rest for 5 minutes.

On a floured surface roll out each ball of dough so that it forms an 8" round. *(If the dough shrinks back to a smaller or irregular size, cover it, let it rest for 3 minutes, and roll it out again).*

makes 4 rounds

Stuffed Grape Leaves
Yalanchi Sarma

1 quart water
8 ounces preserved grape leaves, stems removed
1 cup cooked rice
1 medium onion, grated
2 tablespoons fresh parsley, minced
2 tomatoes, finely chopped
1 teaspoon dried mint
½ teaspoon allspice
1 clove garlic, minced
1 lemon, juiced
water (as needed)

In a medium saucepan place the water and bring it to a boil. Remove the pan from the heat and add the grape leaves. Let the grape leaves sit in the hot water for 10 minutes. Remove them from the water and set them aside.

In a medium bowl place the cooked rice, onions, parsley, tomatoes, dried mint, allspice, and garlic. Mix the ingredients together well. Let the mixture sit for 2 hours.

In the center of each grape leaf place a small amount of the rice mixture. Fold the bottom of the grape leaf up and the sides over. Roll the grape leaf up.

Line the bottom of a large saucepan with some of the grape leaves. Place the rolled grape leaves on top, seam side down, so that they are tightly packed.

Sprinkle on the lemon juice. Add enough water to cover the rolled grape leaves. Place an oven-proof plate on top of the rolled grape leaves to press them down. Cover the pot and bring the liquid to a boil over high heat. Reduce the heat to low and simmer the rolled grape leaves for 45 to 60 minutes, or until most of the water is absorbed. Let them sit for 1 hour before serving.

serves 4

"We buy the grape leaves that are sold just for stuffing, because they are very fine and thin, with no large and tough veins. It is a special kind of grape leaf that is grown just for the leaves, and not for the grapes. A lot of them are grown in Fresno. Many Armenians live there, and they are really into their grape leaves!"

"You need to let the rolled grape leaves cool to lukewarm before you serve them, because this will give them a stable texture. If you try to eat them when they are too hot, they will just fall apart."

"These work very well for parties.....they are a great finger food and people love them. There is a lot of labor involved in making them, but it's fun to do and the end result is worth it."

"Yalanchi Sarma means 'deceiving sarma', because this dish tastes like a meat dish, but it has no meat."

Cheese and Spinach Borag

4	cups spinach, blanched, drained, and chopped
1	pound Monterey Jack cheese, grated
1/3	cup cream cheese
1	egg, beaten
1	tablespoon fresh parsley, chopped
1	dash cayenne pepper
1/2	teaspoon salt
1/4	teaspoon pepper
1	package phyllo dough
1/2	cup butter *(or as needed)*, melted
1	cup milk
1	egg

In a medium bowl place the blanched spinach, Monterey Jack cheese, cream cheese, the first beaten egg, parsley, cayenne pepper, salt, and pepper. Mix the ingredients together so that they are well blended.

On a buttered, flat baking pan place 2 sheets of the phyllo dough. Brush on the melted butter. Repeat this process until half of the phyllo dough is used. Spread on the cheese-spinach mixture. Place 2 sheets of the phyllo dough on top. Brush on the melted butter. Repeat this process until the rest of the sheets are used. Carefully slice the layers into squares.

In a small bowl place the milk and the second egg, and beat them together. Generously brush the mixture on top of the squares.

Preheat the oven to 350°. Bake the squares for 30 to 40 minutes, or until they are a light golden brown.

serves 8

"When I was a boy in Lebanon we would have this on weekends as a special treat. You couldn't buy phyllo dough that was pre-made in the store like you can here, so it took a long time to make."

"After you make this you serve it immediately, while it is still crispy. You can't refrigerate this, so plan on eating the whole thing when you make it."

"My father was very involved in the creation of the recipes for the restaurant. He would put the combinations of the food together and then my mother would perfect them. His creativity and her technical ability made them a great team!"

"The doors are always open in our restaurant so that the air is fresh. The color scheme is relaxing and we play classical music. When people eat here I want them to relax, to enjoy the space around them, and to savor every bite."

Neighborhood Church, Palos Verdes

Pascal
Newport Beach

With its superb French Provençal cuisine and its fresh, elegant decor, Pascal is a bright new star among the top Southern California restaurants.

Chef and owner Pascal Olhats says, *"I named this after my 3-year-old daughter, Magali. When I told her about it she said, 'I don't like scampi!' It has a wonderful aroma when you are preparing it, but it must be served immediately."*

Scampi Magali

16	large shrimp, peeled and deveined
	salt
	pepper
½	cup flour *(or as needed)*
2	tablespoons clarified butter, melted
3	tablespoons Pernod
1	teaspoon garlic, finely chopped
⅓	cup dry white wine
½	cup heavy cream
2	medium tomatoes, peeled, seeded, and diced
¼	cup fresh basil leaves, thinly sliced
2	tablespoons clarified butter

Season the shrimp with the salt and the pepper. Lightly flour the shrimp.

In a large sauté pan place the first 2 tablespoons of clarified butter and heat it on medium until it is hot. Add the shrimp and cook them for 2 minutes on each side, or until they are nicely browned. Remove the shrimp and keep them warm.

Add the Pernod to the sauté pan and flambé it. Add the garlic and the white wine. Cook the ingredients for 2 to 3 minutes, or until the liquid is reduced to ⅓.

Add the heavy cream and cook it for 3 to 5 minutes, or until the liquid is reduced to ⅓.

Add the tomatoes, basil, and the second 2 tablespoons of clarified butter. Stir them in well. Cook the sauce for 1 minute. Season it with the salt and the pepper. Pour the sauce over the shrimp.

serves 4

Warm Duck Fillet Salad with Haricots Vert

1	cup olive oil
1	clove garlic, crushed
¼	cup shallots, chopped
2	tablespoons fresh thyme, chopped
2	tablespoons fresh basil, chopped
2	tablespoons fresh parsley, chopped
1	pound duck tenderloin
	salt
	pepper, freshly ground
2	tablespoons sherry wine vinegar
¼	cup red wine vinegar
½	teaspoon salt
¼	teaspoon pepper, freshly ground
¾	cup walnut oil
2	pounds haricots vert (or baby green beans), **ends snipped off, and cooked al dente** (see chef's comments on this page for instructions)
4	large mushrooms, peeled and julienned
2	medium tomatoes, peeled, seeded, and diced
2	shallots, minced
1	head radicchio, minced

In a medium bowl place the olive oil, garlic, the ¼ cup of chopped shallots, thyme, basil, and parsley. Mix the ingredients together well.

Add the duck to the bowl and marinate it for 1 hour. Remove the duck from the marinade and season it with the salt and the pepper.

In a medium large skillet place 3 tablespoons of the duck marinade and heat it on high until it is hot. Add the duck and sauté it for 2 minutes on each side, or until the skin is crispy and the duck is medium rare.

Remove the duck from the skillet and let it rest for 5 minutes. Cut the duck into thin slices.

Deglaze the skillet with the sherry wine vinegar.

(continued on next page)

"This dish goes together very quickly. It makes a wonderful luncheon salad. Or, it would be perfect for a Sunday brunch."

"Haricots vert are small green beans that are rather hard to find in this country. You may use regular string beans instead, but if you do so you should cut them into 3 or 4 pieces, slice them in half, remove the beans from the inside, and remove any strings."

"The only trick to this dish is the cooking of the beans. Drop them into salted, boiling water and cook them for 4 to 5 minutes. Remove one and taste it to see if it is cooked, but slightly crunchy. If so, remove the beans with a slotted spoon and place them in ice water. It is important to salt the water when you blanch vegetables because this helps to develop their flavor."

"This is a mild dish and the radicchio gives it a little bit of bitterness. The purple color looks very pretty with the green color of the beans."

In a small bowl place the deglazing sherry wine vinegar, red wine vinegar, the ½ teaspoon of salt, and the ¼ teaspoon of pepper. Mix the ingredients together well. While whisking constantly, slowly dribble in the walnut oil.

In a large bowl place the cooked haricots vert, mushrooms, tomatoes, the 2 minced shallots, and the radicchio. Add the walnut oil vinaigrette and toss the ingredients until they are well combined.

On each of 4 individual serving plates place the haricots vert salad. Arrange the duck slices on top.

serves 4

"Sometimes it is hard to find a duck tenderloin, which is the part under the breast. You may substitute a duck breast if you wish, but it will take longer to cook. If you do so, then sauté it until the skin is crispy, and then bake it in the oven for about 12 minutes at 425°."

"I have been asked for this recipe many times, but I have never given it out before now. It is so good that you can just drink it.....it's better than a Bloody Mary!"

"I like to serve this in the summertime when good tomatoes are available. I pour it over some lettuce with thinly sliced tomatoes, and maybe some Roquefort cheese.....it's really wonderful!"

"This will keep very well in the refrigerator. You should let it warm to room temperature and then whisk it right before you use it."

Tomato Salad Dressing

1	large, ripe, beefsteak tomato, peeled and chopped
½	cup red wine vinegar
½	bunch fresh tarragon, coarsely chopped
	salt *(to taste)*
	pepper *(to taste)*
1½	cups olive oil
1	tablespoon fresh basil, chopped
1	tablespoon fresh parsley, chopped

In the bowl of an electric mixer place the tomatoes, red wine vinegar, tarragon, salt, and pepper.

Mix the ingredients on medium speed for 5 minutes.

While continuing to mix the ingredients, slowly dribble in the olive oil.

Strain the dressing.

Add the basil and the parsley, and stir them in.

Pascal

Fettucini au Roquefort

1	cup dry white wine
½	medium onion, finely chopped
¾	cup Roquefort cheese, crumbled
¼	cup Parmesan cheese, freshly grated
⅛	teaspoon black pepper, freshly ground
½	cup heavy cream
1	pound fettucini, cooked al dente
¼	cup pine nuts, toasted
2	tablespoons parsley, chopped

In a medium saucepan place the white wine and bring it to a boil over medium heat.

Add the onions, Roquefort cheese, Parmesan cheese, and pepper. Cook the ingredients for 4 to 6 minutes, or until the liquid is reduced by ½.

Add the heavy cream and stir it in. Cook the sauce for 4 to 6 minutes, or until it is reduced by ½. Strain the sauce.

In a large, warmed bowl place the cooked fettucini and the sauce. Toss the ingredients together so that the pasta is well coated with the sauce.

Add the pine nuts and parsley, and toss the ingredients together well.

serves 4

"This is a rich dish that is not too good for you cholesterol watchers. But if you are going to splurge, this is a great way to do it!"

"The key to the success of this recipe lies in the Roquefort cheese.....it must be real Roquefort and it must be of a very high quality."

"You can toast the pine nuts by tossing them in a heated skillet. Keep them moving constantly and don't let them burn."

"This whole dish takes only 7 or 8 minutes to prepare. You will hardly miss any of your TV show because you practically can make it during the commercial. You will look like a genius!"

Grilled Tuna with Garlic, Lemon, and Tomato

"Here is a light, healthy dish that is perfect for a backyard barbecue. We barbecue a little bit in France, but not like you do in the United States. In France we don't have all of the high tech barbecue equipment..... our technique is much more primitive. We make a fire with wood and some paper, so it takes a long time to get it ready for grilling."

6	8-ounce tuna fillets
½	cup olive oil
3	tomatoes, peeled, seeded, and diced
1	shallot, finely diced
1	clove garlic, finely diced
1	sprig fresh sage
1	sprig fresh parsley
1	sprig fresh tarragon
1	sprig fresh chervil
½	teaspoon salt
½	teaspoon pepper
1	lemon, juiced

Brush the tuna with some of the olive oil. Cook the tuna on a hot grill (or broil it) for 1 to 2 minutes on each side, or until it is seared.

In a large skillet place the remainder of the olive oil and heat it on medium high until it is hot. Add the tomatoes, shallots, garlic, sage, parsley, tarragon, chervil, salt, and pepper. Sauté the ingredients for 2 to 3 minutes.

Add the tuna. Sprinkle the lemon juice on top. Cook and baste the tuna for 6 to 8 more minutes, or until it is just done.

serves 6

"The interesting thing about this dish is the sauce. It is a simple sauce, but it has a lot of different ingredients and flavors in it. The blend of the olive oil, tomatoes, herbs, and lemon juice is just great!"

Pascal

192

Seafood Fricassee

1   cup dry Chablis
1   shallot, finely chopped
1   dash saffron
     salt *(to taste)*
     pepper *(to taste)*
8   ounces medium shrimp, peeled and deveined
8   ounces large sea scallops
8   ounces King salmon fillets, bones removed, and cut into
       4 strips
8   black mussels, washed and beards removed
½   cup heavy cream
1   bunch fresh dill, chopped
4   tablespoons butter, cut into small pieces
2   tablespoons butter
1   leek, washed and julienned

In a large sauté pan place the wine, shallots, saffron, salt, and pepper. Bring the ingredients to a boil over medium high heat.

Reduce the heat to medium low, add the seafood, and cook it for 2 minutes, or until the mussel shells open. Remove the seafood from the broth and keep it warm.

Cook the broth for 3 to 4 minutes, or until it is reduced to ⅓.

Add the heavy cream and cook it for 1 minute, or until the sauce slightly thickens.

Add the dill and stir it in.

While stirring constantly, add the pieces of butter one at a time. Keep the sauce warm.

In a small sauté pan place the 2 tablespoons of butter and heat it on medium high until it has melted. Add the leeks and sauté them for 3 to 4 minutes, or until they are tender.

On each of 4 individual serving plates place the leeks. Place the seafood on top of the leeks. Spoon on the sauce.

serves 4

"Fricassee is similar to a stew in that a lot of different ingredients are cooked together."

"You should cook this dish for a special occasion because it is very festive and colorful looking. Serve it with a side dish of pasta, and enjoy!"

Pascal

Chicken Breasts Provençal

"The inspiration for this recipe comes from an old classical French Provençal dish. The chicken is first sautéed to get the skin crispy, and then it is braised in the oven with garlic, white wine, herbs, and olives."

4	**8-ounce chicken breasts**
	salt
	pepper
½	**cup flour** *(or as needed)*
2	**tablespoons olive oil**
2	**medium tomatoes, coarsely chopped**
16	**garlic cloves, peeled and blanched**
¾	**cup black olives, pitted and halved**
1	**teaspoon fresh thyme, chopped**
1	**teaspoon fresh rosemary, chopped**
1	**teaspoon fresh tarragon, chopped**
1	**teaspoon fresh parsley, chopped**
1¼	**cups chicken stock** *(recipe on page 297)*
2	**tablespoons clarified butter**

"We blanch the garlic so that the flavor will not be quite so strong. Blanch it in boiling milk for two minutes, and then rinse it."

Season the chicken breasts with the salt and the pepper. Coat the skin *(only)* with the flour.

In a large, oven-proof skillet place the olive oil and heat it on medium high until it is hot. Add the chicken breasts and sauté them for 3 to 4 minutes on each side, or until they are nicely browned and the skin is crispy. Discard the fat from the skillet.

Add the tomatoes, garlic, olives, thyme, rosemary, tarragon, parsley, and chicken stock to the skillet.

Preheat the oven to 400°. Cover the skillet and place it in the oven. Braise the chicken for 12 to 15 minutes, or until it is done.

Remove the chicken from the skillet and keep it warm.

"I designed the entire cuisine at Pascal to please myself, because there is no way I can cook something I don't like."

Place the skillet back on the stove and heat it on medium high. Cook the sauce for 5 to 7 minutes, or until it is reduced to ⅓. Add the clarified butter and stir it in.

On each of 4 individual serving plates place a chicken breast. Cover it with the sauce.

serves 4

Lamb Scallopini Roulade

1   **pound leg of lamb, bone and fat removed, and cut into four 1" thick slices**
     salt
     pepper
16   **fresh basil leaves**
¾   **cup goat cheese**
½   **cup olive oil**
1   **garlic clove, chopped**

Place the lamb slices between 2 sheets of waxed paper and pound them until they are ¼" thick. Season the lamb with the salt and the pepper.

On top of each lamb slice place 4 of the basil leaves. Spread the goat cheese on top.

Roll up each lamb slice and tie it securely with kitchen twine.

In a medium bowl place the olive oil and garlic. Add the rolled lamb and marinate it for 20 minutes at room temperature. Turn the lamb over once.

Remove the rolled lamb from the marinade and season it with more of the salt and the pepper.

Grill *(or broil)* the marinated rolled lamb for 6 to 7 minutes, or until the desired doneness is achieved. Turn the lamb rolls so that they cook evenly on all sides.

Remove the strings from the lamb rolls and cut them into ¾" slices.

serves 4

"Here is a light, simple dish that tastes delicious and is easy to make. It also tastes very good cold, so you can make it way ahead of time.....even the day before."

"I came up with this recipe because we were going to have a picnic at the Hollywood Bowl. I sliced the lamb rolls paper thin and served them with some goat cheese, salad, and a good Bordeaux. We had candles and good music, and the whole experience was really excellent!"

"A great way to serve these lamb rolls is to have them warm, and then put them on top of a cold salad."

Poached Salmon in Champagne Dill Sauce

4	**6-ounce salmon fillets**
½	**cup flour** *(or as needed)*
2	**tablespoons clarified butter**
2	**shallots, chopped**
1	**quart champagne**
½	**bunch fresh dill** *(stems left on)*
1	**cup heavy cream**
2	**tablespoons butter, cut into small pieces**
½	**bunch fresh dill, stems removed, and chopped**

Lightly coat the salmon fillets with the flour.

In a large sauté pan place the clarified butter and heat it on medium high until it is hot. Add the salmon fillets and sauté them for 1 minute on each side.

Add the shallots and champagne. Cover the pan and poach the salmon *(at a simmer)* for 4 to 5 minutes, or until it is just done. Remove the salmon and keep it warm.

Add the first ½ bunch of dill to the liquid in the sauté pan. Cook the mixture on medium high for 6 to 8 minutes, or until the liquid is reduced to ⅓. Add the heavy cream, stir it in, and boil the sauce for 2 minutes.

Remove the sauce from the heat. While stirring constantly, add the pieces of butter one at a time. Strain the sauce.

Add the second ½ bunch of chopped dill to the sauce and stir it in.

On each of 4 individual serving plates pour some of the sauce. Place a salmon fillet on top of the sauce.

serves 4

"This is a quick and easy dish to prepare. You can add some caviar on top of the salmon to make the presentation more elegant."

"You sauté the salmon very fast, just to sear it so that the juices are sealed in and the flavor is maintained. When you poach the salmon be sure that you do not let the liquid boil."

"The French love to make sauces with champagne. Champagne has yeast in it and this gives the sauce a different flavor than you would get by using white wine."

"If you use champagne and it is good, then save some for yourself. If you are cooking by yourself, make a toast to the chef!"

Pascal

Snow Eggs in Vanilla Sauce

3	egg whites
1	teaspoon powdered sugar
⅛	teaspoon lemon juice
1⅓	cups milk
1	vanilla bean
3	egg yolks
2	teaspoons sugar
⅔	cup low fat yogurt
4	tablespoons powdered sugar
2	tablespoons water
2	tablespoons toasted slivered almonds

In a medium bowl place the egg whites and beat them for 4 to 6 minutes, or until stiff peaks are formed. While beating constantly, slowly add the 1 teaspoon of powdered sugar and the lemon juice. Set the egg white mixture aside.

In a large, shallow saucepan place the milk and the vanilla bean. Heat the milk on low until it reaches a simmer. Remove the vanilla bean. Keep the milk hot.

Place the egg white mixture in a pastry bag with the large, plain tip.

Pipe out 12 large egg-shaped forms. One at a time, drop each egg into the milk. Simmer it very gently for 4 minutes on each side. (Do not let the milk boil.) Drain the snow eggs on paper towels. Set the milk aside and keep it hot.

In a medium bowl place the egg yolks and the sugar, and mix them together until they are well combined. While whisking constantly, slowly add the hot milk to the egg yolk mixture.

Place the egg-milk mixture in the top of a simmering double boiler. While stirring constantly, cook the mixture for 8 to 10 minutes, or until it has thickened.

Remove the sauce from the heat. Add the yogurt and stir it in. Strain the sauce and let it cool. Chill the sauce in the refrigerator.

(continued on next page)

"This is a beautiful dessert that is not overly sweet or heavy. After you have finished eating it you will have a good feeling, and while you are eating it you will be in heaven!"

"The snow eggs look like little balls of snow, and they float in the vanilla sauce. It's a very French dish that I learned how to make when I was working in Leon, France. People come to the restaurant just for this dessert."

"You might need a little bit of practice to make the eggs, so don't be disappointed if some of the eggs go flat. Don't worry, it's only egg whites! Just try it again."

Pascal

"There are three completely different textures in this dessert.....the crunchiness of the caramel, the cold smoothness of the vanilla sauce, and the lightness of the snow eggs."

"I believe in cooking to make other people happy, and at the same time cooking makes me happy. I love to create, to use fresh ingredients, and to come up with new ideas."

"Our cuisine is from the south of France, but it is adapted to more modern tastes and it includes California ingredients. Southern California has wonderful weather and our food reflects this by being light and refreshing. Yet, it also is sophisticated in its flavors and aromas. I want my food to stimulate all of the senses."

In a small saucepan place the 4 tablespoons of powdered sugar and the water. Heat the mixture on low until the sugar is dissolved. Increase the heat to medium and boil the mixture for 2 to 3 minutes, or until it is caramel colored. Remove the caramel mixture from the heat.

On a non-stick baking sheet drop small, pea-sized mounds of the hot caramel mixture. Let the caramel set for 8 to 10 minutes, or until it has hardened.

On each of 4 individual serving plates ladle on the vanilla sauce. Place 3 snow eggs on top. Sprinkle on the hardened caramel pieces and the toasted slivered almonds.

serves 4

Entrance Detail, Balboa Island

Patrick's Roadhouse
Santa Monica

Famous, funky, and fun, Patrick's Roadhouse serves great homemade food that is equally loved by movie stars, locals, and tourists.

Menu

Patrick's Chicken Salad

Farmer's Breakfast

Basic Omelets

Lorraine Omelet

Eggs McKarageorgevitch

Rockefeller, Hughes, Getty, Onassis Burger

Corned Beef and Cabbage

Irish Stew

Patrick's Meat Loaf

Easy Banana Cream Pie

Owner Bill Fischler says, *"I think that this chicken salad tastes the best if it is served on sourdough bread. The capers give it a nice tang.....but make certain that you buy imported capers from Greece or Italy. Don't use the domestic ones."*

Patrick's Chicken Salad

2	cups white meat of chicken, cooked, skin and bones removed, and diced
1	cup mayonnaise
2	tablespoons chives, diced
1	cup celery, finely diced
⅓	cup red bell pepper, finely diced
⅓	cup green bell pepper, finely diced
⅓	cup yellow bell pepper, finely diced
	salt *(to taste)*
	pepper *(to taste)*
1	tablespoon capers

In a medium bowl place the chicken, mayonnaise, chives, celery, red bell peppers, green bell peppers, yellow bell peppers, salt, and pepper. Mix the ingredients together so that they are well blended.

Cover the bowl and place it in the refrigerator for 1 hour.

Add the capers and stir them in before you are ready to serve the salad.

serves 4

Farmer's Breakfast

2	tablespoons olive oil
2	Idaho potatoes, thinly sliced and lightly steamed
4	strips bacon, diced
4	slices Canadian bacon, julienned
2	sausages, sliced
2	cloves garlic, finely diced
1	large onion, chopped medium
12	mushrooms, sliced
1	green bell pepper, diced
1	red bell pepper, diced
1	teaspoon chile powder
1	teaspoon cumin
1	teaspoon paprika
1	tablespoon catsup
4	**Basic Omelets** *(recipe on next page)*

In a large skillet place the olive oil and heat it on medium high until it is hot. Add the potatoes and sauté them for 5 to 7 minutes, or until they are nicely browned. Set the potatoes aside and keep them warm.

In another large skillet place the bacon, Canadian bacon, and sausage. Sauté the ingredients until they are done *(reserve 2 tablespoons of the grease)*. Drain the meat on paper towels, set it aside, and keep it warm.

In the skillet with the 2 tablespoons of reserved grease place the garlic, onions, mushrooms, green bell peppers, and red bell peppers. Sauté the vegetables for 3 to 4 minutes on medium high heat, or until the onions are translucent.

In a medium bowl place the sautéed vegetables. Add the chile powder, cumin, paprika, and catsup. Mix the ingredients together so that they are well blended. Set the mixture aside and keep it warm.

Place each flat Basic Omelet on a warm dish. Layer the potatoes, meat mixture, and vegetable mixture on ½ of the omelet. Fold the omelet over the top of the ingredients.

serves 4

"Arnold Schwarzenegger gave me this recipe. It is a German dish and his mother used to make it. Arnold was the first of my famous customers. He has been a good friend of mine for 12 years and he has helped to make this restaurant into what it has become."

"This is one of the heartiest, most delicious omelets you will ever eat. Arnold's mother says that this breakfast builds big men!"

"We use only kosher sausages or hot dogs, because this way we know that the meat in them is pure meat, with no undesirable by-products."

"I take personal pride in the food that we produce because it is all homemade. A lot of our recipes have come from our customers, or more accurately, from their mothers."

Basic Omelets

6	eggs
½	cup cream
½	teaspoon salt
⅛	teaspoon paprika
2	tablespoons butter

In a medium bowl place the eggs, cream, salt, and paprika. Whip the ingredients together so that they are well blended.

For each omelet, place ¼ of the butter in a medium sauté pan and heat it on low until it has melted and is hot. Add ¼ of the egg mixture and cook it for 5 minutes, or until it is firm. Tilt the pan occasionally so that the uncooked part of the egg runs to the bottom of the pan.

Remove the omelet and place it on a warm plate. Add the ingredients you are serving it with *(if any)*, and fold it over.

serves 4

Lorraine Omelet

1	tablespoon vegetable oil
1	tablespoon butter
10	mushrooms, sliced
1	small onion, finely diced
2	Basic Omelets *(recipe above)*, cooked
4	slices bacon, cooked and crumbled
4	ounces cream cheese
½	cup Monterey Jack cheese, grated

In a small skillet place the oil and butter, and heat them until the butter has melted and is hot. Add the mushrooms and onions, and sauté them for 3 to 4 minutes, or until the onions are clear.

Place a warm, flat omelet on each of 2 individual serving plates. In the center of the omelet add, in this order, the sautéed mushrooms and onions, bacon, cream cheese, and Monterey Jack cheese. Fold the sides of the omelet over the top.

serves 2

"People come here because of the food, the location, and because of all the other people. There is an expression..... 'people generate people.' You can go to a restaurant that has the best food in the world. But if it is empty you won't enjoy it nearly as much as you would in a place that was filled with the talk and laughter of other people."

"This is the number one best seller in the restaurant. The flavor is such that everyone reacts to it in the same way..... and that reaction is pure ecstasy!"

"The secret to the success of this recipe lies in the cream cheese. You must buy it from a Jewish deli and it must be the very best that is available. There are various qualities of cream cheese, and if you pick a low quality one, then it will melt and have an undesirable taste. A good quality one will have a wonderful richness to it."

Eggs McKarageorgevitch

2	tablespoons clarified butter
4	eggs
2	Thomas English muffins, split and toasted
4	round slices Canadian bacon, grilled
4	slices Monterey Jack cheese
2	black olives, pitted and halved

In a large skillet place the clarified butter and heat it on medium until it is hot. Add the eggs and fry them sunny side up.

Place the split, toasted English muffins on each plate. On each muffin half place a slice of Canadian bacon, a fried egg, and a slice of Monterey Jack cheese.

Place the plate under the broiler for 30 seconds, or until the cheese melts.

Place an olive half on top.

serves 2

"The title of this recipe is a play on words. I love to visit restaurants everywhere, and I try to learn from each place I go. One time I went to McDonalds and I saw that they were serving a terrible breakfast called Eggs McMuffin. So I came back here, and the chef and I created our own version of the dish. We wanted to call it Eggs Mc.....something.....but we needed a last name for it. So we decided to choose the most outrageous, unlikely name that we could..... one that made absolutely no sense whatsoever! Finally we came upon the Yugoslavian last name of 'Karageorgevitch', and decided that it was perfect. So that's how Eggs McKarageorgevitch was born."

"I have found that nothing compares to Thomas English Muffins. They are not paying me to say this, but I firmly believe that they are the best."

"You must use the real kind of Canadian bacon. It cannot be the square cut; it must be the round cut."

Rockefeller, Hughes, Getty, Onassis Burger

1	pound fresh ground beef, shaped into 4 patties
1	tablespoon olive oil
12	mushrooms, sliced
4	hamburger buns, buttered and heated
4	slices Monterey Jack cheese
4	tablespoons sour cream
4	tablespoons Romanoff caviar

Grill the hamburger patties for 3 to 4 minutes on each side, or until the desired doneness is achieved.

In a small skillet place the olive oil and heat it on high until it is hot. Add the mushrooms and sauté them for 3 to 4 minutes, or until they are tender.

On each of 4 individual serving plates place the 2 halves of the hamburger bun. On one half place, in this order, the beef patty, the slice of cheese, and the mushrooms. On the other half place the sour cream and the caviar.

serves 4

"You can see that we give equal time to all of these rich people in the title of the recipe. The title is not meant to imply that these men ate our burgers, but rather the amount of money that they had in their bank accounts! This doesn't mean that the hamburger is very expensive, but rather that it has a very rich taste to it.....it is absolutely delicious!"

"If you are going to make hamburgers, then make sure that the meat is freshly ground and do not use lean meat.....use meat that has a 14% fat content. The fat is necessary to get that really delicious flavor, and most of it cooks out."

"My own personal favorite kind of hamburger is just a plain, basic hamburger.....nice and simple, for the simple minded!"

"Working here is not work to me.....it is like giving a party everyday. I feel sorry for anyone who has to go to work and hates what he does."

Corned Beef and Cabbage

1	**4-pound beef brisket**
	boiling water *(as needed)*
4	**bay leaves**
1	**tablespoon peppercorns**
2	**pounds sauerkraut**
6	**medium potatoes, peeled and quartered**
6	**medium carrots, cut into 8 wedges**
10	**small white onions, peeled**
1	**head cabbage, quartered**

In a large, heavy pot place the brisket and cover it with boiling water. Let the meat simmer on low heat for 8 to 10 hours. Strain out the water.

In the same pot with the brisket add the bay leaves, peppercorns, and sauerkraut. Add more boiling water so that the ingredients are covered. Simmer them for 3 hours, or until the brisket is tender. Remove the brisket and set it aside.

To the same pot add the potatoes, carrots, and onions. Simmer the vegetables for 15 minutes.

Add the cabbage and simmer it for 15 minutes, or until all of the vegetables are tender.

Slice the brisket and place it in the middle of a large serving platter. Arrange the vegetables around the slices of meat.

serves 8

"You must buy the absolute first cut of brisket. We cook it with sauerkraut, which might not sound too good to a lot of people, but the flavor seeps into the meat and makes it taste absolutely delicious!"

"I got this recipe from my mother. I remember watching her make it when I was a little boy."

"I love what I do and most of the kids who work here with me love what they do. The 'esprit d'corps' is better at Patrick's Roadhouse than it is in the French Foreign Legion!"

Irish Stew

2	**pounds lamb, cut into 1½" cubes**
4	**tablespoons Worcestershire sauce**
4	**tablespoons soy sauce**
2	**cups water**
10	**small white onions, peeled**
1	**pound carrots, quartered**
3	**pounds russet potatoes, peeled and sliced**
1	**tablespoon Old Bay Seasoning** (or to taste)
6	**bay leaves**
1	**teaspoon whole cloves**
	salt (to taste)
	pepper (to taste)
	boiling water (as needed)
2	**tablespoon flour dissolved in 2 tablespoons water**

In a medium bowl place the lamb, Worcestershire sauce, soy sauce, and 2 cups of water. Stir the ingredients together. Cover the bowl and place it in the refrigerator. Let the lamb marinate overnight. Remove the lamb and discard the marinade.

In a large, heavy saucepan place the lamb, onions, carrots, potatoes, Old Bay Seasoning, bay leaves, cloves (put the bay leaves and cloves in a cheesecloth bag so that they can easily be removed), salt, and pepper. Add enough of the boiling water to cover the ingredients.

Bring the water to a boil again over high heat. Reduce the heat to low, and simmer the ingredients for 3 hours, or until the meat is tender. Remove the bay leaves and cloves.

Add the flour and water mixture, and stir it in to thicken the sauce.

serves 6 to 8

"Use an old, cast iron pot if you have one. Throw everything into it.....lots of carrot, onions, potatoes, whatever! You want to build up an aroma that is so delicious that, if you could bottle it, you could sell it as a perfume."

"A true Irish stew is made with lamb. Ninety-nine people out of a hundred don't know this, and they make it with beef. Then it's a goulash, not an Irish stew!"

"The minute that you walk into this restaurant you can feel a warmth that wraps itself around you and makes you feel comfortable. We are a very homey place and we serve good simple food that appeals to healthy appetites."

"The name of the restaurant is after my son, Patrick. I named it after him because at the time I felt that it might help protect him from the trauma of my divorce."

Patrick's Meat Loaf

2	pounds lean ground beef
2	eggs, beaten
8	saltine crackers, crumbled
½	teaspoon salt
½	teaspoon pepper
2	hard-boiled eggs, peeled and sliced

In a medium bowl place the ground beef, beaten eggs, saltine crackers, salt, and pepper. Mix the ingredients together with your hands so that they are well combined.

Place half of the meat mixture on the bottom of a lightly oiled loaf pan. Layer the sliced hard-boiled eggs on top. Place the remainder of the meat mixture on top.

Preheat the oven to 375°. Bake the meat loaf for 1 hour, or until it is done. Strain off any grease.

serves 4

"This is a German recipe. It may sound rather simple and uninteresting, but I guarantee you that this is one of the best tasting meat loaves that you will ever eat. The hard-boiled eggs give it a wonderful flavor."

"The saltine crackers are what bind the ingredients. You may have to use more or less than what the recipe calls for, so use your own judgment."

"I just do what I do and I do it well. Patrick's Roadhouse has been in existence for 18 years. People come here and they love the food. We have a following that is incredible."

"We have a lot of movie stars who live here and come to the restaurant to eat. Goldie Hawn, who is such a beautiful and unaffected person, drives by once or twice a week. We have a stop light in front of the restaurant and if I see her in her Rolls Royce convertible waiting for the red light to change, then I will run out and give her a cup of coffee."

"We use manufacturer's cream instead of regular whipping cream. This type of cream is thick, rich, and delicious, and I love it! It has about a million calories in it, but I don't care. Make sure that you eat this pie the day that you make it. The cream will not taste as good if it sits overnight."

"I believe that everything that happens in life is part of a grand plan, including the way Patrick's Roadhouse came into existence. Years ago I was getting a divorce and I was very depressed. I did not get custody of the children and only could see them on the weekends. When they were with me I would bring them to the beach. One Saturday I bought them a hot dog at this little hot dog stand. It was just a terrible hot dog! The next day, I decided to buy another hot dog there, just to give it another chance, and it was just as rank. So I said to the cook, 'This is the worst hot dog that I have ever tasted in my life!' He said, 'Well, if you know so much then why don't you buy the place?' So I bought it for $2,500. I was in the right place at the right time, and I never would have believed that we could have grown into what we are today."

Easy Banana Cream Pie

1	package LeGout Instant Vanilla Pie Filling, **prepared**
1	**teaspoon nutmeg**
½	**teaspoon vanilla extract**
1	**pie shell, pre-baked**
2	**bananas, sliced**
1	**cup manufacturer's cream** (or heavy cream), **whipped**

In a medium bowl place the prepared vanilla pie filling. Add the nutmeg and vanilla, and stir them in.

Line the bottom of the pie shell with ½ of the banana slices. Add the pie filling. Place the remainder of the banana slices on top.

Spread the whipped cream on top of the pie.

serves 8

Greek Bust, J. Paul Getty Museum, Malibu

Pavilion
Newport Beach

Offering a gourmet California cuisine in the lovely vanilla-toned dining room, the Pavilion is an oasis setting in the elegant Four Seasons Hotel.

Chef Bill Bracken says, "Everybody loves corn chowder, and even though this recipe is not really traditional, I believe that it is one of the best that you will ever taste. Serve it as soon as it is made."

Corn Chowder with Smoked Shrimp

2   tablespoons butter
1   small onion, finely diced
2   stalks celery, finely diced
1   leek, finely diced
2   jalapeño chile peppers, finely minced
4   cloves garlic, minced
6   cups fresh corn kernels
3   quarts chicken stock *(recipe on page 297)*
½   cup butter
     salt *(to taste)*
     white pepper *(to taste)*
3   cups heavy cream, whipped
8   large shrimp, smoked, peeled, deveined, and thinly sliced

In a large saucepan place the 2 tablespoons of butter and heat it on medium high until it has melted. Add the onions, celery, leeks, jalapeño chile peppers, and garlic. Sauté the vegetables for 3 to 4 minutes, or until they are tender.

Add the corn *(reserve ½ cup of the kernels for a garnish)* and chicken stock. Simmer the ingredients for 30 minutes, or until the liquid is reduced by ⅓. Let the soup cool slightly.

In a blender place the ½ cup of butter and the soup. Blend the ingredients on high speed for 2 to 3 minutes, or until the soup is very smooth. Strain the soup, return it to the saucepan, and bring it to a boil. Season it with the salt and the pepper. Add the whipped cream and gently stir it in. Bring the soup to a boil and immediately pour it into 8 individual soup bowls. Garnish the soup with the slices of smoked shrimp and the reserved corn kernels.

serves 8

Young Spinach Leaves with Goat Cheese Croutons in Garlic Vinaigrette

Young Spinach Leaves with Goat Cheese Croutons

4	ounces goat cheese
1	ounce Boursin
1	ounce Brie
1	French baguette, cut into ¼" thick slices
1½	pounds baby spinach, stems removed, washed, dried, and torn
	Garlic Vinaigrette *(recipe follows)*
16	cherry tomatoes, halved

In a small bowl place the goat cheese, Boursin, and Brie. Mix the cheeses together so that they are well blended.

Spread the cheese mixture on top of the bread pieces. Place them under a broiler so that the bread is slightly browned.

In a medium bowl place the spinach. Add the Garlic Vinaigrette and toss it in well.

On each individual serving plate place the spinach. Place 3 of the bread pieces on top. Garnish the salad with the cherry tomatoes.

serves 8

Garlic Vinaigrette

1	bulb garlic, peeled, blanched *(see chef's comments on this page)*, and finely minced
¼	cup red wine vinegar
2	tablespoons rice wine vinegar
1	tablespoon Dijon mustard
2	tablespoons fresh parsley, chopped
	salt *(to taste)*
	pepper *(to taste)*
1	cup olive oil

In a small bowl place the garlic, red wine vinegar, rice wine vinegar, mustard, parsley, salt, and pepper. Whisk the ingredients together. While whisking constantly, slowly dribble in the olive oil.

"This salad is on our menu and people love it. They especially love the croutons, which are spread with a mixture of three cheeses. The goat cheese is crumbly and you can't spread it, so that is why we mix it with the Boursin and Brie, which are creamy. The predominant flavor, however, is that of the goat cheese. You can serve these croutons with any kind of a salad, but they are especially good with spinach."

"A lot of people are afraid of something that is called 'Garlic Vinaigrette' because they think 'Uh-oh, garlic!.....I eat this and I'll have bad breath for the rest of the night!' But we blanch the garlic first, and this reduces the strong flavor. To blanch it you should put the cloves in a pot of cold water, bring them to a boil, and then remove them immediately. You don't want to blanch it too long or else you will lose all of the flavor. You also could roast the garlic, which would give the dressing a different flavor. You should roast the whole bulb, with the skins on, and then peel it."

Marinated Grilled Veal Chops with Buttered Beans, Southwestern Risotto, and Poblano Pepper Jus

Marinated Grilled Veal Chops with Buttered Beans

8	veal chops, cleaned
2	cups olive oil
2	cloves garlic, chopped
2	tablespoons fresh basil
1	tablespoon fresh rosemary
2	tablespoons fresh thyme
1	teaspoon fresh cumin seeds, roasted
12	whole peppercorns
1	lemon, juiced
12	ounces green beans, ends snipped off
12	ounces yellow wax beans, ends snipped off
4	tablespoons butter
	salt *(to taste)*
	white pepper *(to taste)*
	Southwestern Risotto *(recipe on next page)*
	Poblano Pepper Jus *(recipe on page 213)*

In a large bowl place the veal chops, olive oil, garlic, basil, rosemary, thyme, cumin seeds, peppercorns, and lemon juice. Place the bowl in the refrigerator and marinate the veal for 48 hours.

In a large pot of boiling, salted water place the two kinds of beans. Blanch them for 5 to 6 minutes, or until they are tender. Plunge them into ice water. Drain the beans.

In a large skillet place the butter and heat it on medium high until it has melted. Add the beans and toss them in the butter so that they are well coated. Season them with the salt and the white pepper.

Grill the marinated veal chops for 4 to 5 minutes on each side, or until they are medium rare.

(continued on next page)

Pavilion

In the center of each individual serving plate place a veal chop. Place a serving of the Southwestern Risotto on the side *(at 2 o'clock)*. Arrange the buttered yellow and green beans on the other side *(at 10 o'clock)*. Ladle the Poblano Pepper Jus on the remaining empty part of the plate *(at 6 o'clock)*.

serves 8

Southwestern Risotto

4	cups chicken stock *(or as needed)* – *(recipe on page 297)*
2	cups white rice
3	tablespoons olive oil
1	red bell pepper, seeded and thinly sliced
1	green bell pepper, seeded and thinly sliced
1	yellow bell pepper, seeded and thinly sliced
2	cups heavy cream
1	teaspoon Cajun spice
1	teaspoon chile powder
1	teaspoon cumin
1	teaspoon garlic powder
1	teaspoon cayenne pepper
½	cup Parmesan cheese, freshly grated

In a medium large saucepan place the chicken stock and the rice. Bring the liquid to a boil on high heat. Cover the pan and reduce the heat to low. Simmer the rice for 30 to 40 minutes, or until it is tender *(add more stock if it is needed)*. Set it aside.

In a large skillet place the olive oil and heat it on medium high until it is hot. Add the bell peppers and sauté them for 3 to 4 minutes, or until they are tender.

In a medium large saucepan place the heavy cream and bring it to a boil. Add the cooked rice, sautéed bell peppers, Cajun spice, chile powder, cumin, garlic powder, and cayenne pepper. Stir the ingredients together until the rice binds together.

Add the Parmesan cheese and stir it in.

"This risotto has a lot of flavors in it, as you can tell by looking at the ingredients. You can use the Italian long grain rice, if you want, but we just use regular rice that is cooked in several stages. This is really a showcase dish!"

"At home when I cook chicken I always save the bones and freeze them. Then, when I have accumulated a large amount, I throw them in a big pot with a lot of vegetables and let everything cook for 3 or 4 hours. I strain the stock and pour it in soda bottles with screw caps, and then freeze it. When I am ready to use the stock I pop the bottle (with the cap removed) in the microwave, and I'm ready to go! I like this because the soda bottles line up on the door of the freezer, and it's really handy."

"If you don't want to make your own chicken stock there are some good quality chicken bases available in the gourmet section of the better grocery stores. If you buy a chicken base you should always check the ingredients. If salt is the first ingredient, then don't buy it! You want one that lists chicken meat first."

"People in Southern California are not really into heavy sauces. This one is nice and light, but at the same time it is full of flavor. Also, it's very quick and easy to make, and it goes well with a lot of different things."

"To make a double brown chicken stock you should roast some chicken bones in the oven, and then cook them with some regular chicken stock that is reduced again by half. This darkens the stock and gives it a nice, rich flavor."

"If you ask me how I like living in Southern California, I really can't answer, because I am here cooking in the restaurant all of the time. So I could just as well be in southern Michigan. I never go to the beach, although I did drive by it the other day, so I know that it's still there! But I'm not complaining, because I truly do love cooking and I would rather do that than anything else."

Poblano Pepper Jus

2   **cups double brown chicken stock** *(see chef's comments on this page)*
    salt *(to taste)*
    white pepper *(to taste)*
2   **dried poblano chile peppers, seeds removed**
¼   **stick butter, cut into small pieces**

In a small saucepan place the double brown chicken stock. Heat it on low until it simmers. Season the stock with the salt and the white pepper.

Add the dried poblano chile peppers. Let the ingredients simmer for 3 minutes.

While whisking constantly, add the pieces of butter one at a time.

Strain the sauce.

Pacific Blue Fin Tuna with Stewed Tomatoes, Baby Zucchini, and Balsamic Herb Jus

Pacific Blue Fin Tuna with Stewed Tomatoes and Baby Zucchini

2	tablespoons extra virgin olive oil
½	onion, thinly sliced
3	cloves garlic, chopped
10	Roma tomatoes, peeled, cut in half, and seeded
1	tablespoon fresh basil, chopped
1	tablespoon fresh oregano, chopped
	salt (to taste)
	pepper (to taste)
18	baby zucchini, ends cut off
4	tablespoons butter
3	pounds Blue Fin tuna, cut into 18 medallions
3	tablespoons extra virgin olive oil
	Balsamic Herb Jus (recipe on next page)
6	sprigs fresh thyme

In a large skillet place the 2 tablespoons of olive oil and heat it on medium high until it is hot. Add the onions and garlic, and sauté them for 3 to 4 minutes, or until the onions are tender.

Add the Roma tomatoes and cook them for 6 to 8 minutes, or until they are cooked down. Add the basil, oregano, salt, and pepper. Stir the ingredients together. Set the mixture aside and keep it warm.

In a large pot of salted, boiling water place the baby zucchini. Blanch them for 4 to 6 minutes, or until they are tender. Remove them and plunge them into ice water.

In another large skillet place the butter and heat it on medium high until it has melted. Add the blanched zucchini, salt, and pepper. Toss the zucchini so that they are well coated with the butter. Set them aside and keep them warm.

Season the tuna medallions with the salt and the pepper.

(continued on next page)

"We change the menu frequently, but some of the dishes are so popular that we never remove them, and this is one of those dishes. If I ever eat in the dining room, which I usually don't because I am in the kitchen cooking, this is what I will eat. It is light, healthy, and delicious."

"Everybody has their own theory about garnishing, but I believe that whatever you use should be something that you can eat, and it should be something that relates to the plate."

In another large skillet place the 3 tablespoons of olive oil and heat it on high until it is hot. Add the tuna medallions and sauté them for 30 seconds to 1 minute on each side, or until they are brown on the outside and pink on the inside.

In the center of each individual serving plate place ⅓ cup of the stewed tomatoes. Lean 3 of the tuna medallions against the tomatoes (at 12, 4, and 8 o'clock). Place 1 zucchini in between each of the tuna medallions. Spoon the Balsamic Herb Jus on top of the fish. Place a sprig of the thyme on top of the tomatoes.

serves 6

Balsamic Herb Jus

2	tablespoons extra virgin olive oil
10	large shallots, thinly sliced and separated into rings
6	ounces enoki mushrooms, bottom part of the stems cut off
¾	cup tomatoes, peeled, seeded, and diced
½	cup balsamic vinegar
1½	cups double brown chicken stock (see chef's comments on page 213)
1	tablespoon fresh thyme, chopped
1	tablespoon fresh parsley, chopped
1	tablespoon fresh tarragon, chopped
1	tablespoon fresh chives, chopped
	salt (to taste)
	pepper (to taste)
2	tablespoons extra virgin olive oil

In a medium size saucepan place the first 2 tablespoons of olive oil and heat it on medium high until it is hot. Add the shallots, enoki mushrooms, and tomatoes. Sauté the ingredients for 2 to 3 minutes, or until the shallots are just tender.

Add the balsamic vinegar. Reduce the heat to low and simmer the ingredients for 3 to 5 minutes, or until it is reduced by ¼.

Add the chicken stock and simmer it for 6 to 8 minutes, or until it is reduced by ⅓.

Add the thyme, parsley, tarragon, chives, salt, pepper, and the second 2 tablespoons of olive oil. Stir the ingredients together. Serve the sauce at once.

Black Angus Tenderloin with Aromatic Herb Crust and Whiskey Sauce

Black Angus Tenderloin with Aromatic Herb Crust

12 ounces bone marrow, soaked in ice water for 24 hours and drained
2   tablespoons fresh rosemary, finely chopped
4   tablespoons fresh parsley, finely chopped
3   tablespoons fresh thyme, finely chopped
1   tablespoon garlic, finely chopped
2   shallots, finely chopped
    salt *(to taste)*
    white pepper *(to taste)*
½   cup bread crumbs *(or as needed)*
3   pounds Black Angus tenderloin, cut into twelve 4-ounce medallions
2   tablespoons olive oil
2   tablespoons Dijon mustard
    Whiskey Sauce *(recipe on next page)*
12 sprigs watercress

In a medium bowl place the bone marrow and beat it with an electric mixer *(with a paddle)* on high speed for 3 to 4 minutes, or until it is creamy.

Add the rosemary, parsley, thyme, garlic, shallots, salt, and white pepper. Mix the ingredients together on low speed so that they are well blended.

Slowly add the bread crumbs and blend them in until the mixture reaches a consistency that can be molded. Set it aside.

Season the medallions with the salt and the white pepper.

In a large skillet place the olive oil and heat it on high until it is very hot.

Add the medallions and sauté them for 2 to 3 minutes on each side, or until they are well browned on the outside and medium rare on the inside.

Lightly brush the sautéed medallions with the mustard.

(continued on next page)

"Here is a really wonderful recipe that takes some time to make, although it is not hard to do. The crust is made with bone marrow, which has a rich, delicious taste."

"For the bone marrow you need to get veal leg bones from your butcher. Have him chop them into 2-inch pieces. You just push the marrow right out. Bone marrow is really unique. When you whip it, it gets really creamy. You can spread it right on a piece of bread and eat it. Unfortunately, it is a fat, but it is certainly a flavorful one!"

"When you add the bread crumbs you have to use your judgment as to how much to use. The mixture must be moist, but it should not stick to your hands. Remember that when you broil the medallions, the marrow will melt and just the bread crumbs and herbs will be left on top. So there must be enough of the bread crumbs in the mixture to make a crust that will brown."

Mold the herbed marrow mixture into ¼" thick patties that are
the shape of the medallions. Place the molded patties on top of
each medallion.

Place the medallions under a preheated broiler so that the crust
browns.

On each of 6 individual serving plates place ¼ cup of the
Whiskey Sauce. Place 2 medallions on top. Garnish the dish with
2 sprigs of the watercress.

serves 6

Whiskey Sauce

2	**tablespoons butter**
8	**shallots, finely diced**
½	**cup whiskey**
2	**cups veal stock** *(recipe on page 151)*
	salt *(to taste)*
	cracked black pepper *(to taste)*
¾	**stick butter, cut into small pieces**

In a medium saucepan place the 2 tablespoons of butter and
heat it on medium high until it has melted. Add the shallots and
sauté them for 2 to 3 minutes, or until they are tender.

Add the whiskey and cook it for 4 to 6 minutes, or until it is
almost dry.

Reduce the heat to medium low. Add the veal stock and cook it
for 12 to 15 minutes, or until it is reduced by ½.

Add the salt and the pepper, and stir them in.

While whisking constantly, add the pieces of butter one at a time.

Grilled Swordfish with Fried Cabbage and Ginger-Thyme Sauce

Grilled Swordfish with Fried Cabbage

4	cups olive oil
2	cups red cabbage, sliced ¼" thick
2	cups green cabbage, sliced ¼" thick
2	tablespoons black sesame seeds
3	tablespoons black sesame oil
	salt *(to taste)*
	pepper *(to taste)*
6	7-ounce swordfish fillets, 1½" thick
	Ginger-Thyme Sauce *(recipe on next page)*
6	sprigs fresh thyme

In a large saucepan place the oil and heat it on medium high until it is hot *(350°)*. Add the red and green cabbage and deep-fry it for 2 minutes, or until it is brown. Remove the cabbage and drain it on paper towels.

In a medium bowl place the fried cabbage, sesame seeds, sesame oil, salt, and pepper. Toss the ingredients together well.

Season the swordfish fillets with the salt and the pepper. Place them on a hot grill that has been brushed with olive oil. Cook them for 3 to 4 minutes on each side, or until they are cooked throughout and still moist in the middle.

At the top of each individual serving plate place the fried cabbage. Lean a fish fillet against the cabbage. Ladle on the Ginger-Thyme Sauce so that it is in front of the fish.

Garnish the dish with a sprig of thyme.

serves 6

"Here is another fish dish that never leaves the menu. It's easy to make and it is uniquely flavorful."

"I saw fried cabbage served somewhere, and I thought that it would be an unusual thing to serve with the swordfish. Every other restaurant in Southern California does a swordfish, and I wanted to do something different. When you toss it with the black sesame oil and sesame seeds you get a really delicious, nutty-like flavor."

Ginger-Thyme Sauce

6	**shallots, finely chopped**
6	**cloves garlic, finely chopped**
½	**cup fresh ginger, peeled and chopped**
7	**ounces rice wine vinegar**
¼	**cup heavy cream**
1¾	**sticks butter, cut into small pieces**
2	**tablespoons fresh thyme, chopped**
	salt (to taste)
	pepper (to taste)

In a medium saucepan place the shallots, garlic, ginger, and rice wine vinegar. Heat the ingredients on low and simmer them for 6 to 8 minutes, or until the liquid is almost gone.

Add the heavy cream and simmer it for 4 to 6 minutes, or until it is reduced by ½.

While whisking constantly, add the pieces of butter one at a time.

Strain the sauce.

Add the thyme, salt, and pepper, and stir them in.

"This sauce is rich and full-flavored. It goes beautifully with the swordfish, which is a strong tasting fish. You don't want to serve a sauce that is too light and delicate. The ginger and thyme blend really well with the butter and the cream."

"The Pavilion is not a trendy restaurant where you must have a wild looking outfit and a hairdo that's out of sight. Rather, it is a place where you can enjoy excellent food and feel that you are getting your money's worth."

Pier, Manhattan Beach

Rebecca's

Venice

Festive, fun, and friendly, Rebecca's serves an upscale, modern Mexican cuisine that is both imaginative and authentic.

Executive Chef David Millen says, *"This salsa is excellent with all types of fish. Serve it with some grilled scallops for a great appetizer."*

Grapefruit Salsa

6   **pink grapefruits, peeled, sections removed from membranes, and chopped into small pieces**
4   **serrano chile peppers, finely diced**
½   **medium red onion, finely diced**
½   **cup cilantro, chopped**
      salt *(to taste)*

In a medium bowl place all of the ingredients and mix them together well.

Let the salsa sit for ½ hour before serving it.

makes 2 cups

Green Shellfish Soup

2	**quarts fish stock**
1	**quart chicken stock** *(recipe on page 297)*
1	**carrot, peeled and sliced**
1	**turnip, peeled and sliced**
¾	**cup white onions, diced medium**
1	**cup leeks, washed and sliced** *(both green and white parts)*
4	**cloves garlic**
3	**bay leaves**
10	**whole black peppercorns**
1	**teaspoon dried Mexican oregano**
1	**teaspoon fresh oregano**
3	**poblano chile peppers, deep-fried and peeled**
1	**bunch parsley, stems removed**
2	**bunches cilantro, stems removed**
4	**cloves garlic**
½	**bunch epazote**
½	**cup white onion, diced medium**
¼	**cup olive oil**
40	**clams** *(in shells)*
40	**medium shrimp, peeled and deveined**
	salt *(to taste)*

In a large saucepan place the fish stock and chicken stock. Bring the liquid to a boil. Add the carrots, turnips, the ¾ cup of onions, leeks, the first 4 cloves of garlic, bay leaves, peppercorns, dried oregano, and fresh oregano.

Simmer the vegetables for 30 minutes, or until they are tender.

Strain the broth and reserve the vegetables. Discard the bay leaves and ¾ of the carrot slices.

In a blender place the cooked vegetables, poblano chile peppers, parsley, cilantro, the second 4 cloves of garlic, epazote, the ½ cup of onions, and 2 cups of the broth. Blend the ingredients together until they are smooth. Add more broth if necessary.

Strain the blended mixture through a fine sieve. Push hard to extract all of the liquid and as much of the blended ingredients as possible.

(continued on next page)

"This recipe is a little bit complicated sounding, although it's not hard to make. The basic flavors are cilantro, poblano chiles, and the shellfish. I would say that you have to like cilantro to like this soup."

"Epazote is a Mexican herb that has a distinct flavor all of its own. It is very oily and it smells like resin. In fact, if you can smell it fresh it will remind you of an oil refinery. Now, don't be frightened by my description of it! It will only be a background flavor in the soup, and it will add a lot of character. You should be able to find it in a Mexican market. If not, don't worry. The soup will still be great without it."

In a large saucepan place the olive oil and heat it on medium high until it is hot. Add the blended mixture and cook it for 5 to 7 minutes, or until it slightly thickens.

Add the rest of the broth and the clams. Simmer the soup for 3 minutes, or until the shells begin to open.

Add the shrimp and cook them for 3 minutes, or until they are done.

Add the salt and stir it in.

In each of 8 individual serving bowls place 5 clams and 5 shrimp. Ladle the soup over the shellfish.

serves 8

Stuffed Green Chiles with Walnut Sauce

Stuffed Green Chiles

1	pound ground pork
2	teaspoons garlic, minced
¼	cup white onions, minced
2	cups tomatoes, seeded and diced
½	cup raisins
1	tablespoon green olives *(pimientos removed)*, **minced**
⅓	cup red wine vinegar
1	teaspoon ground cumin
1	teaspoon salt *(or to taste)*
4	pounds lard *(or other shortening)*
4	Anaheim chile peppers
1	cup flour *(or as needed)*
3	eggs, beaten
	Walnut Sauce *(recipe on next page)*
⅓	cup walnuts, chopped
2	tablespoons pomegranate seeds
3	tablespoons cilantro, chopped

In a large sauté pan place the pork and sauté it for 4 to 5 minutes, or until it is partially cooked.

Add the garlic and onions, and stir them in for 4 to 5 minutes, or until the pork is well done.

Add the tomatoes, raisins, green olives, red wine vinegar, cumin, and salt. Stir the ingredients together and let them simmer for 8 to 10 minutes, or until they are almost dry. Set the mixture aside.

In a large saucepan place the lard and heat it on high until it begins to smoke. Very carefully add the whole Anaheim chile peppers *(they might splatter)* and cook them for 1 to 2 minutes, or until the skins are blistered. Turn them occasionally. Remove the chiles and drain them on paper towels.

Make a 2" slit down each chile. Very carefully scoop out the seeds with a small spoon.

(continued on next page)

"People often have the impression that Mexican food consists primarily of melted cheese, beans, rice, guacamole, and salsa. But actually much of Mexican food has complex flavors, as does this recipe. It reflects the influence of the Spanish, who brought over a lot of spices from North Africa."

"I got the idea for this recipe from the classic Mexican dish called picadillo, which is a meat and tomato mixture. There are a lot of interesting flavors in it. You have the sweet from the raisins, the sour from the vinegar, the exotic from the cumin.....and then it is all blanketed in a rich, nutty walnut sauce."

Place the pork mixture in a pastry bag with no tip, and squeeze it into the chiles so that they are filled up. Press the slits closed. Let the chiles rest for 30 minutes so that they become firm.

Dredge the stuffed chiles in the flour and then dip them into the beaten eggs.

Reheat the lard so that it begins to smoke. Very carefully place the stuffed chiles in the hot lard. Cook them for 5 minutes, or until they are golden brown and cooked through. Drain them on paper towels.

On each of 4 individual serving plates place a stuffed chile. Ladle on the Walnut Sauce. Sprinkle on the chopped walnuts, pomegranate seeds, and cilantro.

serves 4

Walnut Sauce

⅓   **cup walnuts** *(or as needed)*, **chopped**
½   **cup Mexican sour cream**
⅓   **cup Queso Ranchero** *(Mexican soft cheese)*
⅓   **cup half and half** *(or as needed)*

In a food processor place the walnuts, sour cream, and cheese. Purée the ingredients together.

With the food processor still running, slowly add the half and half until a sauce consistency is achieved. If it becomes too thin, then add more walnuts and cheese.

"Queso Ranchero is a Mexican soft cheese. If you can't find it, use goat cheese. The Mexican sour cream is like a crème fraîche (there is a recipe for this on page 49). If you want, you can thin down some sour cream with half and half, and use that instead."

"This sauce is delicious. It's creamy, cheesy, and nutty tasting. It's the kind of sauce that would go well with a lot of other dishes."

Sautéed Chilean Sea Bass with Cilantro Butter and Vegetable Escabesche

Sautéed Chilean Sea Bass

4	8-ounce Chilean sea bass fillets
1	tablespoon olive oil
	salt
	pepper
2	tablespoons olive oil
	Cilantro Butter (recipe follows)
	Vegetable Escabesche (recipe on next page)

Lightly brush the sea bass fillets with the 1 tablespoon of olive oil. Season them with the salt and the pepper. In a large sauté pan place the 2 tablespoons of olive oil and heat it on medium high until it is hot. Add the sea bass fillets and sauté them for 3 to 4 minutes on each side, or until they are just done.

On each of 4 warmed individual serving plates pour on the Cilantro Butter. Place a fish fillet on top of the sauce. Place the Vegetable Escabesche on top of the fish.

serves 4

Cilantro Butter

¾	cup fish (or chicken) stock
1½	sticks butter, cut into small pieces
1	bunch cilantro, coarsely chopped
	salt (to taste)
	pepper (to taste)

In a medium saucepan place the fish stock and bring it to a boil over medium high heat. Let the stock boil for 2 minutes, or until it is slightly reduced.

(continued on next page)

"Sea bass is like salmon, in that when you sauté it at a high heat it gets a really good crust on it. This is because it is a rich fish, with a lot of fat in it. Chilean sea bass is recommended because it comes from cold, deep water, and therefore the flesh is firmer."

"This is a sauce that is made with a French technique but uses Mexican ingredients. In France they do use cilantro, but they don't know what it is and they call it coriander."

"I don't cook at home, ever! I cook six days a week and on my day off I go out with my wife to eat at a restaurant, and pay someone else to feed us."

"This is a pickled vegetable dish that has a lot of different tastes. It's crunchy, light, and very refreshing. You can use it with all kinds of fish, and it is great with poultry as well. The tart taste helps to cut the richness of the Cilantro Butter Sauce."

"When you julienne the zucchini you should use the outer green skin and some of the inner white part. You do not go very far into the zucchini at all. The seeds are not touched."

While whisking constantly, add the pieces of butter one at a time. Whisk them in so that they are well incorporated. Add the cilantro and stir it in. Remove the saucepan from the heat.

Pour the sauce into a blender and purée it until it is smooth. Add the salt and pepper, and stir them in. Keep the sauce warm until you are ready to use it.

Vegetable Escabesche

¼	red onion, finely diced
1½	teaspoons oregano, ground in your palm
1½	tablespoons cilantro, chopped
1	clove garlic, crushed
½	cup white vinegar
⅛	cup water
⅛	cup olive oil
2	chipotle chile peppers, finely chopped
1	bay leaf, crushed
1	medium jicama, peeled and julienned
1	medium carrot, peeled, blanched, and julienned
2	zucchini, exterior green skin julienned

In a medium bowl place the red onions, oregano, cilantro, garlic, white vinegar, water, olive oil, chipotle chile peppers, and crushed bay leaf. Mix the ingredients together so that they are well blended.

Add the jicama, carrots, and zucchini. Toss them in so that they are well coated with the marinade. Let the ingredients marinate for 4 to 6 hours before serving.

Rebecca's Sautéed Duck with Fideo

Rebecca's Sautéed Duck

2   duck breasts, split in half, excess fat trimmed off, and bones removed
     salt
     pepper
4   tablespoons vegetable oil
     Fideo *(recipe on next page)*

Lightly score the duck breasts. Season them with the salt and the pepper.

In a large saucepan place the oil and heat it on medium high until it is hot. Add the duck breasts and sauté them for 4 to 6 minutes on each side, or until they are nice and crispy and just done.

Slice the duck into thin pieces.

At the top of each of 4 individual serving plates place the Fideo. Place the sliced duck at the bottom of the plate.

serves 4

"Americans are used to eating Duck à la Orange, where the duck has been baked for 3 hours or so, and it is nice and tender. In this recipe the duck is more chewy, like a steak. It should be cooked medium to medium rare. Remember, duck is a red meat. It is not a white meat, like chicken, where there can be no pink showing."

"Mexican food is very rustic and down to earth. What you order is what you get.....there is no surprise. It is not refined, like French food, where everything is puréed and strained and molded into something that looks different from what it is. If you order black beans, black beans are what you get. They aren't molded to look like a scalloped shell or anything fancy."

Fideo

3	**large tomatoes**
3	**tablespoons light olive oil**
4	**ounces cappellini pasta, broken into 4" pieces**
½	**small white onion, finely diced**
5	**cloves garlic, finely diced**
3	**cups chicken stock** *(recipe on page 297)*
¼	**cup raw fresh peas**
	cracked black pepper *(to taste)*
	salt *(to taste)*
⅓	**cup cilantro leaves**

Place the tomatoes in a baking pan and roast them for 10 to 15 minutes under a preheated broiler, or until they are black. Place the roasted tomatoes in a blender and purée them. Set the purée aside.

In a large sauté pan place the olive oil and heat it on medium high until it is hot. Add the dry pasta and sauté it for 3 to 5 minutes, or until it is golden brown.

Add the onions and garlic, and sauté them for 2 minutes.

Add the roasted tomato purée and cook it for 2 minutes.

Add ⅓ cup of the chicken stock and cook it for 3 to 4 minutes, or until it has reduced so that it is nearly dry.

Add another ⅓ cup of the chicken stock and cook it for 3 to 4 minutes, or until it has reduced so that it is nearly dry.

Add the peas, the remaining chicken broth, and the black pepper. Cook the mixture for 4 to 6 minutes, or until it is nearly dry. Add the salt and the cilantro, and stir them in.

serves 4

"Fideo is pasta, and it is cooked in a way that is similar to making risotto. It has a unique taste because you toast the pasta and it gets a nutty flavor."

"The basis of my recipes comes from various books that have been written on Mexican cooking. I read the recipes, try them out, and adjust them to what I think tastes best."

Crab Taquitos with Chipotle Sour Cream Salsa, Black Bean Purée, and Guacamole

Crab Taquitos

1	tablespoon vegetable oil
⅓	onion, minced
2	serrano chile peppers, minced
1	stalk celery, minced
½	cup heavy cream
1	egg
1	teaspoon paprika
½	bunch cilantro, chopped
	salt *(to taste)*
1	pound snow crab meat
16	corn tortillas, warmed until pliable
4	pounds shortening
½	cup lime juice, freshly squeezed
	Chipotle Sour Cream Salsa *(recipe on next page)*
	Black Bean Purée *(recipe on next page)*
	Guacamole *(recipe on next page)*
2	ripe tomatoes, blanched, peeled, seeded, and minced

In a medium sauté pan place the oil and heat it on medium high until it is hot. Add the onions, serrano chile peppers, and celery. Sauté the ingredients for 3 to 4 minutes, or until they are tender. Set them aside to cool.

In a medium bowl place the heavy cream and the egg, and beat them together. Add the paprika, cilantro, and salt, and mix them in. Add the crab meat and the sautéed vegetables, and fold them in. In each of the warmed tortillas place some of the crab mixture. Roll the tortillas up and secure them with a toothpick.

In a large saucepan place the shortening and heat it on high until it has melted and reaches 375°. Deep fry the rolled tortillas for 2 to 3 minutes, or until they are crisp and golden brown. Drain them on paper towels. Lightly sprinkle the fried taquitos with the lime juice and salt.

On each of 4 individual serving plates spread on the Chipotle Sour Cream Salsa. Place the Black Bean Purée in a bottle with a spout and pour it out to make a design over the salsa.

(continued on next page)

Rebecca's

"Be careful not to get the oil too hot when you deep-fry these.....375° should be the maximum heat. Otherwise, the tortillas will get crisp and done before the crab gets heated. And one thing we don't want is frigid crab!"

"When the taquitos are rolled up, they should look like big, fat cigars. The whole plate is really beautiful looking, with the different colors of all the salsas."

"Lard tastes the best to fry the taquitos in, but you also can use vegetable oil, or shortening, like Crisco. Remove them with a slotted spoon, and be VERY CAREFUL!"

"Southwestern cuisine is not Mexican food at all. Mexicans don't eat ancho chile fettucini with smoked chicken and pine nuts, if you know what I mean. They don't eat that stuff at all!"

Place 4 taquitos in the center of the plate. Place 3 dollops of the guacamole on the edge of the plate (at 12, 4, and 8 o'clock). Sprinkle the minced tomatoes on top of the guacamole.

serves 4

Chipotle Sour Cream Salsa

1　**cup sour cream**
¼　**cup half and half** (or as needed)
2　**chipotle chile peppers**
½　**teaspoon Spanish paprika**
　　salt (to taste)

In a food processor place all of the ingredients. Blend them together so that the mixture is smooth. Add more half and half if it seems too thick.

Black Bean Purée

1　**cup black beans, cooked**
½　**cup chicken stock** (recipe on page 297)
2　**teaspoons Dry Sack sherry**
　　salt (to taste)

In a blender place the cooked black beans and the chicken stock. Purée the beans until they are smooth. Strain the puréed beans. Add the sherry and the salt, and stir them in.

Guacamole

2　**ripe avocados, peeled and pit removed**
4　**teaspoons fresh cilantro, minced**
4　**teaspoons white onions, minced**
2　**tablespoons serrano chile peppers, minced**
　　salt (to taste)

In a small bowl place the avocado, cilantro, white onions, and serrano chile peppers. Mash the ingredients together so that they are well blended. Add the salt.

"We use Spanish paprika in the restaurant because all of our ingredients are authentic. But for the average person making this, any kind of paprika will do. Spanish paprika has a more orange than red color to it."

"Chipotle chiles are jalapeño peppers that have been smoked. You buy them in a can with adobo sauce. Although they are very hot, the sauce is not. I love them, and I eat them right out of the can, but I do not recommend this to most people. After you handle them don't rub your eyes or lick your fingers..... wash your hands well!"

"The flavor of the bean purée is nice and mild. We use it primarily to add color to the plate. Put it in a plastic mustard jar and then squeeze it out into a nice design."

"This is a classic Mexican guacamole recipe. If you add some salsa to it, like a lot of people do, then it is no longer guacamole. Rather, it is guacamole with salsa."

Duck Rellenos with Añejo Cream and Red Sauce

Duck Rellenos

4   duck legs, fat removed, boned, and cut into ⅜" cubes
2   teaspoons light oil
½   teaspoon salt
½   small white onion, diced medium
2   large tomatoes, blanched, peeled, and seeds removed
1   cup water
4   fresh poblano chile peppers
¼   cup Monterey Jack cheese, grated
1   cup flour, seasoned with salt and pepper
3   eggs, beaten
2   pounds lard
    Añejo Cream *(recipe on next page)*
    Red Sauce *(recipe on page 234)*
4   sprigs cilantro

In a medium bowl place the duck, oil, and salt. Toss the ingredients together so that the duck is well coated with the oil.

Heat a cast iron skillet on high until it is hot. Add the coated duck and the onions. While stirring constantly, sauté the duck for 3 to 4 minutes, or until it begins to turn brown.

Add the tomatoes and the water, and bring the liquid to a boil over high heat. Reduce the heat to low and simmer the ingredients for 8 to 10 minutes, or until the duck is tender and most of the liquid has evaporated. Set the mixture aside and let it cool.

Roast the poblano chile peppers over an open flame *(or under a broiler)* until the skin is black all over and blistered. Place the chiles in a plastic bag for 10 minutes. Remove the skins by rubbing them with a dry cloth.

Cut a 3" long slit in the side of each chile, near the top but below the core. Very carefully remove the seed pod with a sharp knife. Rinse the chiles under cold running water to remove any remaining seeds.

(continued on next page)

"For an interesting and great tasting variation on a chile relleno, this recipe is it! It's straightforward and easy to make, and the finished product looks beautiful. The white and red sauces swirled together really do the trick."

"When people eat here I want them to have a good time, and to think that the food is worth the price. They should have a unique experience in eating Mexican food."

"When I go on vacation I take cookbooks with me, and I read them over and over."

Add the Monterey Jack cheese to the cooled duck mixture and fold it in.

Carefully spoon the duck mixture into the chiles so that it is evenly distributed. Press the slits on the chiles shut and wipe off the outsides.

Dredge the stuffed chiles in the seasoned flour. Dip them in the beaten eggs.

In a large, heavy saucepan place the lard and heat it on high until it is hot. Add the stuffed chiles and cook them for 2 to 3 minutes, or until they are lightly browned. Drain them on paper towels.

Preheat the oven to 400°. Place the fried chiles on a flat sheet and bake them for 6 to 10 minutes, or until the filling is hot.

On each of 4 individual serving plates pour on some of the Añejo Cream and the Red Sauce. Swirl the 2 sauces together to make an attractive design. Place one hot relleno in the center of the plate. Garnish the dish with a sprig of cilantro.

serves 4

Añejo Cream

1½   **cups heavy cream**
⅓   **cup Queso Añejo** *(Spanish cheese)*, **grated**
      salt *(to taste)*

In a small saucepan place the heavy cream. Heat it on medium for 5 minutes, or until it is slightly reduced.

Add the Queso Añejo and salt, and stir them in until the cheese has melted.

Pass the sauce through a medium mesh strainer. Keep the sauce warm until you are ready to use it.

"Before you deep-fry these you should test the oil to see if it is hot. Stick something in it, like a piece of lettuce, and if the oil bubbles, then it is ready. The idea with fried food is to cook it and serve it immediately so that it stays crispy."

"Queso Añejo is a Mexican dry cheese that is crumbly. If you can't get it, then substitute feta or goat cheese."

I think that cooking is a lot of fun. It is not boring because there is ample freedom to create what you want. Plus, there are a lot of interesting characters who work in restaurants."

234

Red Sauce

2   tablespoons olive oil
2   serrano chile peppers, sliced medium
½   small white onion, sliced medium
4   large tomatoes, blanched, peeled, seeded, and coarsely chopped
2   large tomatoes

In a medium skillet place the olive oil and heat it on medium high until it is hot. Add the serrano chile peppers and the onions. Sauté them for 3 to 4 minutes, or until the onions are translucent.

Add the chopped tomatoes and simmer them for 15 to 20 minutes, or until they break down to form a sauce-like consistency.

Place the 2 whole tomatoes in a baking pan. Broil them for 15 to 20 minutes, or until they are black all over.

In a blender place the cooked tomato sauce and the blackened tomatoes. Purée the ingredients until a smooth sauce is formed.

makes 1½ cups

"This red sauce is easy to make and you can serve it with a lot of different Mexican dishes, just as a nice side condiment. It adds both color and flavor to whatever you are serving."

"I don't serve anything that I wouldn't want to eat myself. I also don't serve anything unless I honestly think that it is worth the money. There is no way I want a customer to look at a plate and think, 'Wow.....this is really expensive for Mexican food!' Rather, I want the customer to fully appreciate what he or she is eating, and to be satisfied in all ways."

Flan

⅛ **cup sugar**
2 **teaspoons water**
6 **egg yolks**
⅛ **cup sugar**
1 **vanilla bean, split and the inside scraped out**
2 **cups heavy cream**
⅛ **cup sugar**

In a small saucepan place the first ⅛ cup of sugar and the water. While stirring constantly, heat the mixture on medium for 6 to 8 minutes, or until the sugar turns light brown. Pour the caramelized sugar into the bottom of 4 individual ramekins. Set them aside.

In a medium saucepan place the egg yolks and the second ⅛ cup of sugar. Beat them together for 3 to 5 minutes, or until the egg yolks lighten in color and are creamy.

In a small saucepan place the vanilla bean (both the inside and outer part), the heavy cream, and the third ⅛ cup of sugar. Bring the mixture to a boil over medium heat.

While stirring constantly, slowly add the boiling cream to the egg yolk mixture. Place the saucepan on medium high heat and cook it for 3 to 4 minutes, or until the mixture lightly coats a spoon. Pass the custard through a medium mesh strainer, into a bowl.

Preheat the oven to 225°.

Pour the mixture into each of the 4 ramekins. Place them in a baking pan that is half full of boiling water. Place the pan in the oven and bake the custard for 1 hour and 20 minutes. Remove the pan from the oven and let the custard sit in the water for 30 minutes. Place the custard in the refrigerator for several hours so that it is well chilled.

Loosen the flan from the cups with a knife. Invert the flan onto individual serving plates. Scrape out the softened caramel and place it on top. Serve the flan at room temperature.

serves 4

"Flan is basically ice cream that is baked instead of freezing. It requires a certain knack to make it. There are a lot of subtle judgments to be made during the process, like knowing when the sugar is caramelized, how to temper the egg yolks, and when the flan is done. However, I recommend that you just go for it, because how else can you learn?"

"The only way that a restaurant survives is with repeat business. Therefore, the food must be consistent. People come back to eat a certain dish because they liked the way it tasted when they had it before. They remember this very well, and if it is not the same they will tell you, or else never come back again."

"I think that Mexican food is very interesting. There is no end to the possibilities of what you can do with it. I love the way you can taste the flavors of what you are eating, because they are not disguised."

Statue of Surfer, Hermosa Beach

The Rex
Newport Beach

Elegantly decorated in the style of a turn-of-the-century San Francisco bordello, The Rex is one of the top gourmet seafood restaurants in California.

Owner Rex Chandler says, *"This is a classic recipe that has worked in our restaurant for over 18 years. The spinach and Pernod have a cleansing action on the palate."*

Oysters Rockefeller

½   **pound bacon, diced into small pieces**
⅓   **cup onions, finely chopped**
⅓   **cup red bell peppers, finely chopped**
⅓   **cup green bell peppers, finely chopped**
2   **tablespoons Pernod**
    salt *(to taste)*
    pepper *(to taste)*
2   **bunches spinach, stems removed, washed, and chopped**
30   **Bluepoint oysters, thoroughly cleaned, shells opened, and meat removed** *(reserve the shells)*
    Simple Hollandaise Sauce *(recipe on page 131)*
⅓   **cup fresh parsley, finely chopped**

Heat a large skillet on medium high. Add the bacon and cook it for 3 to 4 minutes, or until it is golden brown.

Add the onions, red bell peppers, and green bell peppers. Sauté them for 2 minutes. Add the Pernod, salt, and pepper.

Add the spinach and sauté it for 2 minutes.

On each of 30 half shells place some of the spinach mixture. Place the oyster meat on top. Place more of the spinach mixture on top.

Preheat the oven to 400°. Place the oysters in a baking dish and bake them for 12 minutes.

On each of 6 individual serving plates place 5 of the oysters. Ladle on the Simple Hollandaise Sauce. Sprinkle on the chopped parsley.

serves 6

Doryman Crab Cakes
with Lobster Sauce

Doryman Crab Cakes

8	ounces Maryland Blue Crab meat
1	egg, beaten
2	tablespoons green bell peppers, finely chopped
2	tablespoons red bell peppers, finely chopped
2	tablespoons celery, finely chopped
2	tablespoons Parmesan cheese, freshly grated
1	tablespoon flour
6	tablespoons butter, softened
½	teaspoon garlic, finely minced
1	tablespoon dry white wine
½	lemon, juiced
1	cup Waverly Wafers *(or as needed)*, ground
¼	cup vegetable oil *(or as needed)*
	Lobster Sauce *(recipe on next page)*
1	lemon, wedged

In a medium bowl place the crab meat, egg, green and red bell peppers, celery, Parmesan cheese, flour, butter, and garlic. Mix the ingredients together so that they are thoroughly blended.

Add the white wine and lemon juice, and mix them in well.

Form the mixture into cakes. Coat them in the ground Waverly Wafers.

In a large skillet place the oil and heat it on medium until it is hot. Add the crab cakes and sauté them for 2 to 3 minutes on each side, or until they are golden brown.

Serve the crab cakes with the Lobster Sauce and the lemon wedges.

serves 4

"I got the idea for this recipe from Maryland. They have a lot of little home-style cookbooks with a hundred different ways to make crab cakes."

"When the crabs are harvested they are either canned or frozen, because the crab turns bad very quickly. So, unless you can find crab that is extremely fresh, it is better to buy it in vacuum-sealed pouches that are frozen."

"Be sure that you don't get the crab mixture too wet, because the cakes will be doughy inside. Also, the oil shouldn't be too hot because the outside will cook, but not the inside. And, if the oil isn't hot enough, they will be greasy."

Lobster Sauce

2	tablespoons vegetable oil
½	cup onions, finely chopped
½	cup celery, finely chopped
2	cloves garlic, finely chopped
½	teaspoon fresh sweet basil, finely chopped
½	teaspoon fresh oregano, finely chopped
½	teaspoon fresh thyme, finely chopped
¼	teaspoon black pepper
1	bay leaf
½	cup cognac
¼	cup Chablis
1	cup clam juice
¼	cup lobster base
2	cups water
1	cup heavy cream
1	pinch paprika
1	pinch cayenne pepper

In a large sauté pan place the vegetable oil and heat it on medium high until it is hot. Add the onions, celery, garlic, basil, oregano, thyme, pepper, and bay leaf. Sauté the ingredients for 3 to 4 minutes, or until the onions are translucent.

Add the cognac and Chablis, and flambé them. Cook the ingredients for 4 to 6 minutes, or until the liquid is reduced by ⅓.

Add the clam juice, lobster base, and water. Cook the ingredients for 8 to 10 minutes, or until the liquid is reduced by ½.

Strain the sauce. Add the heavy cream, paprika, and cayenne pepper. Cook the sauce for 3 to 4 minutes, or until it is thickened.

"This sauce has a lot of depth to it. Many flavors come through, but the primary taste is that of the lobster. The color of the sauce is reddish and it looks nice next to the golden brown of the crab cakes."

"If you don't want to make this sauce, then you can serve the crab cakes with tartar sauce, like they do in Maryland. Either way, they taste terrific!"

"Each customer has a different perception of what good service is, and it is important that our waiters are sensitive to these differences. Some people want to be fawned over, and others want the waiter to be like a wisp of fresh air that is barely noticed. There is a lot of body language involved. To be a top-notch waitperson takes a lot of experience, but this is the kind of personnel we have at the restaurant."

The Rex

240

Clams Casino

30   **Littleneck clams, thoroughly cleaned, shells opened, and meat removed** *(reserve the shells)*
    Casino Butter *(recipe follows)*
1   **cup Parmesan cheese, freshly grated**
30   **strips of bacon, 2" long**

In each of 30 half shells place a small amount of the Casino Butter. Place the clam meat on top of the butter. Place more of the Casino Butter on top. Sprinkle on the Parmesan cheese. Place a bacon strip on top to cover the clam meat.

Preheat the oven to 500°. Place the clams in a baking dish and bake them for 10 minutes, or until the bacon is crispy.

serves 6

Casino Butter

1   **pound sweet butter**
⅓   **cup red bell peppers, finely chopped**
⅓   **cup green bell peppers, finely chopped**
⅓   **cup red onions, finely chopped**
¾   **cup garlic, finely chopped**
¼   **cup parsley, finely chopped**
1   **dash thyme**
1   **dash oregano**
1   **dash tabasco sauce**
1   **teaspoon Worcestershire sauce**
1   **dash pepper**

In a medium bowl place the butter and gently whisk it until it is fluffy.

Add the remainder of the ingredients and mix them together thoroughly.

"This recipe is similar to escargot in that the primary flavors are garlic and butter. I would say that if you are sensitive to garlic, this probably is not the dish for you."

"Make sure that the bacon piece is big enough to cover the whole top of the clam. The combination of the bacon with the garlic butter and the clam is just outstanding!"

"Most restaurants have a seasoned butter called a 'compound butter'. It has wine, parsley, seasonings, lemon, and garlic in it, and the chef uses it to bring life to certain dishes. Instead of adding a pinch of this and a pinch of that several times, he just adds a dash of the compound butter, and boom, it's done!"

"When you are blending the mixture be careful that you do not over-whip the butter, because if you do, you will get too much air into it, and then it will break down too quickly under heat."

The Rex

Bouillabaisse à la Maison

1	gallon water
½	cup fish base
⅓	cup clam base
1	pinch saffron
2	tomatoes, peeled, seeded, and chopped
16	ounces tomato paste
½	cup Pernod
½	cup Chablis
6	tablespoons garlic butter
½	cup olive oil
1	onion, chopped
4	stalks celery, chopped
2	carrots, chopped
3	cloves garlic, finely chopped
½	teaspoon cracked black pepper
½	teaspoon fennel seeds
3	bay leaves
1½	pounds Manila clams, thoroughly cleaned
2	pounds New Zealand mussels, thoroughly cleaned
3	1-pound lobsters, tails and claws separated
1	pound jumbo shrimp
1	pound crayfish
1½	pounds red snapper, cut into 6 pieces

In a large, heavy saucepot place the water, fish base, and clam base. Bring the liquid to a boil.

Add the saffron, tomatoes, tomato paste, Pernod, Chablis, and garlic butter. Reduce the heat to low and simmer the ingredients for 15 minutes.

In a large sauté pan place the olive oil and heat it on medium high until it is hot. Add the onions, celery, carrots, garlic, cracked black pepper, fennel seeds, and bay leaves. Sauté the vegetables for 4 to 6 minutes, or until the onions are clear. Add the ingredients to the stock and stir them in.

Bring the stock to a boil. Add the clams, mussels, lobster tails and claws, shrimp, crayfish, and red snapper. Cook the fish for 3 to 4 minutes, or until the clams and mussels have opened their shells, and the rest of the seafood is done.

serves 6

*"There is no such thing as a classic bouillabaisse. One time I had a customer who ordered this dish. He indignantly told me, 'This is not the way you make bouillabaisse. In France when I had it, it was different!' So I got out my copy of **Larousse Gastronomique** and showed him that there were 51 recipes for bouillabaisse. He thought that there was only one way to make it, and that was the way he had eaten it in Marseilles. There they serve it with eel, but we don't have eel here. I explained to him that all of the different recipes were based on what fish was available in a particular area. I managed to win him over, and he is still a customer!"*

"Bouillabaisse always has a little saffron in it, which gives it a light orangish-red color. Use it very sparingly, because you can always add more, but once it's in the broth, you can't take it out. If you add too much there is nothing else you can add to offset the flavor."

The Rex

242

Salmon au Poivre with Beurre Rouge Sauce

Salmon au Poivre

6	8-ounce salmon steaks
2	tablespoons olive oil
¼	cup cracked black pepper *(or as needed)*
4	tablespoons olive oil
	Beurre Rouge Sauce *(recipe on next page)*

Rub the salmon steaks with the 2 tablespoons of olive oil. Rub the cracked black pepper into the salmon.

In a large, heavy skillet place the 4 tablespoons of the olive oil and heat it on high until it is very hot. Add the salmon steaks and quickly sauté them for 1 to 2 minutes on each side, or until they are seared.

Place the salmon steaks in a baking dish. Broil the fish for 3 to 4 minutes on each side, or until they are done.

On each of 6 individual serving plates pour ½ cup of the Beurre Rouge Sauce. Place the salmon steak on top.

serves 6

"I created this dish because I love pepper steaks, and I also love my red wine with dinner. I don't eat as much meat as I used to, so I wanted to create a fish dish that I thought would be hearty and substantial enough to stand up against a good glass of red wine, like a good steak will."

"I started my restaurant career at the age of 9. My mother had a restaurant and I used to help her in the kitchen. The pleasure that I received from cooking came from making others happy (I use the past tense because now I don't cook as often as I used to.....I am too involved in the business end of running the restaurant.) I have always loved to see how thrilled people are when I present a beautifully prepared dish. I love the energy and excitement that can be created."

"The secret to this sauce is the grape juice. If you reduce the Cabernet by itself, then it has the tendency to get a little brown. But, by adding the grape juice you get a beautiful, purplish color. It looks outstanding next to the salmon."

"We leave our cold butter out overnight to soften it, which would work for you as well. You can't heat the butter to soften it."

"Excellence of food is paramount in our restaurant.....this is a given. Beyond this, I think that service is the most important factor. How you are treated, how you are understood, how you are taken care of.....these are the key ingredients that separate us from the rest of the field."

Beurre Rouge Sauce

1	cup grape juice *(unsweetened)*
1½	cups Cabernet
2	tablespoons shallots, finely chopped
20	whole black peppercorns
⅔	cup veal stock *(recipe on page 151)*
1½	cups heavy cream
1¼	cups sweet butter, softened and cut into pieces

In a medium saucepan place the grape juice, Cabernet, shallots, and peppercorns. Simmer the ingredients on low heat for 30 to 40 minutes, or until the liquid is reduced by ½.

Add the veal stock and cook the ingredients on medium heat for 8 to 10 minutes, or until it is reduced by ½.

Add the heavy cream and cook the sauce for 8 to 10 minutes, or until it is reduced by ⅓.

While whisking constantly, add the pieces of butter one at a time so that they are well incorporated.

Clams en Brodo con Linguini à la Portofino

2	quarts clam juice
½	cup Chablis
3	tablespoons garlic, crushed
1	large tomato, skin removed, seeded, and chopped
1	lemon, juiced
½	bunch green onions, chopped
½	teaspoon dry sweet basil
½	teaspoon dry oregano
1	teaspoon crushed red chile peppers
3	tablespoons olive oil
3	pounds Manila clams
1¾	pounds Baby Sea clams (canned or frozen)
2	pounds linguini, cooked al dente
¼	cup fresh parsley, finely chopped
¼	cup fresh basil, finely chopped
¼	cup fresh oregano, finely chopped
2	lemons, cut into 8 wedges

In a large saucepot place the clam juice and bring it to a boil over high heat. Add the Chablis, garlic, tomatoes, lemon juice, green onions, dry basil, dry oregano, crushed red chile peppers, and olive oil.

Bring the liquid to a boil again. Add the Manila clams and the Baby Sea clams. Cook them for 3 to 4 minutes, or until the shells have opened.

In each of 6 individual serving bowls place the linguini. Place the clams on top. Ladle on the broth. Sprinkle on the parsley, fresh basil, and fresh oregano. Garnish the dish with a lemon wedge.

serves 8

"This dish is actually a soupy broth that is served with clams and linguini. People absolutely love it and it is one of our top sellers. They come to the restaurant for this dish only."

"We serve this in the terrine that we cook it in. We take the lid off at the table and all of this aromatic steam rolls out. It's heavenly!"

"The flavor is a bit on the spicy side, although you can vary the amount of the crushed red chiles as you wish. We serve it with some extra red chiles on the side. Personally, I like it a bit spicier."

"If a clam is not healthy, then the shell will not open, and it should be discarded. But you should be sure to cook the clams long enough to give them a chance to open."

Rex's Poached Salmon with Raspberry Sauce

Rex's Poached Salmon

6   8-ounce salmon fillets
1   gallon fish stock (see chef's comments on this page for
        instructions)
2   cups Chablis
3   whole lemons, sliced
5   bay leaves
1   bunch fresh dill
½   teaspoon black peppercorns
      Raspberry Sauce (recipe follows)

Preheat the oven to 400°.

In a large poaching pan place the salmon, fish stock, Chablis, lemon slices, bay leaves, fresh dill, and peppercorns. Cover the pan and poach the fish in the oven for 10 minutes.

On each of 4 individual serving plates place ½ cup of the Raspberry Sauce. Place a salmon fillet on top.

serves 4

Raspberry Sauce

1   basket raspberries
2   tablespoons shallots, finely chopped
10   whole black peppercorns
2   cups Chablis
¾   cup heavy cream
1   stick butter, softened and cut into small pieces

In a medium saucepan place the raspberries, shallots, peppercorns, and Chablis. Cook the ingredients over low heat for 45 minutes to 1 hour, or until the liquid is reduced by ⅓. Add the heavy cream and cook the sauce for 15 to 20 minutes, or until it is reduced by ½.

Strain the sauce through a cheesecloth and return it to the saucepan. While whisking constantly, add the pieces of butter one at a time so that each one is well incorporated.

"In poaching the salmon we use a fish stock. Take some water and a bunch of fish bones and fish heads (which you can buy), and add some white wine, bay leaf, and whole peppercorns. Boil the ingredients for 10 or 15 minutes, strain it, and then you are ready to poach the salmon in either a shallow pan or a poaching pan."

"I have always worked with seafood because to me a quality product is the essence of the dish..... it is not the technique. If the seafood is fresh and of top quality, then all that needs to be done is to not overcook it, nor to overly complicate what is already beautiful and flavorful. I like food that is prepared this way, and that is why I love seafood."

"The Raspberry Sauce is very red and it looks striking next to the pink salmon. Serve it on a white plate.....this will make the presentation more dramatic."

"The longer and slower you reduce the sauce, the better the flavor will be. If you could reduce it for 8 hours, then it would be that much better."

House, Manhattan Beach

Rockenwagner
Venice

Modern, yet intimate, Rockenwagner is known for its extraordinary contemporary French cuisine which is perfect in both taste and presentation.

Menu

Home-Cured Tomatoes

White Asparagus Salad with Citrus Vinaigrette

Tomato Sorbet

Baby Lettuce Salad with Warm Lamb Tenderloin and Avocado

Rabbit Salad with Raspberry Vinaigrette

Puréed Red Bell Peppers

Ricotta-Filled Jalapeño Ravioli with Goat Cheese Sauce

Sole Fillets with Crusty Topping in a Beurre Blanc Sauce

Warm Strawberry Tart with Almond Cream

European-trained owner Hans Rockenwagner says, *"These tomatoes are good for many, many things. They are just excellent! After these, you will never again want to buy those bagged dried ones that need to be reconstituted."*

Home-Cured Tomatoes

1	cup of olive oil *(or as needed)*
	salt
	pepper
12	Roma tomatoes, stems removed, cut in half lengthwise, and cored
½	teaspoon fresh thyme, finely chopped
½	teaspoon sugar

Brush some of the olive oil on a baking sheet so that it is well coated. Sprinkle the salt and the pepper on top of the sheet.

Place the tomatoes on the sheet with the cut sides facing up.

Sprinkle on the thyme, sugar, and some more of the salt and pepper.

Preheat the oven to 150°. Bake the tomatoes for 6 to 8 hours, or until they are shrunken and wrinkled.

Place the tomatoes and the rest of the olive oil in an airtight container. Add more olive oil if necessary so that the tomatoes are covered.

Store the tomatoes in the refrigerator until you are ready to use them.

White Asparagus Salad
with Citrus Vinaigrette

White Asparagus Salad

2   **quarts water**
2   **teaspoons salt**
1   **teaspoon sugar**
2   **teaspoons butter**
½   **lemon, juiced**
1   **bunch white asparagus, tough ends cut off, and peeled**
     (store the asparagus in cold water)
12 **Home-Cured Tomatoes** *(recipe on previous page)*
8   **ounces prosciutto, julienned**
     Citrus Vinaigrette *(recipe on next page)*

In a large saucepan place the water and bring it to a boil over high heat. Add the salt, sugar, butter, and lemon juice. Add the asparagus and cook them for 15 to 20 minutes, or until they are tender.

On each of 4 hot, individual serving plates place the white asparagus. Place 3 of the Home-Cured Tomatoes and some of the prosciutto on top. Sprinkle on the Citrus Vinaigrette.

Preheat the oven to 300°. Place the asparagus salad in the oven for 1 minute, or until it is warm. Serve it immediately.

serves 4

"In Europe white asparagus is very popular, but here in this country they are extremely difficult to get. So you may have to use green asparagus. If so, then you do not need to cook them as long. Also, you don't need to peel them."

"The peeling of the white asparagus is very important because the skins are very bitter and tough. Believe me, I can compare them to banana skins!"

"In Europe there is a cult around white asparagus. For instance, the peeling of vegetables is always done by the lowest one in the kitchen.....the one who has just started out. But the peeling of a white asparagus is always done by the top person in the kitchen."

Citrus Vinaigrette

3	oranges, peeled and membranes removed
2	lemons, peeled and membranes removed
1	lime, peeled and membranes removed
½	teaspoon cumin seeds
½	cup olive oil
1	pinch sugar
1	pinch salt
1	pinch pepper
1	dash tabasco

In a blender place the oranges, lemons, and lime. Blend the ingredients for 1 minute.

Add the cumin seeds and blend them in.

While blending constantly, very slowly dribble in the olive oil. Continue to blend the dressing for 3 minutes more, or until it is almost the consistency of a mayonnaise.

Add the sugar, salt, pepper, and tabasco. Stir them in well.

makes 2 cups

"This citrus vinaigrette is very flavorful. The different tastes combine together in a most interesting and pleasing way."

"The number one flavor that comes through is that of the citrus. You can't distinguish the lime, lemon, or orange tastes, but what you do taste is the citrus. And, the cumin seeds and tabasco give it a nice, subtle zip."

"You can use this dressing with many different things. It is especially good with fish, either as a marinade or as a little sauce."

250

Tomato Sorbet

6   **tomatoes, peeled and seeded**
¼   **cup sugar dissolved in ¼ cup boiling water**
1   **lemon, juiced**
1   **tablespoon tomato paste**
1   **tablespoon chives, chopped**
     salt *(to taste)*
     pepper *(to taste)*
6   **leaves butter lettuce**
6   **tablespoons sour cream**
6   **basil leaves**

In a blender place the tomatoes, sugar-water mixture, lemon juice, and tomato paste. Purée the ingredients together until the mixture is smooth.

Pour the purée into a medium stainless steel bowl. Add the chives, salt, and pepper. Stir the ingredients together well.

Place the bowl in the freezer. Remove it every 5 minutes and briskly whisk the mixture. Do this for 30 minutes, or until it is the consistency of a sherbert. If ice crystals form, blend the mixture a second time.

On each of 6 individual serving plates place a leaf of the butter lettuce. Place a serving of the tomato sorbet on top. Place a dollop of sour cream on top. Garnish the dish with a basil leaf.

serves 6

"This is so easy to prepare, but it also is something that is out of the ordinary. If you serve it to guests, they will say, 'Wow! This is great! How in the world did you make this?' "

"You can serve this in between courses, as a palate cleanser, as an appetizer, or as a garnish to a salad. Here in the restaurant we serve it with warm sweetbreads and a salad. It goes particularly well with slightly bitter greens such as watercress, arugula, or Belgian endive lettuce, preferably tossed with a balsamic vinaigrette."

"It is important to remove the sorbet from the freezer every 5 minutes and whisk it, because it will start to freeze on the outside, and you want to mix that frozen part in. The more often you take it out and whisk it, the better the consistency will be. Also, the bigger bowl that you use, the bigger the surface there will be for it to freeze, so the whole freezing and whipping process will go much faster."

Baby Lettuce Salad with Warm Lamb Tenderloin and Avocado

3	tablespoons olive oil
4	lamb tenderloins, cleaned
¼	cup red wine vinegar
2	cloves garlic, puréed
¾	cup olive oil
	salt *(to taste)*
	pepper *(to taste)*
4	cups mixed baby lettuce, torn
1	avocado, peeled, pitted, and sliced
2	teaspoons cracked black pepper

In a roasting pan place the 3 tablespoons of olive oil and heat it on medium high until it is hot. Sear the lamb tenderloins on all sides.

Preheat the oven to 450°. Place the roasting pan with the lamb in the oven. Roast it for 4 to 5 minutes, or until it is medium rare. Remove the lamb from the oven. Let it rest for 5 minutes and then slice it into medallions. Set it aside.

In a small bowl place the red wine vinegar, garlic, the ¾ cup of olive oil, salt, and pepper. Whisk the ingredients together so that they are well blended to make a vinaigrette.

In a medium bowl place the mixed baby lettuce. Dribble on some of the vinaigrette and toss it well so that the leaves are evenly coated with the dressing.

On each of 4 individual serving plates place the lettuce. Place the avocado slices on top. Sprinkle on the cracked black pepper. Place the lamb medallions on top of the salad.

serves 4

"This is one of the appetizers that we serve at the restaurant. It is very well loved by our customers."

"The warm meat of the lamb contrasts so nicely with the crispness of the salad. And the vinaigrette gives it a nice tang. This is a fairly mild dish that is not too filling. If you increased the portions it would be good for a nice, light meal."

"I came up with the idea for this recipe because we needed to do something creative with our leftover lamb tenderloins. This is a perfect example of necessity being the mother of invention!"

"Many of the better markets carry a mixture of baby greens that you can buy. It's really wonderful!"

Rabbit Salad with Raspberry Vinaigrette

Rabbit Salad

1	2½-pound rabbit
8	large basil leaves
	salt *(to taste)*
	pepper *(to taste)*
3	tablespoons olive oil
10	sprigs mache lettuce *(or other tender lettuce)*
1	head radicchio, leaves separated and torn
	Raspberry Vinaigrette *(recipe on next page)*

Separate the hind legs from the body of the rabbit. Remove the main bones and butterfly the leg meat. Remove the bones from the rabbit tenderloin *(ask your butcher to do this).*

Wrap the boned tenderloins in the basil leaves. Wrap the butterflied leg portions around the tenderloins. Tie the meat up in several places with kitchen twine.

Season the rabbit with the salt and the pepper.

In a small roasting pan place the olive oil. Heat it on medium high until it is hot. Sear the rabbit on all sides.

Preheat the oven to 400°. Place the pan with the seared rabbit in the oven and roast it for 10 minutes, or until it is done.

Remove the rabbit from the oven and snip off the twine. Cut the rabbit into medallions and keep them warm.

In a medium bowl place the mache and radicchio. Sprinkle on the Raspberry Vinaigrette and toss it with the lettuce.

On each of 4 individual serving plates place the tossed salad. Artfully arrange the rabbit medallions on top.

serves 4

"The hardest thing about this recipe is the boning of the rabbit, which is not easy. So that is why I suggest having your butcher do it. Bring this cookbook and show him the recipe. Thank goodness for your friendly, local butcher!"

"By butterfly, I mean you have to make some slices almost completely through the meat, and then fan it out into a butterfly shape."

"Some people are afraid to eat rabbit, and they say, 'Oh, I don't want to eat Bugs Bunny!' So if you feel this way, then you can substitute chicken for the rabbit. But actually, rabbit is somewhat similar to chicken. It may be a little tougher, but it is a very mild and wonderful meat."

"The quality of the raspberry vinegar must be very good so that the flavor is intense, but at the same time mild. A cheaper vinegar will be too sharp tasting. The nuttiness of the walnut oil combines pleasantly with the raspberry flavor of the vinegar."

Raspberry Vinaigrette

½	**cup walnut oil**
4	**tablespoons raspberry vinegar**
¼	**teaspoon salt**
⅛	**teaspoon pepper**

In a small bowl place all of the ingredients. Whisk them together until they are well blended.

makes ¾ cup

"The ingredients in this recipe are Italian in flavor. It is so simple, but adds a wonderful accent to whatever dish you are serving.....both in its color and in its taste. It can turn an ordinary plate into something really special!"

Puréed Red Bell Peppers

2	**red bell peppers**
⅛	**cup olive oil**
	salt *(to taste)*
	pepper *(to taste)*
1	**dash tabasco sauce**

Roast the red bell peppers over an open flame so that they blacken. Remove the charred skin and the seeds.

In a blender place the bell peppers, olive oil, salt, pepper, and tabasco sauce. Purée the ingredients together.

Ricotta-Filled Jalapeño Ravioli with Goat Cheese Sauce

Ricotta-Filled Jalapeño Ravioli

1	**pound Jalapeño Pasta Dough** (recipe on next page)
1	**pound ricotta cheese**
¼	**cup Parmesan cheese, freshly grated**
4	**eggs**
1	**bunch parsley, chopped**
	black pepper, freshly ground (to taste)
	Goat Cheese Sauce (recipe on next page)

Roll out the Jalapeño Pasta Dough until it is very thin. Cut the dough into 2" squares.

In a medium bowl place the ricotta, Parmesan, eggs, parsley, and pepper. Mix the ingredients together so that they are well blended.

On one square of the ravioli dough place a small amount of the cheese filling. Moisten the edges around the filling with some water. Place another square of dough on top. Pinch the edges together tightly so that the ravioli is well sealed. Repeat the process until all of the ravioli are made.

In a large saucepan place 4 quarts of water and bring it to a boil. Add the ravioli and boil them for 5 to 7 minutes, or until they are cooked al dente. Drain the ravioli.

Place the ravioli in the Goat Cheese Sauce and simmer them for 1 minute.

serves 4

"When you cook the ravioli you should drop them in boiling water and wait until they rise to the surface. Leave them there for 30 seconds to 1 minute, and then remove them."

"My Italian mother-in-law is always experimenting with pastas, and she came up with this recipe. My wife and I have dinner at her house all of the time. I love her food and decided to use this pasta in our restaurant. She and I talk about food and cooking constantly. I am lucky to have such a great mother-in-law who I enjoy so much."

Jalapeño Pasta Dough

4	eggs

4   eggs
12 jalapeño chile peppers, halved and seeded
1   tablespoon salt
1   tablespoon olive oil
1   pound semolina flour
4   cups all-purpose flour *(or as needed)*

In a food processor place the eggs, jalapeño chile peppers, salt, and olive oil. Blend the ingredients together until the mixture is smooth *(use the steel knife blade or the pasta blade)*.

With the food processor still running add the semolina flour.

Add enough of the all-purpose flour so that the dough becomes heavy, like a pie dough.

Let the dough rest for 2 hours.

Goat Cheese Sauce

2   tablespoons butter
5   shallots, chopped
2   cloves garlic, minced
1½ cups heavy cream
5   ounces mild goat cheese, broken into small chunks
1   tablespoon white wine vinegar
   salt *(to taste)*
   pepper *(to taste)*

In a small pan place the butter and heat it on medium high until it has melted. Add the shallots and sauté them for 2 minutes.

Add the garlic and sauté it for 2 to 3 minutes.

Add the heavy cream and bring it to a boil.

While stirring constantly add the small chunks of cheese, one at a time. Lower the heat and continue to stir the sauce until the cheese has melted and is well incorporated.

Add the vinegar, salt, and pepper, and stir them in.

"Make certain that the jalapeño peppers are really well puréed. The color of the dough will be very bright green. It will almost look like you added food coloring."

"The dough will have a moderate sting to it, but it will not be too spicy. It's a great change from ordinary pasta."

"When you add the semolina flour and the all-purpose flour, the whole mixing process should not take too long, or else the dough will get sticky and it will be difficult to work with. If this happens, then cover the dough with some plastic wrap and let it sit for an hour or so."

"This is another recipe from my mother-in-law. It's just delicious with the ravioli!"

"A nice, mild goat cheese that you can use is Montrachet. Goat cheese is readily available in most stores. However, if you can't find it you can substitute blue cheese or else use more of the Parmesan. It won't be the same, but it will still taste good."

Sole Fillets with Crusty Topping in a Beurre Blanc Sauce

Sole Fillets with Crusty Topping

4	6-ounce sole fillets
6	ounces French bread, crust removed, and cubed
5	ounces smoked salmon, chopped
¼	cup butter
1½	tablespoons horseradish
1	lemon, juiced
1	pinch cayenne pepper
	salt *(to taste)*
	pepper *(to taste)*
	Beurre Blanc Sauce *(recipe on next page)*

Place two of the sole fillets flat on a board. Place the other two sole fillets on top. Roll them up from the head to the tail, and then cut them in half so that each roll makes 2 serving pieces. Secure them with a toothpick and set them aside.

In a food processor place the bread, smoked salmon, butter, horseradish, lemon juice, cayenne pepper, salt, and pepper. Blend the ingredients together so that a paste is formed.

In a slightly oiled baking pan place the rolled fillet halves. Place a small patty of the paste, ¼" thick, on top of each piece.

Place the fillets under a preheated broiler for 2 to 3 minutes, or until they are brown and crispy. Remove the pan from the oven.

Preheat the oven to 350°. Set the pan back in the oven and bake the fish for 2 to 3 minutes, or until they are heated through.

On each of 4 warmed, individual serving plates place the Beurre Blanc Sauce. Place one rolled sole fillet on top.

serves 4

"This is a recipe that I used to make when I was working at a restaurant in Germany. It's an interesting combination of flavors.....there's the snap of the horseradish, the heat of the cayenne pepper, the tang of the lemon, all against the background flavor of the sole. The flavor of the paste accommodates the sole.....it is not too overpowering."

"At our restaurant we change the menu for each season. In the summer we feature lobster, in the fall we do wild mushrooms of all kinds, in the winter we have wild game, and in the spring it's white asparagus."

Beurre Blanc Sauce

2	teaspoons butter
6	shallots, finely chopped
2	cups dry white wine
1	cup heavy cream
2	sticks butter, cut into small pieces
¼	teaspoon lemon juice, freshly squeezed
	salt *(to taste)*
	pepper *(to taste)*

In a small saucepan place the 2 teaspoons of butter and heat it on medium high until it has melted. Add the shallots and sauté them for 2 to 3 minutes.

Add the white wine and cook it for 8 to 10 minutes, or until it is almost evaporated.

Add the cream and let it cook for 2 to 3 minutes. Reduce the heat.

While whisking constantly, slowly add the butter pieces, one at a time.

Add the lemon juice, salt, and pepper. Whisk them in.

"When you add the butter be sure that the heat isn't too hot. The sauce should be just simmering. If you need to reheat the sauce then you should do it very gently in a double boiler. Otherwise, the sauce might break. You will know if this happens because it will look just terrible!"

"This is a very classical sauce. It is the basis for a lot of other sauces. When you eat it, it tastes light, but actually it is very rich. You may vary the sauce by adding fresh herbs, caviar, parsley, or even the Puréed Red Bell Peppers (recipe on page 253)."

Warm Strawberry Tart
with Almond Cream

Warm Strawberry Tart

8   ounces prepared puff pastry
      Almond Cream *(recipe on next page)*
2   baskets fresh strawberries, stems removed, and washed
2   egg yolks, beaten
2   teaspoons powdered sugar *(or as needed)*
4   mint leaves

Roll out the puff pastry with a rolling pin so that it is ⅛" thick. Let it rest for 5 minutes. Cut out four 4" rounds.

Place the pastry rounds on a lightly buttered cookie sheet.

Form the Almond Cream into small mounds, 2" in diameter, and place them in the center of the pastry rounds.

Completely cover the almond cream mounds with the strawberries *(with the tip ends up)*.

Brush the exposed part of the pastry rounds with the beaten egg yolks, being careful not to get any of it on the pan.

Preheat the oven to 350°. Bake the tarts for 6 to 7 minutes, or until they are slightly browned. Remove the tarts from the oven.

Sprinkle the powdered sugar on top. Garnish the tarts with the mint leaves.

serves 4

"This is a wonderful dessert. It tastes light and refreshing when you eat it, although the flavor is decadent! Serve it with some vanilla ice cream..... outstanding!"

"Sometimes we make this with apples. You peel them, cut them into thin slices, and arrange them in circles on top of the mound. Then sprinkle on some cinnamon and sugar."

"I like to use ordinary things and then make them extraordinary. For example, rather than using exotic items, like tiny baby vegetables, I would rather use regular full-grown vegetables and prepare something very unusual with them."

"A striking presentation of the dish is particularly in vogue right now. We have always considered this to be one of our top priorities. The chefs put a lot of effort and time into how the plate looks when it leaves the kitchen and goes to the customer. But, to back up a beautiful looking plate you also must have a good product. The flavors must be incredible in order to match the beauty."

"People feel comfortable in our restaurant, but, really, it is the food that draws them here."

Almond Cream

1	cup almonds, ground
½	cup butter, softened
¾	cup sugar
4	egg yolks
½	teaspoon almond extract

In a food processor place all of the ingredients. Mix them together for 5 to 7 minutes, or until a paste is formed.

Place the almond cream in the refrigerator for ½ hour before using it.

Artist, Laguna Beach

Royal Khyber
Newport Beach

Hailed as one of the most beautiful restaurants in America, the Royal Khyber serves an Indian cuisine that is both authentic and delicious.

Menu

Kachumbar Salad

Naan Indian Bread

Chicken Tikka

Stuffed Potato Patties with Mint Chutney

Tandoori Chicken with Mango Chutney

Fenugreek Chicken

Aromatic Garam Masala

Chicken Tawa Masala

Makhani Gravy

Masala Lamb Chops

Indian Rice Pudding

Owner Arun Puri says, *"This salad is very healthy and refreshing. In the summertime the people in India eat it every day with their lunch."*

Kachumbar Salad

2	medium onions, chopped medium
1	large tomato, seeds removed, and chopped
1	medium cucumber, peeled, seeds removed, and chopped medium
4	serrano green chile peppers, seeds removed, and finely chopped
1	tablespoon fresh mint, chopped
2	tablespoons fresh coriander, chopped
4	tablespoons lemon juice, freshly squeezed
½	teaspoon salt
1	lemon, cut into 4 wedges

In a medium bowl place all of the ingredients except for the lemon wedges. Mix them together well.

Place the bowl in the refrigerator for ½ hour.

Serve the salad with the lemon wedges.

serves 4

Naan Indian Bread

4	cups flour
1	teaspoon salt
¼	teaspoon baking powder
1	cup water *(or as needed)*
1	egg
2½	teaspoons sugar
2	tablespoons yogurt
3	tablespoons milk
5	teaspoons vegetable oil
1	teaspoon Kalonji *(onion seeds)*
2	teaspoons melon seeds
2	tablespoons butter, melted

In a medium bowl sift together the flour, salt, and baking powder. Make a well in the flour. Gradually add and mix in enough of the water to make a soft dough. Knead the dough.

In a small bowl place the egg, sugar, yogurt, and milk. Whisk the ingredients together. Slowly add the egg mixture to the dough and work it in.

Knead the dough so that it is soft and smooth *(it should not stick to your fingers)*. Cover the dough with a moist cloth and let it sit for 10 minutes.

Add the oil and work it in. Knead the dough and then punch it down. Cover it with a moist cloth and let it rest for 2 hours.

Divide the dough into 6 portions and form them into balls. Flatten each ball slightly, cover them with a moist cloth, and let them rest for 5 minutes.

Flatten out each ball between your palms to form a round disc. Stretch the dough to form an elongated oval.

Preheat the oven to 325°. Sprinkle on the Kalonji and the melon seeds. Place the ovals on a greased baking sheet and bake them for 10 to 15 minutes, or until they are golden brown. Brush on the melted butter.

serves 6

"At the restaurant we bake this bread in an Indian clay oven called a 'tandoor'. It is shaped like an upside down basket, with a hole in the top as well as in the bottom, and there is charcoal underneath. Inside, the temperature is over 600˚. The cook slaps the bread dough on the inside wall of the oven and leaves it there for 60 to 90 seconds while it bakes. Then he removes the bread with a rod that has a hook on the end. It is a most fascinating process to watch!"

"You can make this bread at home and it will taste wonderful, but you cannot duplicate the flavor that we get at the restaurant, because of the difference in the ovens being used."

"The Kalonji and the melon seeds make the bread taste better, and they look pretty. But, you can eliminate them if you wish."

"The staff at the Royal Khyber is instructed to invite our customers to go back to the kitchen and watch the bread being made."

Chicken Tikka

¼	cup yogurt
2½	tablespoons ginger paste *(see chef's comments on page 270)*
2½	tablespoons garlic paste *(see chef's comments on page 270)*
½	teaspoon white pepper
½	teaspoon cumin powder
⅓	teaspoon mace
⅓	teaspoon nutmeg
⅓	teaspoon green cardamom powder
½	teaspoon red chile powder
½	teaspoon turmeric
4	tablespoons lemon juice, freshly squeezed
2	tablespoons flour
½	teaspoon salt
5	tablespoons vegetable oil
1¾	pounds chicken legs, skinned, de-boned, and each leg cut into 4 pieces
¼	cup butter, melted

In a medium bowl place the yogurt, ginger paste, garlic paste, white pepper, cumin powder, mace, nutmeg, green cardamom powder, red chile powder, turmeric, lemon juice, flour, salt, and vegetable oil. Mix the ingredients together so that they are well blended.

Rub the chicken pieces in the yogurt mixture. Let them marinate for 4 hours.

Put the chicken on 6 skewers. Grill the chicken for 6 to 7 minutes. Turn the skewers several times so that the chicken cooks evenly. Baste the chicken with the melted butter while you are grilling it.

serves 4

"This is a succulent and boneless kebab. It is the second most popular appetizer in the restaurant. Americans love it, and they do not have to use their hands to eat it.....they can use a knife and fork. The word 'tikka' means 'boneless and cubed'. In India it is sold on the sidewalks as delicious little snacks."

"Serve this with a side dish of the Makhani Gravy. It is just excellent!"

"People in India eat with their palates. They don't think about whether or not the food is healthy. But the truth is, Indian food is naturally healthy and nutritious. Hardly any cream, butter, or eggs are used, and most of the sauces are prepared with items like fresh onions, tomatoes, garlic, and yogurt. Americans are just beginning to learn how delicious and how healthy our cuisine really is."

Stuffed Potato Patties with Mint Chutney

Stuffed Potato Patties

2¼ **pounds potatoes, boiled, cooled, peeled, and grated**
¼   **cup corn flour**
1   **teaspoon salt**
3   **tablespoons clarified butter, melted**
1   **teaspoon cumin seeds**
1   **cup green peas, cooked and mashed**
4   **teaspoons coriander powder**
1   **teaspoon red chile powder**
½   **cup clarified butter** (or as needed), **melted**
    Mint Chutney (recipe on next page)

In a medium bowl place the grated potatoes, corn flour, and salt. Mix the ingredients together with your hands so that they are well blended.

Divide the mixture into 12 portions and form them into balls. Flatten them into patties and set them aside.

In a medium skillet place the 3 tablespoons of clarified butter and heat it on medium until it is hot. Add the cumin seeds and sauté them for 2 to 3 minutes, or until they begin to crackle.

Add the mashed cooked peas and sauté them for 1 minute. Add the coriander and red chile powder, and sauté the ingredients for 2 minutes. Remove the mixture from the pan and let it cool. Divide it into 12 equal portions.

In the center of each potato patty place a portion of the pea stuffing. Fold the potato patty over the stuffing and then form it into another ball (so that the stuffing is in the center of the potato mixture). Flatten the ball out so that it is ¾" thick.

In a large skillet place the ½ cup of clarified butter and heat it on medium high until it is hot. Add the stuffed potato patties and sauté them for 3 to 4 minutes on each side, or until they are crisp and golden brown. Press them down with a spatula and drain them on paper towels.

Serve the stuffed patties with the Mint Chutney.

serves 4

"These potato patties are a classical Indian snack. They are very popular, especially at tea time. In India there are four meals a day, just like in England. Tea time is at 5 o'clock, and dinner is around 9 o'clock. America is one of the few countries in the world where dinner is eaten early."

"When people come to the restaurant I want them to come with an open mind, and I want them to ask questions. Indian food is very exotic and very complicated. People may not understand it, but they can still enjoy the taste. With experience in eating it, they can start to identify the different ingredients and to understand how it is made."

Mint Chutney

½	**cup fresh mint, chopped**
½	**cup fresh cilantro, chopped**
½	**cup yellow onions, chopped**
2	**tablespoons serrano chile peppers, finely chopped**
½	**cup lemon juice, freshly squeezed**
½	**cup yogurt**
	salt *(to taste)*

In a blender place the mint, cilantro, onions, serrano chile peppers, and lemon juice. Purée the ingredients so that they are of a smooth consistency. Add more lemon juice if necessary.

Add the yogurt and salt, and mix them in.

"This is very simple to make and it is very delicious. You can make it as spicy as you want by varying the amount of the serrano chile peppers. Once you add the yogurt the chutney will not keep for more than a day or two. Before you add the yogurt, however, the ingredients will keep for a long time."

"Mint Chutney is universal, because it can be served with everything. Serve it with any snack items and also with all tandoori dishes (where the food was cooked in a tandoor oven)."

"Indian food is very flavorful, and it is not always hot, as a lot of people think. You can make the food as hot as you like, but the rich flavors are the key element."

"Outside of Indian food, one of my favorites is Italian food. I am trying to learn the tastes of the oregano, basil, and thyme, and to identify them in the dishes that I eat. We don't use these flavors in Indian food."

Tandoori Chicken with Mango Chutney

Tandoori Chicken

1   teaspoon salt
1   teaspoon red chile powder
4   tablespoons lemon juice, freshly squeezed
1   2½-pound chicken, skin removed and 3 deep incisions made on each breast, thigh, and drumstick
1   cup yogurt
½   cup heavy cream
2½   teaspoons ginger paste *(see chef's comments on page 270)*
2½   teaspoons garlic paste *(see chef's comments on page 270)*
1   teaspoon cumin powder
½   teaspoon Aromatic Garam Masala *(recipe on page 269)*
1   teaspoon saffron
1   drop orange food coloring
3   tablespoons butter, melted
      Mango Chutney *(recipe on next page)*

In a small bowl place the salt, red chile powder, and lemon juice. Mix them together to form a paste. Rub the paste evenly over the chicken. Let the chicken rest for 15 minutes.

In a large bowl place the yogurt, heavy cream, ginger paste, garlic paste, cumin, Aromatic Garam Masala, saffron, and orange food coloring. Whisk the ingredients together so that they are well blended. Spread the mixture onto the chicken. Place the chicken in the refrigerator for 4 hours.

Preheat the oven to 350°. In a large baking pan place a rack. Place the chicken on top. Roast it for 10 minutes. Remove the pan from the oven and let the chicken sit for 5 minutes. Baste it with the melted butter.

Return the chicken to the oven and roast it for 30 to 45 minutes, or until it is done.

serves 4

"Tandoori Chicken is the most popular chicken dish in India. It is beginning to be recognized all over the world, like Japanese sushi or American hamburgers."

"If you make this at home it will be absolutely delicious. However, the flavor will not be the same as what you will eat in our restaurant, because we cook the chicken in the tandoor oven, over mesquite coals."

"The tandoor oven is over 2000 years old. When you cook in it there are 3 cooking processes that go on simultaneously..... baking, grilling, and smoking. So this gives the food a very unique flavor which cannot be duplicated. In the villages of India there are large community tandoors, where people bring their dough or meat, and pay a few pennies to have it cooked. Also, a lot of people have their own tandoor in their homes. At our home in India we had a tandoor oven as well as a conventional oven."

Mango Chutney

⅔   cup onions, grated
3   tablespoons ginger paste *(see chef's comments on page 270)*
3½ teaspoons garlic paste *(see chef's comments on page 270)*
2½ pounds mangoes, peeled and finely chopped
6   cups sugar
1   teaspoon Aromatic Garam Masala *(recipe on page 269)*
2   teaspoons red chile powder
15   green cardamom seeds
½   teaspoon cinnamon powder
¼   cup white distilled vinegar
1   teaspoon salt
20   almonds, chopped
⅔   cup raisins

Place the grated onions, ginger paste, and garlic paste in a piece of muslin. Squeeze out the juice into a small bowl and set it aside.

In a medium large saucepan place the mangoes and sugar. Heat them on medium for 10 minutes, or until the sugar is dissolved.

Add the onion-ginger-garlic juice, Aromatic Garam Masala, red chile powder, cardamom seeds, and cinnamon powder. Stir the ingredients together and cook them for 30 to 45 minutes, or until the mixture becomes the consistency of a jam.

Add the vinegar and salt, and cook the mixture for 3 minutes. Remove the pan from the heat.

Add the almonds and raisins, and stir them in.

Place the chutney in a sterilized jar and cover it tightly with a lid.

Let the chutney sit in the refrigerator for 2 days before serving it.

Fenugreek Chicken

1	cup yogurt
1	teaspoon salt
1	2¼-pound chicken, skin removed, and cut into 8 pieces
½	cup clarified butter, melted
	whole garam masala (5 green cardamom seeds, 1 black cardamom seed, 5 cloves, 1 stick cinnamon, 1 bay leaf, and a pinch of mace)
1¾	cups onions, chopped
3	tablespoons garlic, chopped
3	tablespoons fresh ginger, chopped
6	serrano chile peppers, seeds removed, and chopped
½	teaspoon turmeric
1	teaspoon coriander powder
1	teaspoon red chile powder
¼	cup water
1	cup tomatoes, chopped
¾	cup water
2	tablespoons dried fenugreek
2	tablespoons fresh ginger, finely julienned
¼	cup fresh coriander, chopped

In a medium bowl place the yogurt and salt, and whisk them together. Coat the chicken with the marinade and let it sit in the bowl for 1 hour.

In a large saucepan place the clarified butter and heat it on medium until it is hot. Add the whole garam masala and heat it for 2 to 3 minutes, or until it begins to crackle.

Add the onions and sauté them for 4 to 6 minutes, or until they begin to turn brown. Add the garlic, chopped ginger, and serrano chile peppers. Sauté the ingredients for 2 minutes.

In a small bowl place the turmeric, coriander powder, red chile powder, and the ¼ cup of water. Mix the ingredients together so that the spices dissolve in the water. Add the mixture to the sautéed vegetables and stir it in.

While stirring constantly, add the tomatoes and simmer them for 25 to 30 minutes, or until the fat rises to the top. Add some water if necessary to keep the ingredients from sticking.

(continued on next page)

"Fenugreek is a powerful and flavorful herb that comes from India. I know that you can buy it in Indian stores, although I am not sure how available it is in American supermarkets. If you cannot find it, then I would suggest blending basil, thyme, and oregano together. Fenugreek grows in a certain part of India, and it has a distinct flavor that cannot be duplicated anywhere else in the world. This is because of the particular makeup of the soil where it grows. I grow it here at my home in California, and it doesn't taste the same at all."

"When you cover the chicken with a lid at the end of the recipe you are employing an Indian cooking method called 'Dum', which means 'steam'. It is the maturing of a prepared dish. The final cooking occurs with a tight lid on so that the vapor cannot escape. This way all of the aroma is retained, and the flavors of the spices go into the meat."

Add the marinated chicken, the rest of the yogurt in the bowl, and the ¾ cup of water. Bring the liquid to a boil over high heat and cover the saucepan. Reduce the heat to low and simmer the chicken for 15 to 20 minutes, or until it is done. Adjust the seasoning if necessary.

Sprinkle on the fenugreek, ginger juliennes, and coriander. Cover the saucepan with a tight lid and remove it from the heat. Let it sit for 5 minutes before serving.

serves 4

Aromatic Garam Masala

6	ounces green cardamom seeds
4½	ounces cumin seeds
4½	ounces black peppercorns
2	1-inch sticks cinnamon
¾	ounce whole cloves
2	whole nutmeg kernels

Place all of the ingredients in a food processor. Blend them together so that they are a fine powder. (*A mortar and pestle may also be used.*)

Strain the mixture through a fine sieve.

Store the powder in a dry, airtight container.

"A lot of people in this country don't like Indian food because they don't like the curry. The problem is that the curry powders that are sold here are terrible! They are made with a lot of turmeric and paprika, and other items that are cheap. Garam masala is a true curry, and you can see that those spices aren't in it. The curry manufacturers in this country take advantage of the fact that most Americans don't know what real Indian food tastes like, and unfortunately, this has given Indian food a somewhat bad name."

"Garam masala is probably the most important taste in Indian food. It is used to flavor the food after it is cooked. 'Garam' means 'hot inside (the body)', and 'masala' means 'blend of spices'. The two ingredients that create the heat are the cloves and the pepper. The other items add to the flavor. Garam masala is very, very strong, and no Indian can handle eating very much of it, so use it sparingly."

Royal Khyber

Chicken Tawa Masala

2　tablespoons ginger paste *(see chef's comments on this page)*
2　tablespoons garlic paste *(see chef's comments on this page)*
1　teaspoon salt
⅔　cup vegetable oil
1　2¼-pound chicken, skin removed, and cut into 8 pieces
½　cup clarified butter
1　cup onions, chopped
4½　teaspoons fresh ginger, chopped
6　serrano chile peppers, seeds removed, and finely chopped
1　teaspoon red chile powder
1　tablespoon black peppercorns, ground
1½　cups Makhani Gravy *(recipe on next page)*
1　teaspoon Aromatic Garam Masala *(recipe on previous page)*
⅓　cup fresh coriander, chopped

In a small bowl place the ginger paste, garlic paste, salt, and vegetable oil. Mix the ingredients together. Rub the chicken with the marinade and let it sit for 1 hour.

In an extra large skillet place the clarified butter and heat it on medium until it is hot. Add the marinated chicken *(and any leftover marinade)* and sauté it for 10 minutes. Remove the chicken, set it aside, and keep it warm.

Add the onions, ginger, serrano chile peppers, red chile powder, and ground black pepper. Stir the ingredients together for 1 minute. Return the chicken to the skillet and simmer it for 2 minutes *(add some water if the chicken sticks)*.

Add the Makhani Gravy and raise the heat to medium high. While stirring constantly, cook the chicken for 20 minutes, or until it is tender. Add small amounts of water as necessary to keep the ingredients from sticking.

Add the Aromatic Garam Masala and coriander, and stir them in. Adjust the seasoning if necessary.

serves 4

"This dish is served in restaurants in India. It is also served on the sidewalks from little carts where the food is cooked up and served right there. People just gobble it up!"

"To make a ginger paste or a garlic paste, you add a little water to the ingredient in a blender and then purée it."

"There is an Indian culinary term called 'Bhaunao', which refers to a process of cooking the food. It is a combination of light stewing and sautéing. You add small quantities of liquid to ingredients that are cooking on medium high heat. You must stir constantly to prevent the ingredients from sticking or burning. You do this for spices and vegetables, which extracts the flavor and ensures that they are fully cooked. You also do this for the main ingredient, like the meat. The process is complete only when the fat leaves the meat. Almost every recipe needs this cooking process at some stage, if not two stages."

Makhani Gravy

1	quart water
2¼	pounds tomatoes, chopped
6	serrano chile peppers, seeds removed, and finely chopped
1¾	teaspoons ginger paste *(see chef's comments on page 270)*
1¾	teaspoons garlic paste *(see chef's comments on page 270)*
2	teaspoons red chile powder
10	cloves
8	green cardamom seeds
1	teaspoon salt
⅔	cup butter
⅔	cup heavy cream
4½	teaspoons honey
2½	teaspoons fenugreek
1	tablespoon fresh ginger, finely julienned

In a medium large saucepan place the water, tomatoes, serrano chile peppers, ginger paste, garlic paste, red chile powder, cloves, cardamom seeds, and salt. Simmer the ingredients for 30 to 45 minutes, or until a sauce consistency is achieved.

Force the mixture through a strainer and return it to the saucepan. Bring the mixture to a boil. Add the butter and heavy cream, and stir them in.

Add the honey, fenugreek, and ginger. Stir the ingredients together well.

"This is a rich, delicious, and highly flavored gravy. You can mix it with other meats or you can serve it on the side. It's perfect to use with leftover chicken, beef, or lamb."

"When I grew up we had cooks in our home. My grandfather had one philosophy.....one member of the family must always be in the kitchen to supervise the cooking. He was a real stickler about his food, and he enjoyed good eating. I must have inherited his genes, because I am what you might call a gourmet eater! I know about cooking through my eating."

Masala Lamb Chops

2	tablespoons fresh ginger, peeled and finely julienned
1	tablespoon lemon juice, freshly squeezed
2½	pounds spring lamb chops *(2 ribs each)*, cleaned
1	cup onions, coarsely chopped
½	cup tomatoes, chopped
3	tablespoons ginger paste *(see chef's comments on page 270)*
3	tablespoons garlic paste *(see chef's comments on page 270)*
1	cup plain yogurt, whisked
1	teaspoon red chile powder
	salt *(to taste)*
2	teaspoons cumin seeds, finely ground
1	teaspoon Aromatic Garam Masala *(recipe on page 269)*

In a small bowl place the ginger and lemon juice. Let the ginger marinate for 1 hour.

In a large saucepan place the lamb chops, onions, tomatoes, ginger paste, garlic paste, yogurt, chile powder, and salt. Bring the mixture to a boil on high heat. Cover the pan and reduce the heat to low. Simmer the ingredients for 30 to 45 minutes, or until the chops are very tender. Add some water if necessary. Remove the chops and set them aside.

Raise the heat to medium high. While stirring constantly, cook the ingredients for 20 minutes. If necessary add small amounts of water to prevent the ingredients from sticking.

Add the ground cumin and stir it in for 1 minute.

Return the chops to the mixture. Simmer them for 3 minutes.

Add the Aromatic Garam Masala and stir it in. Adjust the seasoning if necessary.

On a large serving platter place the lamb chops. Ladle the sauce over the top. Garnish the dish with the marinated ginger.

serves 6

"I love this dish because it is both very healthy and very flavorful. The main flavor is that of the lamb, but there also are a lot of wonderful spices in it. You can substitute beef for the lamb."

"We developed this dish for our customers who wanted to have meat, but who wanted a low calorie dish. At the restaurant we have designed recipes that I call 'California style Indian food'. They are very light, extremely flavorful, and they have only 800 calories."

"My mother is probably one of the best cooks in the world, but I guess that everybody's mother is!"

Indian Rice Pudding

6¼   **cups milk**
1½   **tablespoons clarified butter, melted**
⅓   **cup Basmati rice** *(or long grain white rice)*, **soaked for 1 hour and drained**
½   **cup sugar**
1   **teaspoon green cardamom powder**
3   **tablespoons almonds, blanched, peeled, and slivered**
2   **tablespoons raisins**
2   **teaspoons saffron, dissolved in 2 tablespoons warm milk**

In a medium saucepan place the milk and bring it to a boil. Remove it from the heat and set it aside. Keep it warm

In a large saucepan place the clarified butter and heat it on medium until it is hot. Add the rice and sauté it for 4 to 5 minutes, or until it begins to turn brown.

While stirring constantly, add the heated milk and bring it to a boil. Reduce the heat to low and simmer the ingredients for 25 to 30 minutes, or until the rice is tender. Stir the rice every 2 to 3 minutes.

While stirring constantly, add the sugar and cook the mixture for 10 to 15 minutes, or until a custard consistency is achieved.

Add the green cardamom powder, almonds, raisins, and the saffron-milk mixture. Stir the ingredients for 1 minute. Serve the pudding hot.

serves 10 to 12

"This dessert is very popular in India, and it is served almost on a daily basis. It is popular with the wealthy as well as the poor."

"The flavor of the saffron is sooooo good, and so powerful! It is the most expensive spice in the world. People get hooked on saffron, the way people get addicted to chocolate."

"When you are cooking the rice in the milk you will see a little film that appears on top. You want to keep on stirring that film into the milk, because it will become the key part of the pudding itself."

"I came to the United States as a student on an engineering scholarship to get my masters degree. Eventually I ended up in Orange County. My friends and I missed Indian cooking, and so we started this restaurant. The interior is designed after a famous 15th century building outside of New Delhi, and it is exquisitely beautiful."

Palm Trees, Laguna Beach

Saddle Peak Lodge
Malibu

Nestled in the beautiful hills of Malibu Canyon, the Saddle Peak Lodge offers an impeccable Americana cuisine served in an atmosphere that is rich with rustic elegance.

Bruce Boyer is the Chef de Cuisine of this outstanding restaurant. He says, *"You should be able to obtain the seaweed from your local fishmonger because the lobsters that he gets come wrapped in it. Otherwise, use some watercress."*

Baked Oysters with Spinach and Wild Fennel

1	**pound spinach, washed and stems removed**
½	**cup fennel, chopped**
½	**pound butter, softened**
¼	**cup shallots, minced**
1½	**teaspoons nutmeg**
	salt *(to taste)*
	pepper *(to taste)*
2	**tablespoons Pernod**
16	**oysters on the half shell**
1	**cup seaweed** *(see chef's comments on this page)*
16	**drops Pernod**

In a food processor place the spinach and fennel, and purée them together. Place the purée in a medium bowl.

Add the butter, shallots, nutmeg, salt, pepper, and the 2 tablespoons of Pernod. Mix them together well.

Roll the butter up in wax paper to form a log. Freeze the butter.

Preheat the oven to 300°. Place the oysters in a pan. Place a slice of the frozen butter in the center of each oyster. Bake the oysters for 15 minutes.

On each of 4 individual serving plates place a portion of the seaweed. Place the oysters on top. Place a single drop of the Pernod on top of each oyster.

serves 4

Salmon Carpaccio with Horseradish Cream Sauce

Salmon Carpaccio

8   ounces salmon, sliced paper thin
1   teaspoon onions, finely chopped
1   teaspoon chives, finely chopped
1   teaspoon capers
1   teaspoon cornichons (*gherkins pickled in vinegar*), **finely chopped**
4   sprigs watercress
    Horseradish Cream Sauce (*recipe follows*)

Sprinkle the salmon with the onions, chives, capers, and cornichons. Roll up each salmon piece and place it on a piece of wax paper. Roll the wax paper around the salmon. Using your fingers, gently roll the salmon back and forth so that it becomes thinner and somewhat elongated.

Remove the wax paper and cut the rolled salmon into 1" pieces.

Place the rolled salmon pieces on individual serving plates with the cut ends up. Garnish each plate with a sprig of watercress. Serve the salmon with the Horseradish Cream Sauce.

serves 4

Horseradish Cream Sauce

½   cup mayonnaise
¼   cup sour cream
¼   cup yogurt
⅓   cup Dijon mustard
¼   cup horseradish
⅛   cup lemon juice, freshly squeezed
1   dash Louisiana Sauce (*or tabasco*)

In a medium bowl place all of the ingredients and blend them together well.

"Have your fishman slice the salmon as thin as possible, so that it is almost transparent. Use the salmon within hours after purchasing it, because it is raw."

"The salmon becomes slightly cured because of the cornichons and the capers, both of which are marinated vinegar products."

"We use yogurt in this recipe to lower the cholesterol. It's a wonderful sauce that you can use with many things, such as a dip for raw vegetables, or as an accompaniment to roast beef."

California Sweetbreads in the Green with Port Wine Sauce

California Sweetbreads in the Green

1	**quart water**
1	**cup red wine vinegar**
2	**pounds sweetbreads**
2	**eggs**
1	**cup water**
	salt
	pepper
½	**cup flour** *(or as needed)*
1	**cup parsley, finely chopped**
3	**tablespoons butter** *(or as needed)*
	Port Wine Sauce *(recipe on next page)*

In a medium saucepan place the 1 quart of water and the red wine vinegar, and bring them to a boil. Add the sweetbreads and poach them for 5 minutes.

In a small bowl place the eggs and the ½ cup of water, and beat them together to make an egg wash.

Season the sweetbreads with the salt and the pepper. Dust them with the flour and then dip them into the egg wash. Coat them with the chopped parsley.

In a large skillet place the butter and heat it on medium until it has melted. Add the coated sweetbreads and sauté them for 4 to 5 minutes on each side, or until they are nicely browned.

Serve the sweetbreads with the Port Wine Sauce.

serves 4

"Sweetbreads are not very popular in this country, although they are used extensively in Europe. They have a wonderful, delicate flavor, and the texture is very unique."

"Some Americans really enjoy sweetbreads, and I included this recipe because one can search through a hundred cookbooks and not find a single recipe for them."

"If you don't like the idea of sweetbreads, then you can substitute a veal scallopini. The texture and taste will be different, but it still will be delicious!"

"The menu of this restaurant was designed for the ambiance of the dining room and the style of the building. It is very rustic, and yet very elegant. Both cowboys and movie stars love to eat here."

278

Port Wine Sauce

1	**teaspoon butter**
1	**tablespoon truffles** *(or domestic mushrooms)***, finely sliced**
1	**quart brown stock** *(recipe on next page)*
1	**cup port wine**
2	**ounces brandy**
3	**ounces butter, cut into small pieces**

In a small sauté pan place the 1 teaspoon of butter and heat it on medium high until it has melted. Add the truffles and sauté them for 1 to 2 minutes, or until they are tender.

In a medium saucepan place the sautéed truffles, brown stock, port wine, and brandy. Cook the ingredients on medium high heat for 15 to 20 minutes, or until the liquid is reduced by half.

Strain the sauce through a fine sieve and return it to the saucepan

While whisking constantly, add the pieces of butter one at a time.

makes 1 cup

"This sauce will go well with other kinds of meat, such as beef or veal. It's very basic and very delicious."

"Truffles are a fungus, so if you substitute domestic mushrooms (which I suspect most people will do) then you get a fair trade off of flavors. The sauce won't be as good as it could be, but to be realistic, truffles are hard to come by."

"Warning! Never substitute margarine for butter in the sauces that you make!"

Brown Stock

2	pounds veal bones
2	tablespoons vegetable oil
2	carrots, very coarsely chopped
2	onions, quartered
1	stalk celery, very coarsely chopped
1	leek, very coarsely chopped
1	cup tomato paste
1	teaspoon dry thyme
2	sprigs parsley
3	whole cloves
1	quart red wine
2	gallons water

Preheat the oven to 375°. Place the veal bones on a baking sheet and roast them for 30 to 45 minutes, or until they are nicely browned (*do not let the bones touch each other*).

In a large stockpot place the vegetable oil and heat it on medium high until it is hot. Add the carrots, onions, celery, and leeks. Sauté the ingredients for 3 to 4 minutes, or until the onions are transparent.

Add the roasted veal bones and the remainder of the ingredients. Stir everything together well.

Simmer the stock for 24 hours.

Strain the stock through a fine sieve.

makes 1 quart

"Get the veal bones from your local butcher. Try to get good leg bones with the joints. This way you will get a lot of the bone marrow, which really adds to the flavor of the stock."

"The Saddle Peak Lodge started out as a small restaurant that served hamburgers and hot dogs. A lot of people who were out hiking or horseback riding would come here to eat. Also, there used to be a lot of filming done around here for motion pictures, so all of the famous movie stars would eat here as well."

"We use quality products, take no shortcuts, and make very few mistakes! Our goal is to be better than our competition, and to give our customers an experience they will remember."

Saddle Peak Lodge

Kick Ass Chile
in the Saddle Peak Manner

1   tablespoon vegetable oil
5   pounds chile meat, very coarsely ground
1/3   cup bacon grease
1   large onion, diced medium
2   green bell peppers, seeded and finely diced
12   ounces canned diced tomatoes *(including the liquid)*
8   ounces canned green chile peppers, diced
8   ounces tomato paste
2   cups coffee
1/4   cup chile powder
1½   tablespoons cumin
½   teaspoon crushed red pepper *(or to taste)*
3   tablespoons cocoa powder
2   bay leaves
1   orange, halved
1   cup cheddar cheese, grated
1   cup onions, minced
½   cup pickled jalapeño chile peppers

In an extra large skillet place the vegetable oil and heat it on medium high until it is hot. Add the chile meat and sauté it for 8 to 10 minutes, or until it is browned. Drain off the grease.

In a large saucepan place the bacon grease and heat it on medium high until it is hot. Add the diced onions and the green bell peppers. Sauté them for 3 to 4 minutes, or until they are tender.

Add the browned meat, diced tomatoes, green chile peppers, tomato paste, coffee, chile powder, cumin, crushed red pepper, cocoa powder, and bay leaves. Mix the ingredients together well and cook them over medium heat for 10 minutes.

Preheat the oven to 350°. Pour the chile into a large baking pan. Place the 2 orange halves on top of the chile, face down. Bake the chile for 1¼ hours.

Remove the orange halves and the bay leaves. Serve the chile in individual serving bowls. Sprinkle on some of the cheese, minced onion, and pickled jalapeño chile peppers.

serves 10 to 12

"We have been working on this chile dish for the last six years to get it to this state. It's spicy, good, and people love it! We make a hundred pounds of it a week..... that's how popular it is."

"Let the chile sit for a day or two before eating it, and it will taste even better!"

"The cocoa powder adds both flavor and color to the chile. And the orange rind gives it a unique taste that people find hard to identify."

"If you want to reheat the chile, then use coffee instead of water. I know this sounds strange, but I promise you that it will taste better if you do."

"A classic mom's apple pie would be the fitting end to any of these recipes."

Lacquered Long Island Duckling with Wild Rice Griddle Cakes

Lacquered Long Island Duckling

1	cup soy sauce
1	quart sherry
½	cup honey
¼	cup ginger root, freshly grated
¼	cup brown sugar
2	bay leaves
2	Long Island ducks
3	tablespoons arrowroot, dissolved in 3 tablespoons sherry
	Wild Rice Griddle Cakes *(recipe on next page)*

In a large bowl place the soy sauce, sherry, honey, ginger root, brown sugar, and bay leaves. Mix the ingredients together well. Add the ducks and make certain that they are completely covered by the marinade *(make a proportionately larger amount of the marinade if necessary)*. Cover the bowl and refrigerate the ducks for 3 to 4 days.

Preheat the oven to 300°. Place the ducks and the marinade in a roasting pan. Bake the ducks for 1 hour, or until they are deeply browned. Baste the ducks every 5 minutes *(without fail)*.

Remove the ducks and let them rest for 30 minutes.

Split the ducks in half.

Place the roasting pan with the marinade on top of the stove. Remove the bay leaves and strain off the grease. Heat the marinade on medium until it is hot. Add the arrowroot-sherry mixture, and stir it in so that the liquid becomes somewhat thickened to make a sauce.

Preheat the oven to 375°. Place the duck halves on a baking sheet and cook them for 10 minutes, or until they are reheated.

Serve the ducks with the sauce and the Wild Rice Griddle Cakes.

serves 4

"This is a fantastic dish! The ducks are just permeated with the flavor of the marinade. Be sure that the ducks are completely submerged in the liquid."

"The average supermarket will have Long Island ducks in the frozen food department. Be sure that they are completely thawed out before you put them in the marinade."

"This is not a difficult dish to prepare, but it does require a lot of attention when you are baking the ducks because you must constantly baste them."

"By cooking the ducks slowly, the grease will come out from under the skin, so the finished product will be relatively grease-free. But there will be a lot of grease in the pan, so be sure to remove it before you thicken the sauce."

Saddle Peak Lodge

Wild Rice Griddle Cakes

1	**tablespoon butter**
1	**teaspoon shallots, finely diced**
1	**pound wild rice, cooked**
1	**tablespoon parsley, chopped**
½	**cup walnuts, crushed**
1	**cup Bèchamel Sauce** *(recipe on next page)*
½	**teaspoon salt**
¼	**teaspoon pepper**
½	**cup bread crumbs** *(or as needed)*
3	**tablespoons vegetable oil** *(or as needed)*

In a large saucepan place the butter and heat it on medium high until it has melted. Add the shallots, wild rice, parsley, walnuts, Bèchamel Sauce, salt, and pepper. Mix the ingredients together thoroughly.

Let the rice cool for 1 hour.

Pat the rice into cakes, approximately 1½" in diameter and ½" thick. Coat the patties with the bread crumbs. Place them in the refrigerator for ½ hour.

In a large skillet place the oil and heat it on medium low until it is hot. Fry the patties for 1 to 2 minutes on each side, or until they are nicely browned.

serves 4 to 6

"This is an original recipe of the restaurant. Wild rice goes really well with duck, as well as other game birds This is just a variation of serving it in a way that is unique to our menu."

"The bread crumbs will be better if you make your own, but they must be ground very fine. I recommend using fresh bread that you dry out in the oven, and then grating or blending it."

Bèchamel Sauce

2	**tablespoons butter**
2	**tablespoons flour**
1	**cup milk**
1	**teaspoon sherry**
1	**dash nutmeg**
	salt (to taste)
	pepper (to taste)

"In our restaurant we take exotic foods and put them into the milieu of the American palate so that nothing is over-powering. We try to take the harsh, musky taste out of the game meats so that one's palate is not assaulted. So, we take exotic products and make them un-exotic. They only sound exotic when you tell your friends what you had to eat here last night!"

In a medium saucepan place the butter and heat it on medium until it has melted. Add the flour and stir it in for 4 to 6 minutes, or until the flour taste is gone.

While stirring constantly, slowly add the milk. Continue to stir the sauce until it reaches a boil and thickens.

Add the sherry, nutmeg, salt, and pepper. Stir them in well.

makes 1 cup

Boar Chops with Indian Peaches and Spatzle

Boar Chops

4	6-ounce boar chops *(or pork chops)*
12	ounces papaya nectar
2	tablespoons olive oil
8	Indian Peach halves *(recipe follows)*
4	tablespoons sour cream
4	lingonberries
	Spatzle *(recipe on next page)*

In a large bowl place the boar chops and the papaya nectar. Cover the bowl and place it in the refrigerator. Marinate the boar chops for 2 to 3 days.

In a large skillet place the olive oil and heat it on medium until it is hot. Add the boar chops and fry them for 5 minutes on each side, or until they are cooked medium *(or to your desired taste)*.

Fill each Indian Peach half with a dollop of sour cream. Sprinkle some lingonberries on top.

On each of 4 individual serving plates place 1 boar chop, 2 halves of the Indian Peaches, and a serving of the Spatzle.

serves 4

Indian Peaches

2	cups rosé wine
2	tablespoons honey
2	tablespoons brown sugar
1	stick cinnamon
4	peaches, peeled, halved, and pitted

In a medium saucepan place the rosé wine, honey, brown sugar, and cinnamon. Stir the ingredients together.

Bring the liquid to a boil over medium high heat. Add the peaches and cook them for 10 to 15 minutes, or until they are tender *(do not cook them to the point that they disintegrate)*.

"Boar is particularly difficult to find. There are a few specialty shops that carry it, but it is not something that you can get by going to your favorite market and telling the butcher, 'Okay, give me a couple of good boar chops!' Pork is a very adequate substitute."

"The flavor of boar is mild.....it's like a musky tasting pork. By marinating the boar in the papaya nectar, the musky taste is removed. Also, the enzymes from the papaya nectar tenderize the meat. If you substitute pork, then just marinate it for 1 day."

"You can find lingonberries in the gourmet food section. It is okay to substitute fresh raspberries or another kind of berry. What you want to achieve is a tart counter-flavor to the game meat."

Spatzle

2	cups flour
4	eggs, beaten
½	teaspoon nutmeg
1	teaspoon salt
1	teaspoon oil
	milk *(as needed)*
1	gallon water
2	teaspoons salt
1	tablespoon butter
¼	teaspoon nutmeg

In a medium bowl place the flour, eggs, the ½ teaspoon of nutmeg, the 1 teaspoon of salt, and the oil. Mix the ingredients together thoroughly. Add enough of the milk so that the dough is slightly thicker than that of a heavy pancake batter.

In a large pot place the water and bring it to a boil. Add the 2 teaspoons of salt.

Place a large colander *(with holes ⅛" in diameter)* on top of the pot with the boiling water. Place the dough in the colander and press it through the holes with a rubber spatula. Boil the spatzle for 1 minute. Drain the spatzle and then plunge it into a bowl of ice water. Drain the spatzle again and set it aside.

Preheat the oven to 350°.

In a medium baking dish place the butter and the ¼ teaspoon of nutmeg. Place the baking dish in the oven so that the butter melts. Add the cold, drained spatzle and toss it in the butter.

Bake the noodles for 15 minutes, or until they are hot and puffy.

serves 4

"This is very easy to make. When you push the dough through the holes the noodles will be thin and itty-bitty, and you'll probably say to yourself, 'Well, I don't think these look very good at all!' But then when you put them in the oven with the butter, they will become nice and puffy and wonderful looking."

"The only trick is in getting the dough to the right consistency, which you might have to experiment with."

"Have your ice water ready before you boil the noodles."

Saddle Peak Lodge

Malibu Lagoon, Malibu

Sausalito South
Manhattan Beach

Offering a Continental seafood cuisine, Sausalito South is adorned with rich stained glass windows, oak woodwork, and shiny brass.....like a typical San Francisco restaurant.

Menu

Ceviche

Cauliflower Soup

Chilled Fusilli Pasta with Chicken and Cilantro Pesto

Warm Bay Scallop Salad with Balsamic Vinaigrette

Sautéed Sea Bass Veracruz Style

White Chocolate Mousse

Executive Chef Robert Serna says, *"I got this recipe from a lady in Acapulco. Ceviche is a very popular seafood cocktail down there. People will sell it to you right on the beach. Serve this with some crackers, avocado, and a wedge of lemon. It's light, refreshing, and delicious."*

Ceviche

1	pound sea bass, diced into ¼" pieces
¾	cup lime juice, freshly squeezed
2	tomatoes, peeled, seeded, and diced
½	bunch cilantro, chopped
¼	onion, chopped
2	serrano chile peppers, seeded and diced
⅛	teaspoon ground oregano
1	tablespoon olive oil
1	cup clam juice
	salt *(to taste)*
	white pepper *(to taste)*

In a medium bowl place the sea bass and the lime juice. Gently toss them together. Cover the bowl and refrigerate it for 12 hours.

Place the marinated fish in a colander and let it drain for 1 hour.

In another medium bowl place the remainder of the ingredients and mix them together.

Add the fish and gently mix it in.

Chill the ceviche for 2 hours.

serves 4

Cauliflower Soup

2	**tablespoons olive oil**
2	**small white onions, thinly sliced**
3	**small leeks** *(white part only)*, **chopped**
2	**shallots, chopped**
2	**quarts chicken stock** *(recipe on page 297)*
2	**large cauliflowers, cut into florets**
1	**cup heavy cream** *(or as needed)*, **heated**
	salt *(to taste)*
	white pepper *(to taste)*
1	**cup chicken stock** *(recipe on page 297)*
16	**asparagus tips**

In a medium sauté pan place the olive oil and heat it on medium until it is hot. Add the onions, leeks, and shallots. Sauté the vegetables for 3 to 4 minutes, or until they are tender *(do not let them get brown)*.

In a large saucepan place the sautéed vegetables, the 2 quarts of chicken stock, and the cauliflower. Bring the liquid to a boil and then reduce the heat to low. Let the ingredients simmer for ½ hour, or until the cauliflower is tender.

Place the ingredients in a blender and purée them. Strain the mixture.

Add the heated heavy cream in small amounts and stir it in until the desired consistency is achieved.

Season the soup with the salt and the white pepper.

In a small saucepan place the 1 cup of chicken stock and heat it until it simmers. Add the asparagus tips and cook them for 3 to 5 minutes, or until they are just tender *(do not overcook)*. Drain the asparagus.

In each of 6 individual serving bowls ladle in the soup. Place the asparagus tips on top.

serves 6

"There are a lot of recipes for cauliflower soup, and this particular one was developed by my son, Robert. The nice thing about it is that you can take this recipe and substitute asparagus or broccoli for the cauliflower. If you do this, then use the green part of the leeks instead of the white part, and add some celery. But if you make the cauliflower soup you should use the white part of the leeks because you want the soup to be pure white."

"We garnish the cauliflower soup with some asparagus tips to give it color. It's also nice to add some finely ground hazelnuts."

"When you purée the ingredients you should be very careful because they will be hot. Just fill the blender halfway, and hold the lid on tightly with your hands. When you add the cream the purée will get a nice, rich texture. The soup should be of a medium thick consistency. If it is too thin, then the asparagus tips will sink to the bottom of the bowl."

"This soup is also excellent chilled. Add some yogurt and stir it in. This adds a nice extra flavor that tastes good with the cold cauliflower."

Chilled Fusilli Pasta with Chicken and Cilantro Pesto

4	chicken breasts
4	bunches cilantro
4	cloves garlic
½	cup sliced almonds, blanched
4	serrano chile peppers *(or to taste)*, seeded
½	cup olive oil
1	cup mayonnaise
1	pound fusilli pasta, cooked al dente, drained, and chilled

Preheat the oven to 375°. Place the chicken in a baking pan and roast it for 15 to 20 minutes, or until it is done. Remove the chicken and let it cool. Remove the skin and shred the meat. Place the shredded meat in the refrigerator so that it chills.

In a food processor *(or blender)* place the cilantro, garlic, almonds, and serrano chile peppers. Blend the ingredients together.

With the food processor still running, slowly dribble in the olive oil to make a pesto.

Place the pesto in a bowl. Add the mayonnaise and whisk it in.

In a large bowl place the chilled pasta, shredded chicken, and the cilantro pesto. Mix the ingredients together well. Place the pasta in the refrigerator for 1 hour.

serves 4

"You can make this dish with lobster or shrimp, or any other kind of meat that you like. I love recipes like this where you can take the basic idea, but then substitute another main ingredient, depending on what you are in the mood for, or what is left over in the refrigerator."

"Instead of a basil pesto we are using a cilantro pesto. We add the mayonnaise to bind everything together and to give the pesto a smooth consistency."

"At the restaurant we garnish this dish with some roasted tomatoes, white asparagus, and black olives. The visual beauty of the plate is outstanding."

"You can use pine nuts instead of the almonds, although they cost about four times as much. The flavor of the nuts does not really come through because it is overpowered by the cilantro, so to me it is a waste to use pine nuts. I would rather save them for a dish where you can really appreciate their flavor."

Warm Bay Scallop Salad with Balsamic Vinaigrette

Warm Bay Scallop Salad

2	tablespoons olive oil
3	cloves garlic, finely chopped
1	tablespoon shallots, finely chopped
2	pounds bay scallops
½	cup white wine
⅓	cup unsalted butter
2	heads romaine lettuce, washed, torn, and dried
4	bunches spinach, stems removed, washed and dried
¾	cup Balsamic Vinaigrette *(recipe on next page)*
½	cup feta cheese, crumbled
½	cup pine nuts, roasted
2	cups tomatoes, peeled, seeded, and wedged

In a large skillet place the olive oil and heat it on medium until it is hot. Add the garlic and shallots, and sauté them for 10 seconds.

Add the bay scallops and sauté them for 2 to 3 minutes, or until they are halfway done.

Add the white wine and the butter. Sauté the ingredients for 2 to 3 minutes, or until the butter is melted and the scallops are done. Set the dish aside and keep it warm.

In a medium bowl place the romaine lettuce and the spinach. Add the Balsamic Vinaigrette and toss it in well.

On each of 8 individual serving plates place the salad greens. Place the bay scallops on top. Sprinkle on the feta cheese and the roasted pine nuts. Place the tomato wedges around the edge of the plate.

serves 8

"Here is a light, elegant salad that tastes wonderful and is easy to make. You can substitute shrimp, veal, or lamb for the scallops. Or, if you want to be extravagant, you can use lobster."

"There are no secrets to making this. Just don't overcook the scallops..... cook them so that they are medium rare. Have all of your ingredients ready, sauté the scallops, toss the lettuce with the dressing, put the scallops on the lettuce, and garnish the plate with the feta cheese, pine nuts, and tomatoes..... you see how simple it is to make!"

"Cooking is like music. You combine different ingredients together to create a dish, just as you combine different notes together to create a melody."

"We have a lot of specials that we change each day, so we are always trying to come up with dishes that are new and different. That is the motivation for the creation of this salad."

"My son, Robert J. Serna, is my Sous Chef. I wanted him to be a doctor or an engineer, but he didn't like that.....he wanted to be a chef, like his father. So I am training him, and he is excellent! He has helped to develop many of our recipes."

"The dressing is very basic, and you can use it on any green salad. Add some fresh herbs to change the flavor."

"I was born and raised in Mexico City, where I used to be an accountant for a large firm. But I didn't like the pressure and tension involved in the work, especially at the end of the year. So my wife and children and I moved to the United States. I was seeking a complete life-style change. I had always enjoyed cooking, so I got a job in a restaurant. I started out as a dishwasher, and within the year I was a line cook. Eventually I trained with many different European chefs."

Balsamic Vinaigrette

2	tablespoons Dijon mustard
1	cup balsamic vinegar
2	cups vegetable oil
1	tablespoon shallots, minced
1	teaspoon lemon juice, freshly squeezed
	salt *(to taste)*
	white pepper *(to taste)*

In a medium bowl place the mustard and whisk it.

Add the balsamic vinegar and whisk it in.

While whisking constantly, slowly dribble in the vegetable oil.

Add the shallots, lemon juice, salt, and white pepper. Whisk them in well.

makes 3 cups

Sautéed Sea Bass Veracruz Style

6	8-ounce sea bass fillets, boned
	salt
	pepper
¼	cup flour (or as needed)
3	eggs, beaten
4	tablespoons olive oil
3	tablespoons unsalted butter
2	tablespoons capers, drained
24	large green olives (stuffed with pimientos), halved
1	red onion, sliced into thin rings
¼	cup canned jalapeño chile peppers, sliced
2	cups tomatoes, peeled, seeded, and chopped

Season the sea bass fillets with the salt and the pepper. Dust them with the flour. Dip them in the beaten eggs.

In a large skillet place the olive oil, and heat it on medium high until it is hot. Sauté the floured sea bass fillets for 4 to 6 minutes on each side, or until they are just done. Set them aside and keep them warm.

In a medium skillet place the unsalted butter and heat it on medium high until it is hot. Add the capers, green olives, onion rings, jalapeño chile peppers, and tomatoes. Sauté the ingredients for 1 to 2 minutes, or until they are hot.

On each of 6 warmed individual plates place a sea bass fillet. Place the sautéed mixture on top.

serves 6

"I love sea bass. Once I went to a seminar and learned that there are over 250 kinds of sea bass in the world. I'm sure that not many people know this fact..... it is a little amazing!"

"My mother used to make this with dried cod in Mexico. She let it soak in water overnight so that it would reconstitute. Then she would serve it with these sautéed vegetables. My father loved this dish so we had it a lot. I got the idea to make it with fresh fish instead, and it tastes great!"

White Chocolate Mousse

5	ounces white chocolate
3	egg yolks
4	tablespoons sugar
⅓	cup Frangelico
2	tablespoons lemon juice, freshly squeezed
2	sheets clear gelatin
¼	cup water
3	cups heavy cream, whipped

In the top of a simmering double boiler place the white chocolate and melt it. Keep it warm.

In the top of another simmering double boiler place the egg yolks, sugar, Frangelico, and lemon juice. While whisking constantly, cook the ingredients for 5 minutes, or until the mixture thickens and is smooth *(with no lumps)*.

Add the melted chocolate to the egg yolk mixture and stir it in.

In another small saucepan place the gelatin and the water. Heat them slightly and mix them together so that the gelatin is totally dissolved. Let the mixture cool to room temperature. Add it to the egg yolk-chocolate mixture and stir it in well.

Carefully fold the whipped cream into the mixture. Place the mousse in the refrigerator for 1 hour, or until it is firm.

serves 8

Beach Scene, Redondo Beach

Sorrento Grille
Laguna Beach

With-it, upbeat, exciting! These are words to describe the feeling of the Sorrento Grille, a popular Laguna Beach restaurant that serves a contemporary Italian cuisine.

Owner Dean Betts says, *"Crostini is a thin toast. We make a lot of other crostinis and this is the big winner. Try to get a chewy, country style sourdough bread if possible."*

Crostini with Grilled Eggplant and Goat Cheese

2	tablespoons extra virgin olive oil
4	slices sourdough bread
1	clove garlic
1	tablespoon garlic purée
¼	cup extra virgin olive oil
1	small eggplant, sliced into four ½" thick pieces
4	tablespoons goat cheese, crumbled
2	Roma tomatoes, sliced

Brush the 2 tablespoons of olive oil on both sides of the bread slices. Grill *(or broil)* them for 1 to 2 minutes on each side, or until they are crisp and brown. Rub both sides with the clove of garlic.

In a small bowl place the garlic purée and the ¼ cup of olive oil, and mix them together. Dip the eggplant slices into the olive oil mixture so that they are well coated.

Grill *(or broil)* the eggplant slices for 1 to 2 minutes on each side, or until they are tender and golden brown.

Place the goat cheese on top of the toasted bread. Add the grilled eggplant and the sliced tomatoes.

serves 4

Italian Sausage, Pepper, and Polenta Soup

5	**Italian sausages, sliced**
2	**quarts chicken stock** *(recipe on next page)*
½	**cup olive oil**
1	**green bell pepper, seeds removed, and julienned**
1	**red bell pepper, seeds removed, and julienned**
1	**yellow bell pepper, seeds removed, and julienned**
1	**small yellow onion, sliced**
5	**cloves garlic, chopped**
	salt *(to taste)*
	pepper *(to taste)*
8	**slices Classic Polenta, ½" thick** *(recipe on next page)*
2	**tablespoons mozzarella cheese, grated**
2	**tablespoons parsley, chopped**

In a large skillet place the sausage and heat it on medium high. Cook the sausage for 6 to 8 minutes, or until it is nicely browned. Drain off the oil.

Add enough of the chicken stock to cover the sausage. Bring the liquid to a boil and then reduce it to a simmer. Cook the sausage for 5 minutes. Remove the sausage and set it aside. Reserve the stock.

In another large skillet place the olive oil and heat it on medium high until it is hot. Add the 3 kinds of julienned bell peppers, onions, and garlic. Sauté the vegetables for 2 to 3 minutes, or until they are just tender. Set them aside.

In a large saucepan place the remainder of the chicken stock, including the part that the sausage was cooked in. Heat the stock on medium high until it is hot. Add the salt and the pepper.

In each individual serving bowl place, in this order, the sautéed vegetables, sausage, Classic Polenta, chicken stock, mozzarella cheese, and parsley.

serves 8

"Our previous chef, Rosanne Ruiz, developed this recipe. When she first told me about it I said, 'No, I don't think so.....it doesn't sound too good.' But she went ahead and made it anyway, and she made me taste it. As it turned out, I just loved it!"

"This is more than just a soup.....it actually is a meal in itself. You have carbohydrates from the polenta, protein from the sausage, and then there are the vegetables. It's simple to make and tastes delicious!"

"In Italy many children are raised on polenta, and it is always a challenge for their mothers to come up with interesting ways to serve it. One favorite way is to fry it in olive oil with onions and garlic, and then put cheese on top."

Classic Polenta

2	**cups water**
1	**cup polenta** *(yellow corn meal)*
¾	**cup butter**
	salt *(to taste)*

In a medium saucepan place the water and bring it to a boil. While stirring constantly, slowly add the polenta. Continue to cook and stir the polenta on medium low heat for 30 minutes.

Add the butter and the salt. Stir and cook the polenta for another 15 minutes.

Place the polenta in a baking pan and refrigerate it for 1 hour, or until it becomes firm.

serves 8

Chicken Stock

4	**pounds chicken pieces** *(backs, wings, feet)*
4	**quarts cold water**
3	**carrots, diced**
2	**onions, diced**
1	**stalk celery, diced**
1	**tablespoon thyme**
3	**bay leaves**
1	**tablespoon black peppercorns**
¼	**teaspoon salt**

In a large saucepan place all of the ingredients. Loosely place a lid on top. Bring the liquid to a boil on high heat. Reduce the heat to low and simmer the ingredients for 2 hours.

Strain the stock. Let it cool to room temperature. Place it in the refrigerator.

"The secret to making good polenta is to keep on stirring it. It takes a good, strong arm to make polenta because you have to stir it for 45 minutes. Stir and scrape the bottom of the pan so that it doesn't stick and get thick. After it is done it will be like a thick cream of meal. Be sure to use coarse grain polenta."

"After you refrigerate the polenta and it becomes firm, you can cut it into pieces and either grill, bake, or fry them."

"When you bring the broth to a boil, foam will appear on top. The foam should be skimmed off. You can let the stock simmer for up to 8 hours, and it will be even better. I just said 2 hours in this recipe because that is about the minimum time, and I didn't want to scare off the average home cook!"

"The canned chicken stocks tend to be too salty, but they can be used in a pinch. It's a good idea to freeze the stock in ice cube trays and then you can just pop out the cubes as you need them."

Caesar Salad with Garlic Croutons

Caesar Salad

½   cup extra virgin olive oil
1   cup olive oil
1½   teaspoons kosher salt
2   tablespoons balsamic vinegar
¼   cup red wine vinegar
6   anchovy fillets, finely chopped
2   tablespoons Parmesan cheese, freshly grated
2   teaspoons lemon juice, freshly squeezed
1   tablespoon garlic purée
1½   teaspoons parsley, finely chopped
12   Garlic Croutons (recipe follows)
2   hearts romaine lettuce, washed, dried, and torn

In a medium jar with a lid place the 2 olive oils, kosher salt, balsamic vinegar, and red wine vinegar. Shake the ingredients together so that they are well blended. Set the vinaigrette dressing aside.

In a large salad bowl place the anchovies, Parmesan cheese, lemon juice, garlic purée, parsley, and Garlic Croutons. Toss the ingredients together well.

Add the lettuce and ½ cup of the vinaigrette dressing. Toss the ingredients together well.

serves 4

Garlic Croutons

2   tablespoons olive oil
2   slices sourdough bread, cut into ½" cubes
1   clove garlic

In a medium bowl place the olive oil. Add the bread cubes and toss them in the oil so that they are well coated.

Preheat the oven to 350°. Place the bread cubes on a baking sheet. Toast the bread cubes for 10 minutes, or until they are crisp and golden brown. Rub each bread cube on all sides with the clove of garlic.

"The taste of the anchovies is just a background flavor that mainly gives some saltiness to the salad. People normally aren't too fond of anchovies, but everyone goes crazy over this salad, so they must add a taste that is important. What this tells me is that the poor anchovy is battling a lot of prejudice, and people might like them better than they think they do."

"A Caesar salad should be made right before you are ready to serve it so that the garlic and other ingredients are fresh, and you can clearly taste each one. The only thing that can be made ahead of time is the vinaigrette dressing. It's really fun to make this at the table if you are having a nice dinner party."

"It takes a lot of work for our cooks to prepare the garlic croutons because we make hundreds of them, and each one must be hand-rubbed with the garlic cloves. But, it is worth it because they taste so good."

Sorrento Grille

Fettucini, Prawns, and Prosciutto with Basil

"The flavors in this dish are scrumptious! It is simple to make and there is no danger of the sauce breaking or separating. We use fresh pasta and it takes only 45 seconds to cook it. Serve this dish immediately!"

3	cups heavy cream
1	pinch crushed red pepper flakes
1	pinch black pepper
1	tablespoon parsley, chopped
4	ounces prosciutto, cut into bite-size pieces
16	prawns, peeled and deveined
1	pound fettucini, cooked al dente
1	tablespoon olive oil
2	tablespoons garlic purée
8	leaves fresh basil

In a large sauté pan place the heavy cream, red pepper flakes, black pepper, and parsley. Cook the ingredients on medium high heat for 4 to 5 minutes, or until the liquid is reduced by ½.

Add the prosciutto and prawns, and cook them for 2 to 3 minutes, or until the prawns are just done.

Add the fettucini and toss it in so that it is well coated with the sauce.

Add the olive oil and garlic purée, and toss them in.

On each of 4 individual warmed serving plates place the fettucini. Garnish each plate with 2 basil leaves.

serves 4

"In Italy cheese is not normally used in seafood dishes, so it is not included in this recipe. Also, it is not a good idea to use cheese in a dish that has cream in it, because together they tend to form a glob. However, Americans are used to having cheese with their pasta, so we serve some freshly grated Parmesan cheese on the side."

Sorrento Grille

Pasta Puttanesca

½   cup extra virgin olive oil
2   tablespoons fresh basil
2   garlic cloves
1   shallot, coarsely chopped
¼   cup capers, rinsed and drained
2   tablespoons Calamata olives, pitted
4   anchovy fillets, rinsed and drained
3   tomatoes, peeled, seeded, and diced
12   ounces angel hair pasta, cooked al dente
2   tablespoons Parmesan cheese, freshly grated

In a food processor place the olive oil, basil, garlic, shallots, capers, Calamata olives, and anchovy fillets. Blend the ingredients for 15 to 20 seconds, or until they are roughly chopped. Let the mixture sit for 6 hours in the refrigerator so that the ingredients marinate.

In a large skillet place the marinated olive oil mixture and heat it on medium until it is hot. Add the diced tomatoes and the pasta, and toss them in well.

Garnish the pasta with the Parmesan cheese.

serves 4

Fresh Egg Pasta

3   cups all purpose flour
4   eggs
1   tablespoon olive oil
½   teaspoon salt

In a medium bowl place all of the ingredients and knead them together with your hands for 10 minutes. Wrap the dough in plastic wrap and place it in the refrigerator for 1 hour.

Roll the dough out on a floured board so that it is very thin. Let it sit for 30 minutes.

Roll the dough up so that it forms a scroll. Slice the dough to the preferred width.

"Our chef, Duilio Valenti, brought this recipe from Italy, and it has proved to be an excellent contribution to our menu. It is a very old and authentic recipe that became popular in the red light district of town. The men would make it for the 'ladies of the night' to eat while they were working, because it was really quick and simple to put together."

"Summertime is when this tastes the best, because that is when you can get the best tomatoes."

"The highest quality Parmesan cheese comes from Parma, Italy. The aging process is strictly controlled, as well as the quality of milk that is used. When you buy your Parmesan cheese look for one that says 'Parmesan Regginiano'."

"It is no big deal to make your own pasta, although most people think that it is. If you own a pasta making machine, then it will be all that much easier! We do not use semolina flour because we want our pasta to be nice and light."

Marinated Rosemary and Garlic Chicken with a Brick

2   chickens, halved
2   tablespoons garlic purée
2   tablespoons fresh rosemary, chopped
2   cups olive oil

In a large bowl place the chicken, garlic purée, rosemary, and olive oil. Cover the bowl and let the chicken marinate for 24 hours in the refrigerator. Turn the chicken occasionally.

In a large sauté pan pour ¼ cup of the marinade and heat it on medium until it is hot. Place the chicken in the pan, skin side down. Place a brick that is wrapped in foil on top of the chicken. Fry the chicken for 5 to 7 minutes, or until it is brown. Turn the chicken over and place the brick back on top. Fry it for 7 to 8 minutes, or until it is brown. Turn the chicken back over to the skin side and fry it for 1 to 2 minutes more.

serves 4

"There is a great story behind this recipe, which came from our previous chef, Rosanne Ruiz. She was visiting her girl-friend, Vicki, in San Francisco. They were in the kitchen of Vicki's 84 year-old grandmother who was making dinner for them. There was a frying pan on the stove with a huge brick in it. Rosanne was flabber-gasted to think that she was cooking a brick. So she asked the grand-mother (who was affectionately called 'Grambo' and always wore a red bandana around her neck) what on earth she was doing. The grandmother said something like, 'SQUASHIZZI!' It turned out that she was cooking chicken and she was using the brick to squash it down flat. Rosanne has been using this technique in her own cooking ever since, and it works great!"

"The skin comes out very crispy and the meat is moist and tender inside. It's a wonderful, flavorful recipe that could not be simpler to make. Plus, the brick on top makes for a great conversation piece."

Tirami-Su (Pick-Me-Up)

¾   cup Kahlua
2   cups espresso
50   **Ladyfingers** *(recipe on next page)*
3¾   cups Marscapone *(Italian sweet cream cheese)*
2½   cups heavy cream
1   cup sugar
½   cup cocoa powder

In a medium bowl place the Kahlua and espresso, and mix them together. Add the Ladyfingers and let them soak for 30 seconds. Squeeze out the liquid and set them aside.

In a food processor place the Marscapone, heavy cream, and sugar. Whip them together until the mixture thickens. *(Do not over-whip or else the cream will turn to butter.)*

In a 9½" springform pan place ¼ cup of the cream mixture. Spread it around so that it covers the bottom of the pan.

Layer the Ladyfingers on the bottom of the pan so that it is completely covered.

Add ¼ of the cream mixture and spread it around evenly.

Cover the cream with a layer of the Ladyfingers.

Cut some Ladyfingers in half and line the sides of the pan with them.

Repeat the layering process twice more. Pour the last ¼ of the cream mixture on top.

Sprinkle on the cocoa powder.

Cover the dish and refrigerate it for 3 hours.

serves 8

"Marscapone is a sweet, Italian cream cheese. It is almost like butter, it is so rich and good. You can find it in a deli store."

"This is an Italian dessert and it really is fantastic. It is on our menu and we dare not take it off! Usually Tirami-Su calls for rum, but we use Kahlua because we think that it tastes much better. You definitely will feel the 'pick-me-up' effect after you get hit with all of that espresso, sugar, and cocoa powder!"

"One taste of this and you will feel like you have died and gone to heaven!"

Ladyfingers

"It's very easy to make ladyfingers, and they come out perfect every time. Let them cool before you start using them in the Tirami-Su."

4	large egg whites
⅓	cup cake flour
3	large egg yolks, beaten
½	cup sugar
½	tablespoon vanilla
½	cup powdered sugar

In a medium bowl place the egg whites and beat them for 4 to 5 minutes, or until soft peaks are formed.

Sift the flour into the egg whites and gently fold it in during the sifting.

In a small bowl place the egg yolks, sugar, and vanilla. Beat the ingredients together so that they are well blended.

Add the egg yolk mixture to the egg whites, and gently fold it in.

Place the batter in a pastry bag with a plain tip.

Squeeze out the batter onto a buttered and floured baking sheet into cakes that are 1" wide and 2" long. Leave a 1" space between the cakes.

Preheat the oven to 350°. Sprinkle the powdered sugar on the cakes. Bake the ladyfingers for 20 minutes, or until they are done.

"We have an open kitchen, and so people are always watching the cooks prepare the food. On Fridays around 5 o'clock they start to sweat and their hearts start to beat fast because they know that it's almost time for them to perform. It's like stage fright and it is really exciting!"

Brick Steeple, Malaga Cove, Palos Verdes

Towers
Laguna Beach

Located at the top of the famed Surf and Sand Hotel with a panoramic view of the Pacific coastline, Towers serves a superb French Provençal cuisine in a striking, art deco setting.

Menu

Celery Root and Fennel
Soup with Toasted Hazelnuts

Grilled Scallops
with Baked Tomato and
Basil Vinaigrette

Fresh Bean Salad with
Shallot Vinaigrette

Grilled Swordfish with
Tomato Pepper Ragoût

Towers' Duck with
Honey Cilantro Sauce and
Stir-Fry Vegetables

Duck Stock

Crème Brulé

Pavé au Chocolate with
Coffee Sauce

Executive Chef Jack Kenworth says, *"This is a wonderful soup! It's very tasty, healthy, and low in calories. There is no cream in it.....the potatoes are what make it thick."*

Celery Root and Fennel Soup with Toasted Hazelnuts

4	tablespoons butter
1	large onion, chopped
4	large bulbs celery root, peeled, cut into 1" cubes, and tossed with fresh lemon juice
1	large russet potato, peeled and cubed
6	cups chicken stock *(recipe on page 297)*
2	small fennel bulbs, trimmed and sliced
	salt *(to taste)*
	black pepper, freshly ground *(to taste)*
1	pinch nutmeg
½	cup hazelnuts, toasted and chopped

In a large saucepan place the butter and heat it on medium high until it has melted. Add the onions and sauté them for 2 to 3 minutes, or until they are translucent.

Rinse and drain the celery root. Add it to the onions.

Add the potatoes and chicken stock. Bring the liquid to a boil. Add the fennel and simmer the ingredients for 15 to 20 minutes, or until the vegetables are tender.

Place the soup in a blender and purée it until it is smooth. Season the purée with the salt, pepper, and nutmeg. Strain the purée.

Serve the soup with the toasted hazelnuts sprinkled on top.

serves 6 to 8

Grilled Scallops with Baked Tomato and Basil Vinaigrette

Grilled Scallops with Baked Tomato

6	large tomatoes, blanched and peeled
1	clove garlic, finely chopped
4	tablespoons fruity olive oil
	salt
	pepper
1	pound scallops
	Basil Vinaigrette *(recipe on next page)*

Gently cut off the meaty, outside part of each tomato from the core, so that a long strip is formed. *(See chef's comments on this page.)*

In a small bowl place the garlic and olive oil. Lightly brush the tomato strips with the olive oil-garlic mixture. Sprinkle them with the salt and pepper.

Preheat the oven to 300°. Place a piece of parchment paper in a baking pan. Place the seasoned tomato strips on top of the paper and bake them for 15 to 20 minutes, or until they are limp.

Season the scallops with the salt and the pepper. Grill *(or broil)* them for 4 to 6 minutes, or until they are just done. Rotate the scallops as you cook them.

On each of 6 individual serving plates place a baked tomato strip. Place the scallops partially on top of the tomato, at a diagonal. Gently fold the tomato strip over the scallops, so that they appear to be partially wrapped, in a slightly coiled manner.

Spoon the Basil Vinaigrette on each side of the tomato and scallops.

serves 6

"This is my absolute most favorite recipe! We make it for both lunch and dinner, and it is a big hit with our customers. It looks gorgeous on the plate with the bright green sauce, the red tomato, and the white scallops."

"The only tricky thing about making this is preparing the strip of tomato. It's not hard to do at all, but it is hard to describe the procedure without showing pictures. Basically what you are doing is removing the inner core and seeds from the tomato, and then making one slice down the side of the outer part so that the tomato lies down flat in a strip. Good luck!"

"How many times have you looked at a recipe and said to yourself, 'Oh, no, that's much too difficult to make! I'll never be able to do that!' and so you have failed before you have even tried. So don't let yourself be talked out of doing this one, because it's really terrific. Just jump right in there and do it!"

"Save the inner part of the tomato that you remove for a soup stock or tomato sauce or something. Never let anything go to waste if you can help it."

Basil Vinaigrette

1	bunch sweet basil, leaves removed
	extra virgin olive oil *(as needed)*
	salt *(to taste)*
	pepper *(to taste)*
1	egg yolk
⅓	cup extra virgin olive oil
⅔	cup light olive oil
3	tablespoons champagne vinegar
1	tablespoon red wine vinegar

Blanch the basil leaves in boiling, salted water for 8 seconds. Remove them and immediately plunge them into ice water. Gently squeeze out the water with your hands.

Place the blanched basil in a blender. Pour in enough of the extra virgin olive oil so that the basil is covered. Add the salt and pepper. Purée the ingredients so that a paste is formed. Remove the paste and refrigerate it until it is cold.

In a medium bowl place the egg yolk, the ⅓ cup of extra virgin olive oil, the light olive oil, champagne vinegar, and red wine vinegar. Whisk the ingredients together so that they are well blended.

Add the chilled basil paste and whisk it in. Add more salt or pepper if needed.

"The base of this vinaigrette is an egg yolk. This is what holds the dressing together and gives it a creamy consistency."

"We don't put pine nuts and Parmesan cheese in the paste because that would add too many confusing flavors. What we want here is a strong basil taste and a good, fruity olive oil."

Fresh Bean Salad with Shallot Vinaigrette

Fresh Bean Salad

4	ounces fresh fava beans, shelled, blanched, and peeled
8	ounces fresh haricots vert *(or small green beans)*, **blanched**
8	ounces fresh yellow wax beans, blanched
1	bunch fresh chervil, stems removed
1	bunch opal basil, stems removed and leaves julienned
1	bunch sweet basil, stems removed and leaves julienned
½	bunch fresh tarragon, leaves picked off
¾	pound mixed baby greens
	Shallot Vinaigrette *(recipe follows)*
	salt *(to taste)*
	pepper *(to taste)*

In a large bowl place all of the ingredients except for the Shallot Vinaigrette, and gently toss them together.

Add a small amount of the Shallot Vinaigrette at a time and toss it in, until enough has been added so that the salad is well coated. Add the salt and pepper, and gently toss them in.

serves 8

Shallot Vinaigrette

⅓	cup extra virgin olive oil
⅔	cup light olive oil
4	shallots, finely chopped
3	tablespoons red wine vinegar
1	tablespoon balsamic vinegar
	salt *(to taste)*
	pepper *(to taste)*

In a blender place all of the ingredients and mix them together well.

"People are getting much more sophisticated in their requirements for produce, and grocers are responding to this need by offering more and more exotic items, like the haricots vert. If you can't find them, then use the tiny green beans. There are so many different kinds of beans on the market that you can choose whichever ones are nice and fresh. I chose the ones listed in this recipe because of the contrast in the colors, flavors, and shapes."

"In blanching the beans you should use a lot of salt and water. Blanch just a few beans at a time so that you can move them around in the boiling water. Have an ice water bath ready to plunge the beans into immediately after you remove them from the boiling water. Blanch them only so that they are cooked al dente."

Grilled Swordfish with Tomato Pepper Ragoût

¼ **cup extra virgin olive oil**
2 **cloves garlic, chopped**
1 **onion, thinly sliced**
3 **red bell peppers, roasted, peeled, seeded, and sliced**
3 **yellow bell peppers, roasted, peeled, seeded, and sliced**
3 **tomatoes, blanched, peeled, seeded, and diced**
1 **tablespoon fresh oregano, chopped**
6 **basil leaves**
  salt *(to taste)*
  pepper *(to taste)*
6 **8-ounce swordfish steaks, trimmed**

In a medium skillet place the olive oil and heat it on medium high until it is hot. Add the garlic and onions. Sauté them for 3 to 4 minutes, or until the onions are translucent.

Add the pepper slices and sauté them for 1 to 2 minutes.

Add the tomatoes and oregano. Cover the skillet and reduce the heat. Cook the mixture for 30 minutes, while stirring it occasionally.

Add the basil leaves, salt, and pepper. Stir the mixture and cook it for 3 to 4 minutes more. Set the ragoût aside.

Season the swordfish steaks with the salt and pepper. Grill *(or broil)* them for 3 to 4 minutes on each side, or until they are just done.

On each of 6 individual warmed serving plates place the ragoût. Place a swordfish steak on top.

serves 6

"We serve this dish as a special, and it is always very successful. People who are health conscious especially love it because it is low in fat, low in calories, and yet it is loaded with flavor. In other words, it works!"

"You can serve the ragoût with lamb, chicken, scallops, shrimp, or any other kinds of fresh fish that you want to use. It adds a lot of color and zing to a plate."

"I like to find the tiniest basil leaves possible and then use them whole in the ragoût. They look more attractive this way, and eye appeal is just as important as taste."

Towers

Towers' Duck with Honey Cilantro Sauce and Stir-Fry Vegetables

Towers' Duck

2   **ducks, legs** (with thighs attached) **and breasts removed, excess fat cut off, giblets discarded** (reserve the fat and carcasses)
1   **cup soy sauce**
2   **teaspoons fresh ginger, minced**
     salt (to taste)
     pepper (to taste)
2   **teaspoons olive oil**
     Stir-Fry Vegetables (recipe on next page)
     Honey Cilantro Sauce (recipe on next page)
2   **tablespoons fresh cilantro, chopped**

In a medium bowl place the duck legs, soy sauce, and ginger. Let them marinate for 15 minutes.

Preheat the oven to 500°. Place the marinated duck legs in a pan and bake them for 15 minutes. Remove the pan from the oven and set it aside.

Season the duck breasts with the salt and pepper.

In a large, heavy skillet place the olive oil and heat it on high until it is hot. Place the duck breasts, in the skillet, skin side down, and sauté them for 1 to 2 minutes, or until they are nicely browned. Turn the duck breasts over and sauté them for 1 minute more, or until they are brown.

Place the duck breasts, skin side down, in the pan with the duck legs.

Preheat the oven to 500°. Bake the duck pieces for 8 to 12 minutes, or until they are medium rare (they should be slightly firm to the touch).

Slice the breasts. Separate the legs from the thighs.

On each of 4 individual serving plates place a serving of the Stir-Fry Vegetables. Arrange the sliced duck breast in a semi-circle around the vegetables. Place the duck legs and thighs on the other half of the plate. Ladle on the Honey Cilantro Sauce. Garnish the plate with the fresh cilantro.

serves 4

Towers

"Here is a recipe that has a lot of steps to it, but the end result is dynamite! Take the time to read the instructions through completely before you decide whether or not to attempt it."

"I want to explain to you how to tell when the duck is done, but I can't. I go strictly by feel. Essentially it should be slightly firm to the touch. You're going to have to clone me twenty thousand times and send me along with each book!"

"You let the duck rest for five minutes before slicing it. If you slice it right away, then you will lose all of the natural juices."

310

Honey Cilantro Sauce

4	**tablespoons honey**
4	**shallots, diced**
¼	**cup soy sauce**
1	**cup dry white wine**
4	**tablespoons coriander seeds**
4	**teaspoons fresh ginger, minced**
4	**cups duck stock** *(recipe on next page)*
1	**bunch cilantro, chopped**
	salt *(to taste)*
	pepper *(to taste)*

In a medium saucepan place the honey, shallots, soy sauce, white wine, coriander seeds, fresh ginger, and duck stock. Mix the ingredients together and cook them on medium heat for 20 to 25 minutes, or until the liquid is reduced by ½.

Add the cilantro, salt, and pepper. Let the sauce simmer for another 15 minutes.

Stir-Fry Vegetables

	duck fat *(reserved from Towers' Duck recipe on previous page)*
1	**carrot, julienned**
½	**red onion, julienned**
½	**green bell pepper, julienned**
½	**red bell pepper, julienned**
5	**whole shiitake mushrooms, stems removed, and julienned**
1	**zucchini, julienned**
1	**teaspoon fresh ginger, minced**
¼	**bunch cilantro, leaves removed**
	salt *(to taste)*
	pepper *(to taste)*
¼	**cup duck stock** *(recipe on next page)*

In a large wok place the duck fat and heat it on high until it is hot. Add the carrots, onions, green bell peppers, red bell peppers, mushrooms, zucchini, ginger, and cilantro. Stir-fry the vegetables for 1 to 2 minutes, or until they are just done.

Add the salt and the pepper, and stir them in. Add the duck stock and stir it in.

"This sauce is the perfect complement to the duck.....it has a sweet and somewhat complex flavor. You will notice there is no cream or butter in it, and yet it still tastes rich."

"When I was a kid I worked in restaurant kitchens, and did all of the things that the cooks didn't want to do, like scrubbing pots and pans, and peeling carrots. I kept this up throughout high school because it meant that I had cash and could afford a car and a girlfriend."

"This dish tastes much better if you use the duck fat instead of another kind of oil."

"Use a large skillet if you don't have a wok, although personally I think that there should be a wok in every kitchen."

Duck Stock

2	tablespoons olive oil
2	duck carcasses *(reserved from the Towers' Duck recipe on page 310)*, split in half
2	large onions, coarsely chopped
4	carrots, coarsely chopped
4	stalks celery, coarsely chopped
4	bulbs garlic, cut in half
1	cup dry white wine
4	bay leaves
8	sprigs fresh thyme
4	tablespoons tomato paste
4	quarts unsalted chicken stock *(or as needed)* – *(recipe on page 297)*

Preheat the oven to 500°.

Place a roasting pan on top of the stove on medium heat until it is hot. Add the olive oil and remove it from the heat.

Add the split duck carcasses and roast them in the oven for 10 minutes. Add the onions, carrots, celery, and garlic. Roast the ingredients for another 10 to 15 minutes, or until they are brown. *(Turn and move the ingredients around during the roasting time so that they darken evenly.)*

Remove the duck and vegetables from the pan and set them aside. Strain out the grease. Pat the bottom of the pan dry with paper towels.

Return the pan to the top of the stove and heat it on medium until it is warm. Add the white wine and deglaze the pan.

In a large, heavy saucepan place the wine and the deglazing materials that were scraped from the bottom of the pan. Add the roasted duck bones and vegetables, bay leaves, thyme, and tomato paste. Add enough of the chicken stock so that the ingredients are completely covered, plus 1" more.

Bring the liquid to a boil and skim off any foam that appears on top. Reduce the heat and cook the ingredients on a vigorous simmer for ½ to 1 hour, or until the liquid is reduced by ½. Strain the stock.

makes 8 cups

"We appreciate feedback from the public. The positive feedback keeps us going, and the negative feedback keeps us on our toes."

"I always wanted to be a baseball player when I was growing up and I even got so far as to try out for the Cincinnati Reds. But my mom told me that although I was good, I was not good enough to make it. So she talked me out of trying for the major leagues. Then, when I was in college I majored in history and I wanted to become an historian. But, just like my mom, my history professor talked me out of it. Since then I have often wondered what would have happened if I had pursued either a baseball or history career, but deep down I believe that I was born to be a chef."

Crème Brulé

"This is such a nice dessert. It's easy to make and you can keep it in your refrigerator for up to 3 days. Serve it with some fresh raspberries or some diced pineapple..... it's terrific!"

"I am not a pastry chef, and when I came to work here I was told by my boss that he wanted a crème brulé on the menu. So I fooled around with about 9 or 10 recipes, and for some reason they didn't work for me. Finally I came up with this one. For me, it works. I think that it is fairly foolproof."

"A secret tip to ensure that this custard will come out creamy every time is to vigorously whisk the egg yolks right before you add the cream to them."

"We make a lot of wonderful desserts in our restaurant, but this one is our biggest seller. It's a nice way to finish off a great dinner."

1	quart heavy cream
1	large vanilla bean, cut lengthwise with inside part scraped out
1	pinch salt
8	egg yolks
¾	cup sifted sugar
1	tablespoon powdered sugar *(or as needed)*

In a medium saucepan place the heavy cream, vanilla bean *(both the husk and the inside part)*, and salt. Heat the ingredients on medium until the cream almost reaches the boiling point. Remove the pan from the heat.

In a medium bowl place the egg yolks and the sifted sugar. Whisk them together until a ribbon is formed.

While whisking constantly, very slowly add the warm cream to the egg yolk mixture. Strain the mixture through a large mesh strainer. Skim off any foam that appears on the surface.

Preheat the oven to 300°. Pour the custard into 8 ramekin dishes. Set the dishes in a pan that is ½ full of boiling water. Bake the custard for 1¼ hours, or until it is set.

Let the custard cool. Sprinkle on the powdered sugar.

Place the custard under a preheated broiler for 30 seconds to 1 minute, or until the sugar caramelizes.

serves 8

Pavé au Chocolate
with Coffee Sauce

Pavé au Chocolate

18	ounces semi-sweet chocolate, cut into small pieces
4½	ounces unsalted butter, cut into small pieces
¼	cup Grand Marnier
½	cup sugar
8	egg yolks
8	egg whites
	Coffee Sauce *(recipe on next page)*

In a simmering double boiler place the chocolate and butter pieces one at a time, and stir them until they have melted.

Add the Grand Marnier and stir the sauce for 4 to 6 minutes, or until a ribbon is formed. Set the mixture aside and keep it warm.

In a medium bowl place the sugar and egg yolks. Whisk them together for 4 to 6 minutes, or until a ribbon is formed. Add the mixture to the melted chocolate and stir it in.

In another medium bowl place the egg whites. Beat them for 4 to 5 minutes, or until soft peaks are formed. Gently fold the egg whites into the chocolate mixture.

Pour the chocolate mixture into a buttered, ceramic terrine. Freeze it overnight.

Place the frozen mold in a hot water bath for 30 seconds and shake it loose.

On each individual serving plate pour ¼ cup of the Coffee Sauce. Place a slice of the chocolate pavé on top.

serves 10

"Here is another very simple yet very delicious recipe. The pavé is almost like a frozen chocolate mousse, but it is very dense."

"I studied cooking in France at La Varenne, which is a famous school in Paris. I went over with 9 American women, and it was really a great experience! Every morning I would go to the open air market and purchase fresh fish, vegetables, herbs, or whatever I needed. There was a different vendor for each product and it was all very romantic. I got my first glimpse into what cooking was all about.....I saw the richness and the variety."

Coffee Sauce

6	**egg yolks**
¾	**cup sugar**
2	**cups milk**
2	**tablespoons instant decaffinated coffee**
1	**tablespoon vanilla**
1	**pinch salt**

In a medium bowl place the egg yolks and the sugar. Whip them together for 4 to 6 minutes, or until a ribbon is formed.

In a medium saucepan place the milk and bring it to a boil. Add the decaffinated coffee, vanilla, and salt. Stir the ingredients together.

While stirring constantly, slowly add the egg yolk mixture to the milk.

Return the sauce to a boil for 1 minute more. Place the pan in an ice bath and let the sauce cool.

Chill the sauce and serve it cold.

makes 3 cups

"The coffee sauce has a crème anglaise, or vanilla sauce base. You can add some melted chocolate and swirl it in, for a nice variation."

"I really do love cooking. I like to be in the kitchen, touching the food, smelling it, tasting it, and putting it together in wonderful ways."

Boat Rental Sign, Balboa Island

Valentino
Santa Monica

Famous for its innovative Italian cuisine, Valentino's commitment to excellence assures one a memorable dining experience.

Menu

*Mussels in Basil
with Orange Sauce*

*Rolled Eggplant
Stuffed with Cheese*

Zucchini alla Menta

*Sweet Corn and
Red Bell Pepper Risotto*

*Scallops of Striped Bass
with Tomato*

*Ragû of Wild Games
with Polenta*

Brown Sauce

Chicken with Pine Nuts

*Fresh Fruit and Ice Cream
with Zabaglione*

Owner Piero Selvaggio says, *"When you buy the mussels be sure that the shells are closed. You may serve this dish either hot or cold."*

Mussels in Basil with Orange Sauce

1   **bunch basil, chopped** *(reserve 12 leaves for the garnish)*
2   **oranges, juiced**
½   **teaspoon salt**
¼   **teaspoon pepper**
1   **cup extra virgin olive oil**
36   **large mussels, washed** *(shells on)*
⅔   **cup dry white wine**
1   **orange, cut into 6 wedges**

In a medium bowl place the chopped basil, orange juice, salt, and pepper. While whisking constantly, slowly add the olive oil. Continue to whisk the ingredients for 2 to 3 minutes, or until the sauce thickens.

In a large skillet place the mussels and the white wine. Cover the skillet with a lid and steam the mussels on medium high heat for 2 to 3 minutes, or until the shells open. Immediately remove the mussels. Discard the upper shells.

Place 6 mussels on each individual serving plate. Pour a portion of the sauce over each serving. Garnish each plate with 2 of the basil leaves and 1 orange wedge placed in the center.

serves 6

Rolled Eggplant
Stuffed with Cheese

2	Japanese eggplants, sliced lengthwise into ⅜" thick pieces
2	teaspoons salt
2	tablespoons olive oil *(or as needed)*
4	ounces goat cheese
4	ounces cream cheese
¾	cup red wine vinegar
¼	cup olive oil
2	cloves garlic, minced
½	cup fresh basil, chopped *(reserve 4 leaves for the garnish)*
½	cup fresh parsley, chopped

Place the eggplant in a colander and lightly sprinkle both sides with the salt. Let the eggplant drain for 2 to 3 hours. Pat each slice dry with paper towels.

In a large skillet place the 2 tablespoons of olive oil and heat it on medium high until it is hot. Fry the eggplant slices for 1 to 2 minutes on each side, or until they are golden brown. Drain the eggplant on paper towels.

In a small bowl place the goat cheese and cream cheese, and blend them together.

Put the cheese mixture in a pastry bag and pipe a small amount onto each eggplant slice, lengthwise. Roll the eggplant up so that it is in a jelly-roll form. Place the eggplant rolls in a medium bowl and set it aside.

In another medium bowl place the red wine vinegar, the ¼ cup of olive oil, garlic, chopped basil, and parsley. Whip the ingredients together until they are well blended.

Pour the marinade over the eggplant rolls and refrigerate them for 1 hour.

Slice the eggplant rolls into pinwheels and artfully arrange them on 4 individual serving plates. Garnish each serving with a basil leaf.

serves 4

"This is an original recipe of ours. It makes a wonderful, flavorful appetizer and it's perfect to serve at a nice dinner party."

"You can make this dish way ahead of time, and let it marinate for a longer time."

"If you don't salt the eggplant to draw out the water, then it will taste very bitter."

"You may garnish this dish however you like.....with a sprig of mint or parsley, or maybe some chopped tomatoes."

Zucchini alla Menta

"Zucchini is a very simple vegetable and this is a wonderful way to make it interesting. You may serve this as an appetizer or as a vegetable side dish."

4	small zucchini, thinly sliced
⅓	cup virgin olive oil
10	fresh basil leaves
10	fresh mint leaves
1	clove garlic, chopped
1	teaspoon crushed red pepper
½	teaspoon balsamic vinegar
	salt *(to taste)*
	pepper *(to taste)*

Quickly grill *(or bake)* the zucchini slices until they are barely tender.

Place the zucchini in a small bowl.

In another small bowl place the olive oil, basil, mint, garlic, crushed red pepper, balsamic vinegar, salt, and pepper. Mix the ingredients together well.

Pour the marinade over the zucchini and gently mix it in so that the slices are well coated. Let the zucchini rest for 2 to 3 hours before serving.

serves 6

"Balsamic vinegar has been aged for a long time so that it is almost like sherry. It thickens with the aging and the flavor becomes very intense. Therefore, you must be careful when using it, because a little bit will go a long way. It is like putting black ink into a gallon of water.....just a few drops will change the color! You may use regular red wine vinegar if you don't have the balsamic."

Valentino

Sweet Corn and
Red Bell Pepper Risotto

½	cup butter
1	medium onion, chopped medium
1	pound Aborrio rice, uncooked
1	cup white wine
1	ounce Pernod
2	quarts beef stock
¼	cup Parmesan cheese, freshly grated
6	red bell peppers, roasted, peeled, cut in half crosswise, and seeded
1	cup fresh sweet corn kernels, cooked
¼	cup Parmesan cheese, freshly grated

In a large skillet place the butter and heat it on medium high until it has melted. Add the onions and sauté them for 2 to 3 minutes, or until they are clear.

Add the rice and mix it in well so that each grain is well coated with the butter.

Add the white wine and the Pernod, and stir them in.

Bring the ingredients to a simmer. While stirring constantly, slowly add the beef stock over a 15 to 20 minute period, or until the rice is of a creamy consistency.

Remove the rice from the heat. Add the first ¼ cup of the Parmesan cheese and stir it in.

Dice the bottom halves of the red bell peppers (reserve the top halves).

Add the diced bell peppers and the sweet corn to the rice, and stir them in. Mix the ingredients together well.

Place one serving of the risotto on each of 6 individual serving plates. Place the top half of the reserved bell pepper on top. Sprinkle on some of the second ¼ cup of Parmesan cheese.

serves 6

"A good risotto is one of the master Italian cuisines. In my earlier days I used to say that if a cook comes to work for me, and I don't know him very well, then he will be put to test by making a risotto, because this is something that requires a certain touch."

"Risotto is a little difficult to make. You must leave your guests for the last 15 minutes to complete it, and then you must serve it immediately. However, it is something that is very unique, and it is very rewarding to make. Your guests will definitely appreciate your labor and skill."

"If you have leftover risotto, make rice patties and fry them."

"Italians don't eat corn because it is something that they feed to the chickens. But Americans love corn, especially when it is sweet, tender and juicy. So with this recipe we took a classic Italian dish and gave it a California twist with the corn and red bell pepper."

Scallops of Striped Bass with Tomato

"This is a very elegant presentation of a simple fish. The marriage of the different flavors is quite wonderful."

"You may use any kind of firm, white fish like halibut or swordfish. Don't use salmon!"

"This is a recipe that can easily be made by an average cook. Yet, at the same time, it has a certain creativity and style that elevates it from the ordinary to the excellent."

1	3-pound striped bass *(including the head)*
2	quarts water
1	clove garlic, chopped medium
1	scallion, chopped medium
1	stalk celery, chopped medium
1	carrot, chopped medium
2	tomatoes, peeled, seeded, and chopped
1	bay leaf
½	cup flour *(or as needed)*
3	tablespoons olive oil
1	clove garlic, crushed
⅓	cup dry white wine
¼	cup brandy
1	teaspoon Worcestershire sauce
2	tomatoes, peeled, seeded, and chopped
½	cup sweet butter
6	basil leaves

Remove the scales and head from the fish and place them in a large pot *(reserve the fish)*. Add the water, garlic, scallions, celery, carrots, the first 2 chopped tomatoes, and the bay leaf. Bring the ingredients to a boil and then simmer them for 1 hour. Occasionally skim off the top of the stock. Strain the stock through a cheesecloth and set it aside.

Cut the fish into 6 individual steaks. Thoroughly coat them on both sides with the flour.

In a large skillet place the olive oil and heat it on medium high until it is hot. Add the crushed garlic. Add the floured fish steaks and sauté them for 2 minutes on each side. Add the wine and brandy, and flambé them. Remove the fish steaks *(reserve the liquid)* and place them in a warm, covered dish.

Add the Worcestershire sauce, the other 2 chopped tomatoes, and the butter to the liquid in the skillet. Stir the ingredients over a medium high heat for 1 to 2 minutes, or until the liquid is reduced by ½.

On each of 6 individual serving plates place a fish steak. Spoon the sauce over the top. Garnish the dish with a fresh basil leaf.

serves 6

Valentino

Ragû of Wild Games with Polenta

Ragû of Wild Games

½	cup extra virgin olive oil
½	onion, chopped medium
1	carrot, julienned
2	stalks celery, julienned
2	quail, boned and halved
2	pigeons, boned and quartered
4	rabbit legs, halved
1	teaspoon fresh thyme, finely chopped
1	teaspoon sage
1	cup red wine
1	quart beef stock
½	cup chicken stock *(recipe on page 297)*
½	pound fresh porcini *(or shiitake)* mushrooms, thinly sliced
	salt *(to taste)*
	pepper *(to taste)*
4	cups Quick Polenta *(recipe on next page)*

In a large stockpot place the olive oil and heat it on medium high until it is hot. Add the onions, carrots, and celery. Sauté the vegetables for 3 to 4 minutes, or until they just begin to brown.

Add the quail, pigeon, and rabbit. Sauté the meats for 3 to 4 minutes, or until they are lightly browned.

Add the thyme and the sage, and stir them in.

While stirring constantly, slowly sprinkle in the wine. Continue to stir and cook the ingredients for 5 minutes.

Add the beef stock and the chicken stock, and stir them in. Cover the pot and simmer the ingredients for 20 minutes.

Add the mushrooms and simmer the ingredients for another 10 minutes.

Add the salt and the pepper.

Ladle the Quick Polenta onto 6 individual serving plates. Spoon on the ragû *(divide the game pieces equally)*.

serves 4

"This is a very intriguing dish. It's not at all hard to make, and it makes a wonderful impression on your guests. The wild games give it an exotic aura. It is very rich and very beautiful."

"If you can't find rabbit then use chicken. However, rabbit is up and coming in its popularity, and it is appearing in supermarkets with more frequency. I think that rabbit is a wonderful meat. It is much more flavorful than chicken."

"We do not call our restaurant northern Italian or southern Italian. If anything, we describe ourselves as contemporary Italian. We use all kinds of classical Italian cooking and interpret the dishes in our own way so that they are elevated to a higher level."

"Polenta is a fun thing to do because it is very simple. In this recipe, I have called for instant polenta because it is so much faster to make."

"Nobody really invents cuisine. The ingredients exist and you put them together in tasty and creative ways, just like in painting where you have the basic ingredients of the brushes, canvas, and different colors of paint. How you combine these ingredients together will make the difference between creating something that is ordinary or something that is fantastic."

"This recipe is as simple and as basic as possible. Here in the restaurant we make our own stock for the bouillon and cook it for many, many hours with bones and lots of different ingredients. But the average cook at home can't usually do that. So I recommend sprucing up this recipe with different spices and herbs to your own individual taste."

Quick Polenta

1½   **quarts water**
2   **teaspoons butter**
1½   **cups instant polenta** *(corn meal)*
½   **cup butter**

In a medium large saucepan place the water and bring it to a boil.

Add the 2 teaspoons of butter and stir it in.

Add the polenta and stir it in with a wooden spoon for 5 minutes over medium heat.

Add the ½ cup of butter and stir it in.

serves 4 to 6

Brown Sauce

4   **tablespoons butter**
4   **tablespoons flour**
2   **cups bouillon, heated**
  salt *(to taste)*
  pepper *(to taste)*

In a medium saucepan place the butter and heat it on medium until it has melted. Add the flour and stir it in for 1 minute.

While stirring constantly, slowly add the heated bouillon. Continue to stir until the sauce reaches the boiling point.

Add the salt and pepper, and stir them in.

makes 2 cups

Chicken with Pine Nuts

8	**chicken breasts**
½	**cup flour** *(or as needed)*
½	**cup cooking oil**
⅓	**cup butter**
1¼	**cups pine nuts**
4	**cloves garlic, minced**
1	**cup dry white wine**
2	**lemons, juiced**
1	**bunch parsley, chopped**
2	**cups Brown Sauce, heated** *(recipe on previous page)*
½	**teaspoon salt** *(or to taste)*
¼	**teaspoon pepper** *(or to taste)*

Thoroughly coat the chicken breasts with the flour.

In a large skillet place the oil and heat it on medium high until it is hot. Add the chicken breasts and sauté them for 3 to 4 minutes on each side, or until they are golden brown. Remove the chicken breasts and place them in a large baking dish. Cover the dish and keep the chicken warm.

Drain the oil out of the skillet. Add the butter and heat it on medium high until it has melted. Add the pine nuts and sauté them for 1 to 2 minutes, or until they are golden brown.

Add the garlic and white wine, and cook them for 3 to 4 minutes, or until the wine has evaporated.

Add the lemon juice, parsley, the heated Brown Sauce, salt, and pepper. Stir the ingredients together.

Pour the sauce over the chicken.

Preheat the oven to 350°. Bake the chicken for 15 minutes, or until it is very hot.

serves 8

"This is a wonderful dish that everyone loves. The pine nuts give it a delicious, distinct flavor, and it is very easy to make."

"The flavor of the pine nuts marries very well with the flavors of the lemon and the chicken."

"I believe in growing as a chef by constantly experimenting and by pushing oneself. This means that one must be willing to have failures and make mistakes! Eventually, the great chefs develop a personalized style that is uniquely their own."

Valentino

Fresh Fruit and Ice Cream
with Zabaglione

Fresh Fruit and Ice Cream

6 small figs, halved
1 basket raspberries, washed
1 basket assorted berries, washed
2 kiwi, peeled and thinly sliced
1 papaya, peeled, seeded, and cut into pearls
1 melon, peeled, seeded, and cut into pearls
2 pears, peeled, seeded, and thinly sliced
½ cup currants
   Zabaglione (recipe follows)
6 scoops vanilla ice cream

On each individual serving plate artfully arrange a portion of the fruits.

Gently pour on the Zabaglione.

Place a scoop of ice cream on top.

serves 6

Zabaglione

½ cup sweet Riesling wine
½ cup Strega liqueur
4 eggs
½ cup sugar

In a small bowl place all of the ingredients and mix them together.

Pour the mixture into a steaming double boiler and whisk it for 2 to 3 minutes, or until it becomes creamy.

"This dish is based on a very traditional and old-fashioned Italian dessert, which will always be popular. We have elaborated upon it to make it more creative."

"The mixture of wonderful fruits is almost like a fruit compote, and the ice cream adds a delicious touch. Of course, you can serve this with no ice cream, if you prefer, and it will still be excellent. Also, if you want to serve the Zabaglione by itself, then just put it into fancy glasses."

"I used to be a maître d' at a restaurant where everything was flambé. The Zabaglione was wonderful for putting on a good show at the table. I would whip the ingredients together in a most dignified manner."

"You must have a good arm when you whip this, or otherwise it won't come out right. If you don't have a good arm, then don't make it!"

Valentino

Gazebo, Laguna Beach

West Beach Cafe
Venice

Offering an eclectic Southern California cuisine in a contemporary, comfortable dining room, West Beach Cafe is a hot spot that never seems to lose its sizzle!

Owner Bruce Marder says, *"The lettuces in the salad can be varied. You just want a nice mixture of greens that have a slightly different color and texture to them, so that they will be interesting."*

Mixed Seafood Salad

3	tablespoons olive oil
½	pound calamari, cleaned, skin removed, and cut into ¼" rings
3	tablespoons olive oil
½	pound medium shrimp, peeled and deveined
3	tablespoons olive oil
2	teaspoons garlic, diced
2	teaspoons shallots, diced
¾	pound mussels, scrubbed
¾	pound Manila clams, scrubbed
1½	cups dry white wine
1½	teaspoons fresh tarragon, coarsely chopped
	salt
	pepper
1	head Belgian endive, washed, dried, and cut into 1" pieces
1	small head escarole, washed, dried, and cut into 1" pieces
6	bunches watercress, washed, dried, and large stems removed

In a large skillet place the first 3 tablespoons of olive oil and heat it on high until it is hot. Add the calamari and sauté it for 1 to 2 minutes, or until it is tender. Remove the calamari, set it aside, and keep it warm.

Add the second 3 tablespoons of olive oil to the skillet and heat it on medium until it is hot. Add the shrimp and sauté them for 2 to 3 minutes, or until they are lightly translucent in the middle. Remove the shrimp, set them aside, and keep them warm.

(continued on next page)

328

Add the third 3 tablespoons of olive oil to the skillet and heat it on medium low until it is hot. Add the garlic and shallots, and sauté them for 3 to 4 minutes or until they are tender.

Add the mussels, clams, and white wine to the skillet. Simmer the ingredients for 3 to 4 minutes, or until the shells open. Remove the shellfish, set them aside, and keep them warm.

Add the tarragon to the skillet. Cook the ingredients for 2 to 3 minutes, or until the liquid is reduced by ⅓. Remove the skillet from the heat and let the liquid cool for 2 to 3 minutes. Add the salt and the pepper.

In a large salad bowl place the Belgian endive, escarole, and watercress. Add ¾ of the warmed liquid from the skillet and toss it with the greens.

In a large bowl place the seafood and and the remainder of the liquid. Toss the ingredients together.

On each of 4 individual salad plates place the tossed greens. Artfully arrange the seafood on top.

serves 4

"The neat thing about this recipe is that the juices get extracted from the mussels and clams, and this provides the basis of the dressing for the salad."

"A lot of people don't like the idea of eating calamari. They say, 'Yukkk! I don't want to eat squid!' However, if they tasted it, chances are they would love it, because it really has a wonderful flavor. Cleaning the calamari takes some work, but you also can buy it frozen and already cleaned. If the idea of coping with the calamari seems too awesome, just eliminate it from the salad."

"I believe in keeping cooking simple by not using too many ingredients. I want the essential flavor of the food to be tasted. Also, it's very important to cook the food the correct amount of time. Don't be afraid to constantly taste or test the food for its degree of doneness. Never follow a recipe blindly..... use your own common sense."

Shrimp and Corn Chowder

1½	**cups fresh corn**
2	**cups potatoes, diced into ½" cubes**
1	**quart chicken stock** *(recipe on page 297)*
2	**tablespoons olive oil**
1	**red bell pepper, roasted, skin and seeds removed, and diced large**
1	**green bell pepper, roasted, skin and seeds removed, and diced large**
½	**cup onions, diced large**
½	**cup celery, diced large**
½	**pound small shrimp, peeled, deveined, and tails removed**
1	**teaspoon fresh thyme, chopped**
1	**teaspoon paprika**
	salt *(to taste)*
	pepper *(to taste)*
2	**teaspoons chives, thinly sliced**

In a medium large saucepan place ½ of the corn, ½ of the potatoes, and the chicken stock. Bring the liquid to a boil and then reduce the heat to low. Simmer the ingredients for 15 to 20 minutes, or until the potatoes are tender.

Strain out the vegetables and place them in a blender. Reserve the chicken stock in another container. Add some of the chicken stock to the blender. Purée the ingredients so that a thick soup consistency is achieved. Add more of the chicken stock if necessary. Return the purée to the saucepan and keep it warm.

Place the remaining corn and potatoes in a pot of boiling, salted water. Cook them for 10 minutes, or until the potatoes are tender. Drain the vegetables. Add them to the purée mixture and stir them in.

In a large skillet place the olive oil and heat it on medium high until it is hot. Add the red and green bell peppers, onions, and celery. Sauté the vegetables for 3 to 4 minutes, or until they are tender. Add them to the soup.

Bring the soup to a simmer. Add the shrimp, thyme, paprika, salt, and pepper. Cook the soup for 5 minutes, or until the shrimp are done. Garnish the soup with the chives.

serves 4

"There is no butter or cream in this soup. It's very hearty, tasty, and good for you. It can be served as a first course, or it would be nice for a light meal if you include a crisp, green salad and some good French bread."

"It's a little tricky getting the soup to the right consistency. When you add the chicken stock to the blender go a little bit light at first. You can always add more if you need it. I don't make this soup very thick but you can make it any consistency that you want."

"Waiters are not necessarily professional people. Most of them want to be actors, writers, or artists, and working in a restaurant is just a temporary occupation. Very few Americans have the goal to be a waiter, whereas in Europe to be a professional waiter is a very common and respected occupation. It's funny, because my waiters make a lot of money!"

Ragoût of Turkey Breast and Artichokes with Roasted Red Bell Pepper Sauce

Ragoût of Turkey Breast and Artichokes

¼   **cup olive oil** *(or as needed)*
1½ **pounds turkey breast, boned, skin removed, and cut into 1" cubes**
     salt *(to taste)*
     pepper *(to taste)*
1½ **cups button mushroom caps**
1   **medium red onion, cut into 1" cubes**
4   **large artichoke hearts, cooked and cut into 1" cubes**
⅔   **cup Roasted Red Bell Pepper Sauce** *(recipe on next page)*
⅓   **cup fresh basil, chopped**

In a small bowl place the olive oil, turkey cubes, salt, and pepper. Toss the turkey so that it is well coated with the oil.

Heat a large sauté pan on medium high. Add the seasoned and oiled turkey pieces. Sauté them for 3 to 4 minutes, or until they are nicely browned and halfway done.

Add the mushrooms and red onions. Sauté the vegetables for 3 to 4 minutes, or until they are tender *(add more oil if necessary)*. Let the turkey and the sautéed vegetables sit for several minutes.

Add the artichoke hearts and stir them in.

Add the Roasted Red Bell Pepper Sauce and the basil, and stir them in. Add more salt and pepper if necessary.

serves 4

"This is a great tasting dish, especially because of the roasted bell peppers. Everything is cooked together in the same pan, so all of the different flavors blend together."

"If you are going to serve this on a plate the finished ragoût should be cooked down quite a bit so that no juice seeps out. In this case be careful not to overcook the turkey. If you are going to serve it in a bowl, then it can be juicier and you won't have to cook it so long."

"This recipe calls for 4 large artichoke hearts. I am assuming that you can find fresh artichokes, because the hearts in them will be much larger than the ones you get in a can. If you have to use the canned ones, then double the amount."

Roasted Red Bell Pepper Sauce

1	**pound red bell peppers**
1	**tablespoon olive oil** *(or as needed)*
2	**tablespoons olive oil**
¼	**medium onion, diced**
1½	**cups chicken stock** *(recipe on page 297)*
	salt *(to taste)*
	pepper *(to taste)*

Lightly brush the red bell peppers with the 1 tablespoon of olive oil. Roast them over an open flame until the skins blister and turn black. Remove most of the skin *(leave on some of the black to color the sauce)*. Remove the seeds and discard them. Set the peppers aside.

In a medium saucepan place the 2 tablespoons of olive oil and heat it on medium high until it is hot. Add the onions and sauté them for 3 to 4 minutes, or until they are translucent.

Add the chicken stock and roasted bell peppers, and simmer the ingredients for 20 minutes. Strain the pepper-onion mixture *(reserve the chicken stock)*.

Place the pepper-onion mixture in a blender and purée it. Add the chicken stock a little at a time, until the desired consistency is achieved.

Season the sauce with the salt and the pepper.

"You can do a lot of things with this sauce. Add some lemon juice to it and serve it with fish. Or, you can make a wonderful soup out of it by adding some potatoes and more liquid."

"I got interested in cooking when I was in my early twenties. I was traveling around in Europe and North Africa and I met a bunch of chefs who were camped out on the beach in Morocco. They would make these incredible dishes that would be simmering in a little pot on their camp stove. The aromas were fantastic and I remember thinking, 'Wow! Why does that guy's stuff smell so good?' My eyes were opened to new kinds of food, cooking, and tastes, other than the plain, basic American food that I had eaten all of my life. This experience on the beach led to my decision to become a chef. Before then I had never cooked at all, except maybe to scramble some eggs or grill a steak."

Grilled Chilean Sea Bass with Tomato Eggplant Sauce

Grilled Chilean Sea Bass

4	6-ounce Chilean sea bass fillets, 1" thick
1	tablespoon olive oil
	salt *(to taste)*
	pepper *(to taste)*
	Tomato Eggplant Sauce *(recipe on next page)*

Lightly brush the sea bass with the olive oil. Sprinkle on the salt and the pepper.

Grill the fillets for 3 to 4 minutes on each side, or until they are golden brown on the outside and slightly translucent in the middle.

On each of 4 individual serving plates place a sea bass fillet. Liberally spread the Tomato Eggplant Sauce on top.

serves 4

"This is a very popular dish that is incredibly simple to make. The sea bass can be grilled or sautéed, and other kinds of firm-fleshed fish can be used. It's one of those great dishes that is healthy and delicious, which is what people in Southern California love!"

"I want to make our customers happy, and so I will do whatever possible to satisfy each person's own individual needs."

Tomato Eggplant Sauce

1	**cup virgin olive oil**
3	**cups eggplant, peeled and cut into ½" cubes**
2	**cups tomatoes, peeled, seeded, and chopped**
1½	**tablespoons fresh parsley, finely chopped**
	salt *(to taste)*
	pepper *(to taste)*

In a large sauté pan place the olive oil and heat it on medium until it is very hot. Add the eggplant and cook it for 6 to 8 minutes, or until it is tender. Drain away the excess oil.

Add the tomatoes and cook them for 8 to 10 minutes, or until most of the liquid is cooked out of the mixture.

Add the parsley, salt, and pepper. Stir the ingredients together well.

makes 3 cups

"You can use this sauce on a variety of dishes. It's especially good with a large, tubular pasta, like rigatoni. It's so robust that it is almost like a vegetable dish instead of a sauce."

"If the eggplant is not completely fresh, you should first season it with some salt and then let it sit in a strainer so that the liquid drains out. We have our eggplants delivered to us at the restaurant, and we know that they are ablsolutely fresh. But when you buy them from the super-market it's hard to know for sure. So, to be on the safe side, you probably should do this. Otherwise, the eggplant will taste bitter."

"When you add the eggplant to the oil, be sure that your sauté pan is very hot! The eggplant will soak up the oil, but after it starts cooking it will release a lot of the oil."

Peach Tartlettes Tatin
with Crême Anglaise

Peach Tartlettes Tatin

4   **5" round puff pastry crusts** (⅛" thick), **pricked with a fork**
2   **tablespoons unsalted butter**
4   **tablespoons sugar**
5   **peaches, washed, pitted, and each one sliced into 10 segments**
3   **tablespoons brandy**
      Crême Anglaise (recipe on next page)

Preheat the oven to 350°. Place the puff pastry rounds on a buttered cookie sheet and bake them for 10 to 12 minutes, or until they are just beyond a golden color.

In a large sauté pan place the butter and heat it on medium until it has melted. Add the sugar and stir it in for 6 to 10 minutes, or until it dissolves and turns a caramel color.

Add the peach segments one by one, so that they form a single layer.

Add the brandy and flambé it. Remove the sauté pan from the heat and let the peaches cool.

In each of four 4½" ramekins arrange the peaches. Cover them with a piece of plastic. Firmly press the peaches down with the bottom of a glass. Chill the peaches in the refrigerator for 15 minutes.

Remove the plastic from the peaches. Invert them onto the baked crusts.

Preheat the oven to 350°. Place the tarts on a cookie sheet and bake them for 5 minutes.

On each of 4 individual plates ladle on the Crême Anglaise. Place a warm tart on top.

serves 4

"This is a variation of a classical recipe. Instead of a whole tart there are four individual ones. You can use any fruit that has a good texture and will hold together, such as pears, plums, or apples."

"Be careful when you flambé the brandy. Take the pan off the heat, pour in the brandy, tilt the pan so that the brandy comes to the top edge of the pan, and the flame will come up. Stand back and watch out!"

"When you press the glass on top of the peaches you are removing the air, as well as making the slices more compact and uniform in their shape."

Crême Anglaise

2	**cups heavy cream**
⅓	**cup sugar**
2	**vanilla beans, split**
6	**egg yolks**
⅓	**cup sugar**

In a medium saucepan place the heavy cream, the first ⅓ cup of sugar, and the split vanilla beans. Bring the ingredients to a boil over medium heat.

In a medium bowl place the egg yolks and the second ⅓ cup of sugar. Whisk them together for 4 to 6 minutes, or until they are well combined.

Add a small amount of the hot cream to the egg yolks and whisk it in. While whisking constantly, slowly add the egg yolk mixture to the hot cream. Continue to whisk the mixture for 4 to 6 minutes, or until a spoon is lightly coated.

Strain the mixture through a sieve. Place it in a medium bowl. Place the bowl in an ice bath for 20 minutes and whisk it every 3 minutes, or until it is cool.

Chill the cream in the refrigerator.

makes 3 cups

"Cream sauces are easy to make and they taste so rich and delicious. You get all of the flavors of the vanilla, cream, sugar, and egg yolks. You can add some liqueur to this sauce, like maybe 2 tablespoons of cognac. This will give it another flavor."

"My desire was to go to cooking school in France, and so I worked in Chicago trying to save up the money. Then the thought occurred to me that maybe I could go to cooking school right there, so at least I could begin to learn some things about cooking. I opened up the yellow pages and found a listing for a school in Glenview, Illinois. The chef there was a wonderful person, and he ended up giving me an apprenticeship. I worked at the school every day to pay for my classes.....and that was the beginning of my career!"

"You need a tremendous amount of experience to become a good chef. Each food item has its own unique characteristics, and you need to handle that item many, many times to really understand how to deal with it properly."

Lifeguard Tower, Redondo Beach

Whale & Ale Pub Restaurant

San Pedro

Serving an English cuisine with a California flair, the Whale & Ale Pub Restaurant is the perfect setting for unwinding after a hard day's work. It's fun and relaxing, and the food is great!

Menu

Pickled Eggs

Savory Pâté

Scotch Eggs

Pea Soup with Mint

Stilton Mixed Green Salad with Port Vinaigrette

Banger Blue Pie

Sea Soup

Ale-Battered Shrimp with Spicy Tomato Sauce

Scones

English-born Robert Matthews is the general manager. He says, *"Pickled eggs are popular in English pubs because they stimulate your taste buds, like pretzels, and they make you want to drink more beer. I love them!"*

Pickled Eggs

12	hard boiled eggs, shells removed
1	tablespoon dried red pepper flakes
1	teaspoon mustard seeds
¼	teaspoon celery seeds
¼	cup garlic, minced
2	cups champagne vinegar
½	cup malt vinegar
¾	cup water
1½	teaspoons salt
1½	teaspoons sugar

In a sterilized quart jar pack the hard-boiled eggs. Add the dried red pepper flakes, mustard seeds, celery seeds, and garlic.

In a large saucepan place the champagne vinegar, malt vinegar, water, salt, and sugar. Bring the ingredients to a boil over high heat.

Pour the boiling liquid into the jar and seal it. Let the jar cool to room temperature and then refrigerate it for at least one week.

makes 12 eggs

Savory Pâté

1	tablespoon butter
½	cup shallots, finely chopped
¼	cup brandy
¼	cup port wine
½	pound lean pork, ground medium
½	pound lean veal, ground medium
¼	pound fat back, ground medium
10	chicken livers, finely chopped
1	teaspoon fresh thyme, finely chopped
½	teaspoon fresh chervil (or ¼ teaspoon dried), finely chopped
⅛	teaspoon black pepper, freshly ground
2	medium eggs, beaten

In a medium saucepan place the butter and heat it on medium high until it has melted. Add the shallots and sauté them for 3 to 4 minutes, or until they are translucent.

Add the brandy and port wine, and cook them for 2 to 3 minutes, or until the liquid is reduced by ½.

In a large mixing bowl place the shallots and the reduced liquid. Add the remainder of the ingredients. Mix them together with your hands so that they are well blended.

Preheat the oven to 350°. Place the meat mixture in a lightly greased loaf pan and bake it for 30 minutes, or until it is just done (do not overcook).

Remove the loaf from the oven (leave the meat in the loaf pan), place a heavy object on top of the meat (like a brick), and set it in the refrigerator to cool.

Serve the pâté as a spread for crackers or lightly buttered toast fingers.

serves 8 to 2

"The main trick with this recipe is not to overcook the pâté. You can test its doneness by pushing it down with your finger. It should spring back up, like it is a fairly stiff sponge. If you overcook it, then the meat will crumble."

"The reason for putting the brick (or other heavy object) on top of the pâté is to press the juices back down into the meat."

"This pâté takes some trouble to make, but in my opinion it's well worth the effort because it tastes really great. Your guests will love it!"

Scotch Eggs

1½	**pounds ground lamb**
1½	**teaspoons rosemary, ground**
¼	**teaspoon salt**
½	**teaspoon black pepper**
⅛	**cup dry vermouth**
1½	**teaspoons crushed red pepper**
10	**hard boiled eggs, peeled**
¾	**cup flour** *(or as needed)*
½	**cup buttermilk** *(or as needed)*
¾	**cup bread crumbs** *(or as needed)*
3	**cups vegetable oil**

In a medium bowl place the ground lamb, rosemary, salt, pepper, dry vermouth, and crushed red pepper. Thoroughly mix the ingredients together with your hands.

Divide the ground lamb mixture into 10 equal portions.

Wrap one portion of the lamb mixture around each of the hard boiled eggs. Make sure that the eggs are completely sealed with the meat.

Lightly roll the wrapped eggs in the flour. Dip them in the buttermilk. Roll them in the bread crumbs so that they are well coated.

In a medium saucepan place the oil and heat it on medium high until it is 375°. Deep-fry the coated eggs for 4 to 6 minutes, or until the lamb is firm and dark brown in color.

makes 10 eggs

Pea Soup with Mint

3	tablespoons butter
1	shallot, finely chopped
1¼	pounds frozen petit peas
2	cups chicken stock *(recipe on page 297)*
⅛	teaspoon sugar
¼	teaspoon salt
⅛	teaspoon white pepper
3	tablespoons fresh mint, finely chopped
1	egg yolk, beaten
½	cup heavy cream
4	sprigs fresh mint

In a large saucepan place the butter and heat it on medium high until it has melted. Add the shallots and sauté them for 3 to 4 minutes, or until they are tender.

Add the peas and stir them in so that they are well coated with the butter and shallot mixture. Cover the saucepan and cook the peas for 3 to 4 minutes, or until the butter is absorbed.

Add the chicken stock, sugar, salt, white pepper, and the chopped mint. Stir the ingredients together and let them simmer for 10 minutes, or until the peas are tender. Remove the pan from the heat and let the ingredients cool to room temperature *(reserve ¼ cup of the peas for a garnish)*.

Pour the mixture into a food processor and purée it until it is smooth.

Return the purée to the saucepan and gently reheat it *(do not boil)*. Add the egg yolk and heavy cream, and beat them in well so that the mixture is smooth.

Garnish the soup with the reserved peas and the mint sprigs.

serves 4

"This is an unusual recipe that is simple to make, doesn't take too long, and is easy to reheat. Although I have never tried it, I would imagine that it would freeze very well."

"Pubs in England are like any other eating establishment. Some are awful and some are great.....I suppose it all depends on who is doing the cooking in the kitchen, doesn't it?"

"In England, if you walk into a pub and sit at a table, nobody will serve you. You have to go up to the bar, order your beer and pay for it, and then order and pay for your food. They may bring your food over to your table, or they may call over to you and say, 'Hey! Your food's ready. Come and get it!' So, this is very different from the United States."

Stilton Mixed Green Salad with Port Vinaigrette

Stilton Mixed Green Salad

8	cups mixed greens
2	medium tomatoes, wedged
1	medium avocado, peeled, pitted, and sliced
	Port Vinaigrette *(recipe follows)*
4	teaspoons Stilton cheese, grated

On each of 4 chilled salad plates place a portion of the mixed greens.

Artfully arrange the tomato wedges and avocado slices on top. Drizzle on some of the Port Vinaigrette. Sprinkle on the grated Stilton cheese.

serves 4

Port Vinaigrette

¼	cup Dijon mustard
2	cups olive oil
¼	cup walnut oil
¼	cup safflower oil
¼	cup avocado oil
⅓	cup tarragon vinegar
½	cup lemon juice, freshly squeezed
⅓	cup Tawny Port wine
1	teaspoon salt
½	teaspoon black pepper, freshly ground

In a medium bowl place the mustard. While mixing constantly on low speed, very slowly drizzle in the olive oil, walnut oil, safflower oil, and avocado oil.

Add the tarragon vinegar, lemon juice, Tawny Port wine, salt, and pepper. Mix the ingredients together well.

Chill the dressing in the refrigerator.

makes 3¾ cups

"This salad, with the dressing, has a combination of flavors that has a very stimulating effect on one's taste buds."

"Tarragon vinegar has a very distinct flavor and it is necessary for this recipe. It's very easy to make your own tarragon vinegar. Just buy an ordinary bottle of white wine vinegar, stick a couple of sprigs of fresh tarragon in it, and let it sit for a week."

"For some reason, the avocado flavors from the oil in the dressing and the fresh avocados go together very well with both the port, which is a sweet wine, and the Stilton cheese, which is a sharp, blue cheese."

Banger Blue Pie

2	**8-ounce bangers** *(mild English sausage)*
1	**teaspoon butter**
4	**medium mushrooms**
½	**teaspoon garlic, minced**
1	**tablespoon spinach, chopped**
⅛	**teaspoon salt**
¼	**teaspoon black pepper**
2	**cups half and half**
½	**cup sour cream**
4	**ounces Swiss cheese, grated**
8	**ounces Danish blue cheese**
¼	**cup port wine**
4	**eggs, beaten**
1	**uncooked pie shell with a top**
1	**egg, beaten with 2 tablespoons of water**

Grill *(or broil)* the sausages for 10 to 15 minutes, or until they are nicely browned on all sides. Slice the sausage into ⅜" pieces and set them aside.

In a small saucepan place the butter and heat it on medium until it has melted. Add the mushrooms, garlic, and spinach. Sauté the ingredients for 2 to 3 minutes, or until the mushrooms are tender.

In a medium bowl place the sausage, sautéed vegetables, salt, pepper, half and half, sour cream, Swiss cheese, Danish blue cheese, port wine, and 4 beaten eggs. Mix the ingredients together thoroughly.

In a buttered baking dish place the pie shell and pat it in. Place the sausage mixture into the pie shell and put on the pastry top. Pinch the pie crusts together around the edges.

Preheat the oven to 350°. Brush the top of the pie with the eggwash. Bake the pie for 20 to 30 minutes, or until it is done and the pastry shell is lightly browned.

serves 6

"This is an excellent, typically English dish that is very flavorful. You should serve it with an assortment of fresh fruits, such as melon, grapes, pineapple, and strawberries."

"If you cannot find the banger sausage, then you can substitute a white veal sausage. The main thing is you don't want a sausage that's too spicy."

"Pub food has changed dramatically over the past 20 years. Back then people would drink their beer with a pickled egg and maybe a bag or two of chips. But, because pubs made more money on their food than they did on their beer, they have become much more food oriented than before."

Sea Soup

3	tablespoons butter
1	cup leeks, julienned
1	pound yams, peeled and diced medium
1	pound potatoes, peeled and diced medium
1½	cups clam juice
1	cup frozen corn
12	ounces fresh salmon, diced medium
1	quart heavy cream
1	quart milk
1	teaspoon Worcestershire Sauce
1	teaspoon tabasco sauce

In a large saucepan place the butter and heat it on medium high until it has melted. Add the leeks and sauté them for 4 to 6 minutes, or until they are tender.

Add the yams and the potatoes, and sauté them for 3 to 4 minutes, or until the butter is absorbed.

Add the clam juice and simmer the mixture for 10 to 15 minutes, or until the yams and potatoes are almost cooked.

Add the corn and the salmon and stir them in.

While stirring constantly, pour in the heavy cream and milk, and blend them in well.

Add the Worcestershire Sauce and the tabasco sauce, and stir them in.

Remove the soup from the heat and set it on top of a saucer so that it rapidly cools to room temperature.

Reheat the soup before serving it.

serves 12

"The tricky part in making this soup is to be sure that it cools down quickly. That is why I have you set the pot on top of a saucer.....so that the air circulates all around it. The danger is that the fish will start fermenting. You will know if this happens because froth and foam will appear on the top and the aroma will get very strong."

"This is a rich and amazing soup. One bowl of it and you can forget about eating dinner..... you've had enough! For a nice, simple meal serve it with some good bread and a green salad."

"We call for salmon in this recipe, but you can use any kind of fish that is fresh and good that day."

Ale-Battered Shrimp with Spicy Tomato Sauce

Ale-Battered Shrimp

1	quart large ice cubes
2	cups water
12	ounces ale
2	cups all-purpose flour
1	teaspoon salt
1½	cups egg whites, beaten so that soft peaks form
3	cups vegetable oil *(or as needed)*
1½	pounds large shrimp, shelled and deveined
½	cup flour *(or as needed)*
	Spicy Tomato Sauce *(recipe follows)*

In a large bowl place the ice cubes, water, and ale. Let them sit for 2 hours. Strain out the remaining ice cubes.

In a medium bowl place the 2 cups of flour and the salt. While stirring gently, add enough of the ale-water mixture so that the batter is thick enough to coat the shrimps well. Fold in the beaten egg whites.

In a large saucepan place the oil and heat it on high until it is hot. Dredge the shrimp in the ½ cup of flour and dip them in the batter. Deep-fry the shrimp for 2 to 3 minutes, or until they are crisp and golden brown.

Serve the shrimp with the Spicy Tomato Sauce.

serves 4

Spicy Tomato Sauce

1½	cups ketchup
½	cup chile sauce
½	teaspoon garlic powder
½	teaspoon onion powder
⅛	cup horseradish
⅛	cup lemon juice, freshly squeezed
2	tablespoons Worcestershire sauce

(continued on next page)

"This is a great recipe! It makes a batter that fries up nice and crispy, and doesn't get soggy. The ale is what helps to do this."

"In the restaurant we serve this with a tartar sauce, Spicy Tomato Sauce, and potatoes. People love it!"

"These shrimp are a fairly typical English pub dish. They are one of our most popular items at the restaurant."

"When I want to make a dish, I first visualize it in my mind and then I cook it. Over a period of 5 to 10 years, I learned all of the basic techniques of cooking. Now that I have the basics, I expand upon them to create what I want. The sources of inspiration are endless!"

½   teaspoon tabasco sauce
⅛   cup chile powder
⅛   teaspoon salt
½   teaspoon white pepper

In a medium bowl place all of the ingredients and mix them together well. Cover the sauce and refrigerate it overnight.

Scones

2   cups flour
2½   tablespoons baking powder
1   tablespoon sugar
½   teaspoon salt
2   tablespoons butter, softened
3   eggs
2¾   cups heavy cream, whipped stiff
     strawberry jam
1   cup heavy cream, whipped

In a medium bowl sift the flour and baking powder together with the sugar and salt so that they are well blended.

Work the butter into the flour with a pastry cutter so that the mixture is of a coarse, mealy texture.

Make a well in the center of the flour mixture. Place the eggs in the well. Using your hands, work the eggs into the flour so that a ball is formed.

Make another well in the ball of dough. Place the 2¾ cups of whipped cream in the well and work it in with your hands so that it is completely combined.

On a floured board place the dough and shape it into a square that is 1½" thick. Cut the dough into small squares and place them on a sheet pan.

Preheat the oven to 450°. Bake the scones for 15 minutes, or until they are lightly browned and done. Serve the scones with the strawberry jam and the 1 cup of whipped cream.

makes approximately 40 scones

"Our restaurant is casual, friendly, and a lot of fun. There are enough pressures in life, so when you go out you should relax and enjoy yourself."

"A scone is like a biscuit, only it is lighter and not as crisp. It is a classic English food that is served with afternoon tea."

"You don't need to be careful when you make this recipe. For some reason, the less care you take in making the scones, the better they come out.....within reason, of course. So for those of you who are nervous about trying this recipe, don't worry. Just whip them up, put them in the oven, and be done with it!"

"Originally I wanted to be a farmer in England, but I ended up becoming a chef who was trained in the classical way."

Cliff View, Laguna Beach

Index

COOKBOOK ORDER FORMS

Please send me the book(s) which I have indicated below. For shipping charges I am enclosing $2.75 for the first book, and $1.50 for each additional book.

Quantity	Book Title	Price	Total
_____	Southern California Beach Recipe	$17.95	_____
_____	*Santa Fe Recipe (softbound)	$13.95	_____
_____	**Taos Recipe (softbound)	$11.95	_____
	Shipping total:		_____
	TOTAL AMOUNT ENCLOSED:		_____

Ship to: _____

Address: _____

City: _____

State: _____ Zip: _____

Make check or money order payable to **Tierra Publications**. Send it to:

Tierra Publications
2801 Rodeo Road, Suite B-612
Santa Fe, New Mexico 87505
(505) 983-6300

(Master Card and Visa phone orders accepted)

Please send me the book(s) which I have indicated below. For shipping charges I am enclosing $2.75 for the first book, and $1.50 for each additional book.

Quantity	Book Title	Price	Total
_____	Southern California Beach Recipe	$17.95	_____
_____	*Santa Fe Recipe (softbound)	$13.95	_____
_____	**Taos Recipe (softbound)	$11.95	_____
	Shipping total:		_____
	TOTAL AMOUNT ENCLOSED:		_____

Ship to: _____

Address: _____

City: _____

State: _____ Zip: _____

Make check or money order payable to **Tierra Publications**. Send it to:

Tierra Publications
2801 Rodeo Road, Suite B-612
Santa Fe, New Mexico 87505
(505) 983-6300

(Master Card and Visa phone orders accepted)

Santa Fe Recipe *"A Cookbook of Recipes from Favorite Local Restaurants"* • 300 recipes • 30 restaurants • 305 pages
****Taos Recipe*** *"A Cookbook of Recipes from Restaurants in Taos, New Mexico"* • 170 recipes • 16 restaurants • 177 pages

Notes